Finding JOY

Journey Of You

Ted Kopecko

www.FindingJOY.us

BEST SELLER
PUBLISHING

Finding JOY - Journey Of You

Book Cover Design by Ted Kopecko

Illustrations by Ted Kopecko

Finding JOY

Dedication

God gave me insight and wisdom.

Family and friends gave me inspiration.

Mentors gave me action.

Life gave me fortitude and resilience.

YOU gave me purpose.

Congratulations... on taking your first bold step toward a self-transformative journey and a more abundant life with *Finding JOY... Journey Of You.* We're thrilled for you and committed to supporting your success as you uncover your purpose, elevate your value, and pursue the freedom that comes from living with intention and entrepreneurial spirit.

To enhance your experience with the book, we've created this powerful companion workbook—designed to align with each chapter and guide you through meaningful reflection, actionable exercises, and growth-driven challenges.

Free Workbook. Real Growth. Let's Go.

Fuel your journey with tools that transform. Visit www.FindingJOY.us or scan the code to access your *Finding JOY... Journey Of You* Workbook. Join our JOY community and start designing a life of freedom, purpose, and massive impact.

Contents

Contents

Join Our JOY Community for...
Webinars & Workshops,
Motivation & Mentorship,
Future JOY Speaking Events
JOY Store: Shirts & Fun Stuff

About the Author
Ted Kopecko

As a good steward of society, I worked most of my life away, paying my bills along the way never really questioning the eventual destination. Like most of us, I just figured if I worked long enough and hard enough in my business life as an architect and then as a commercial broker with a weekend off here and there it would somehow all work out. My destination was predetermined by default. This seems to be the pathway that most of us live by, whether we are climbing the corporate ladder or just scraping by, job jumping, living for the weekends, stuck in a work cycle we never intentionally designed or the curve ball life throws at us to derail our path or strike us out of life's game.

As I reflect on my life, from the businesses I've owned to the experiences I've had as a licensed commercial architect, real estate broker, and entrepreneur, one question has always stayed with me: *Why do some people succeed while others don't?* So many of us spend our days working away, going through the motions, never really stopping to think about whether we're on the path we actually want. I've had the privilege of working with so many incredible people, and through it all, I've learned that success isn't about luck or timing - it's about being intentional, about knowing where you're going, and staying true to that course. This book is the culmination of those life lessons, the realization that finding joy comes not just from where we go, but from the path we choose to walk – our innate purpose.

No matter where you find yourself in life. I am excited to share with you these life lessons and experiences to give you a short cut to your life success and give you a new perspective on your destination in finding your purpose, value and freedom.

Let's connect... Message me at www.FindingJOY.us and let's get your journey started!

Acknowledgement

Heartfelt Thanks to These Incredible People for Their Support, Friendship, Wisdom, and Contributions.

Jenna Love-Schrader - Copy Editor
Rob Kosberg - Best Seller Publishing
Bob Harpole - Best Seller Publishing
Andrew Porto - Book Web Site Designer

Dr Scott Kwiatkowski, D.O. - Medical Advisor, AskDr ScottDO.com
Dr Kathy Kopecko, O.D. - Medical Advisor
Nina Johnson, N.C. - Holistic Nutritionist
Angela and Dr Sehr - Business Partners
Steve Hillier - Business Partner
Preston Kopecko - Business Partner
Dan Kennedy - Business Partner

My Book Club - Steve, Heidi, Martina, Nina, Char, Becky, Gretchen, Sue, Dennis, Tony, Tom

Above all, my sincere love and thank you to my family for their unwavering support and love...

Becky, Preston and Daniela
Marianne, Kathy and Hanny
Joan and Ted Sr

Finding JOY

Your Journey Starts Now

The proper function of man is to live, not to exist. I shall not waste my days in trying to prolong them. I shall use my time.

Jack London[1]

Did you know that you hold the keys to your happiness, your purpose, and the freedom that lies within you? You have the power to transform your life and find the journey you've been seeking. This is not hyperbole; it's a reality that you can achieve, but only if your will to change is greater than the influences that are holding you back in life.

The guiding principle of our lives should ideally be the pursuit of JOY... finding the journey of you. However, for many of us, life is a series of fleeting moments of happiness interspersed with daily struggles as we strive to make ends meet with life struggles.

Finding JOY aims to provide a transformative shift in your perspective and mindset on life, the challenges you face, and the people you engage with. Its central theme is to guide you from your current state toward a life imbued with a deeper sense of purpose, fulfillment, and value, ultimately leading you to a life of abundant freedom.

If you find yourself weary of the monotonous cycle of daily life, and you feel a deep-seated conviction that you are destined for a future filled with greatness and abundance, then *Finding JOY* should become your life's mantra. You see, JOY is truly the *Journey Of You*. It is your personal roadmap to discover your *purpose*, recognize your *value*, and achieve your *freedom* before you depart playground Earth.

Are you prepared to embrace a life of abundance and unlock the extraordinary potential within you? I hope you are! *Finding JOY* is designed for the fearless, the unafraid who are eager to make a significant impact in the world. Say yes to change, and let's embark on your transformative life journey toward Finding JOY. So, get in the ride, buckle-up! An amazing journey awaits!

**You are not alone on this journey.
Join Our JOY Community for...**
Webinars & Workshops,
Motivation & Mentorship,
Seminars & Speaking Events
JOY Store for Merch & Fun Stuff!
Let's do this together!

What's on Your Mind?

Whatever the mind can conceive and believe,
it can achieve.

Napoleon Hill[1]

I have often pondered why only a select few of us attain the abundance life has to offer while the majority remain ensnared in the daily struggles of life. If struggle is your chosen motivation for living, then embrace the decisions you've made and drop the complaints. The choices you make in life establish a pattern that shapes your perspective and experience of life. Thus, your decisions can render your life either meaningful or ordinary. You assign value to your time through the choices you make. Remember, the choice is yours, so choose wisely because your time is a valuable and finite resource.

> **"Don't spend time beating on a wall, hoping to transform it into a door."**
>
> Coco Chanel[2]

For the majority of us, we traverse through life with the inherent understanding that there must be more to existence than a monotonous cycle of working to pay bills until we bid farewell to playground Earth. We are cognizant of our potential for a more fulfilling life, yet the path to such a life remains elusive, causing us to fumble through life's challenges, often feeling frustrated and stuck as time passes us by. However, it's crucial to recognize that our frustration can serve as a powerful catalyst for change, propelling us toward a new life trajectory that transcends the mundane and embraces significance. If you find yourself feeling "life-strated," take solace in the fact that you have already embarked on the first step toward discovering your purpose, raising the value of your time, and creating an abundant life.

"Life has no limitations, except the ones you make."
Les Brown[3]

The Journey of Jeff

In the early 1990s, a young man named Jeff was working a lucrative job on Wall Street. He was successful by societal standards, but he felt a nagging dissatisfaction with his direction. His life was a monotonous cycle of work and paying bills, and he knew there had to be more to life than repeating every day in frustration.

He was cognizant of his potential for a more fulfilling life, yet the path to such a life remained elusive. He felt frustrated that life was passing by, and he was going nowhere fast. However, Jeff didn't let his frustration consume him. Instead, he used it as a powerful catalyst for change.

Jeff quit his job and moved across the country to start a small online bookstore from his garage and began to network with people to share his vision. That bookstore eventually became Amazon, one of the most successful companies in the world. The frustration Jeff Bezos felt propelled him toward a new life trajectory that transcended the mundane and embraced significance.

> *"Life's too short to hang out with people who aren't resourceful."*
>
> Jeff Bezos[4]

His story serves as a reminder that feeling life-strated can be the first step in changing your life story. Each one of us harbors an innate greatness like Jeff Bezos. It is our responsibility, in our unique life journey, to discover and unleash this inherent potential. Les Brown, the renowned speaker and mentor, would agree when he stated...

> *"You must remain focused on your journey to greatness."*
>
> Les Brown[5]

What profound insights and mindset did Jeff Bezos possess that the rest of us might have overlooked in our journey through life? He possessed a *growth mindset* that allowed him to look beyond obstacles and self-imposed fear to visualize pathways to obtain solutions. He did not get bogged down with what's not possible but what is, since his fear of staying in a "life-strated" lifestyle was greater than the fear of accepting greater life challenges.

Mindset: Your Cerebral Program

Your mindset is shaped by early life experiences, the environment of your upbringing, and the lessons imparted by family, friends, teachers, and mentors. Much like the hard drive of a computer, the life program that was installed into your cerebral hard drive from birth to adolescence becomes an integral part of your nature. It forms the vast expanse of your reactions, decisions, and choices that shape your life's trajectory. The download of this life program synchronizes your mindset.

Your mindset significantly influences your life's purpose, your perception of the value of time, and ultimately, the degree of freedom you will enjoy in life. Mindset is a powerful tool that can either limit or liberate you, depending on how you choose to develop it.

The significance of mindset cannot be overstated; it serves as your internal compass, guiding your approach to your life's journey. Henry Ford, the visionary founder of Ford Motor Company, summarized mindset perfectly when he said,

> *"Whether you think you can or think you can't, you're right."*
>
> Henry Ford[6]

Ford's statement is a profound reflection on the power of mindset. He understood that your mindset fundamentally shapes your perspective on your life journey. Throughout his own life, Ford viewed challenges not as insurmountable obstacles, but as opportunities to gain experience in problem-solving and success.

> *"Most experts and great leaders agree that leaders are made, not born, and that they are made through their own drive for learning and self-improvement."*
> Dr. Carol Dweck[7]

Your mindset lays the foundation for your life's journey, shaping the ultimate lifestyle you currently enjoy or aspire to achieve. Dictionary.com describes *mindset* as "A fixed mental attitude or disposition that predetermines a person's responses to and interpretations of situations."[8] Essentially, it's the mental software that's deeply ingrained in your nature.

The promising part is that you have the power to install a new, enhanced mindset program onto your cerebral hard drive, altering your life's trajectory from ordinary to extraordinary to exceptional. This process of Finding JOY is applicable regardless of your age. However, the challenging part is that it's not a simple task, but the rewards it brings to your life make it absolutely worthwhile.

> *"The hallmark of successful people is that they are always stretching themselves to learn new things."*
> Dr. Carol Dweck[9]

Dr. Carol Dweck, PhD, a distinguished professor at Stanford University's School of Psychology and the author of *Mindset*, is renowned for her groundbreaking research on the psychology of mindset. She categorized mindset into two distinct personality types: the *fixed mindset* and the *growth mindset*. Her extensive work in this field has significantly contributed to our understanding of human psychology.

"In a fixed mindset," Professor Dweck states, "people believe their basic qualities, like their intelligence or talent, are simply fixed traits. They spend their time documenting their intelligence or talent instead of developing them." Conversely, Professor Dweck adds, "In a growth mindset, people believe that their most basic abilities can be developed through dedication and hard work—brains and talent are just the starting point. This view creates a love of learning and a resilience that is essential for great accomplishment."[10] Simply put, the development of a growth mindset fosters a passion for learning and a resilience to achieve life success and time value.

> *"The unsuccessful person is burdened by learning and prefers to walk down familiar paths. Their distaste for learning stunts their growth and limits their influence."*
>
> John C. Maxwell[11]

In a fixed mindset, an individual perceives their intellect and talent as unchanging, which directly influences their ability to experience new opportunities and life growth. Essentially, a person with a fixed mindset tends to take on tasks or expand their influence only when the perceived risk of failure is minimal or nonexistent.

On the other hand, in a growth mindset, an individual views their ability and talent as their life's uniform, equipping them to play the game of life. Challenges are seen as opportunities for personal development, and failure is viewed as a valuable learning experience. In essence, the fear of failure in a fixed mindset is a dominant personality trait that restricts an individual's capacity to experience personal growth and obtain greater success in life.

> *"Everyone is a mixture of fixed and growth mindsets. You could have a predominant growth mindset in an area, but there can still be things that trigger you into a fixed mindset trait."*
> Dr. Carol Dweck[12]

Are You Leaning Fixed or Growth?

Every individual possesses a unique blend of fixed and growth traits. It's the amount of either fixed or growth trait tendencies that determines a person's mindset outlook as either more fixed or more growth. As polar opposites, all people are on the bandwidth between the two mindsets.

It really comes down to the amount of limiting beliefs you have about your abilities and talents to accept life challenges as exciting or overwhelming. The seeds of limiting beliefs were planted early and sprout in the decisions you make later in life.

> *"You try something, it doesn't work, and maybe people even criticize you. In a fixed mindset, you say, 'I tried this, it's over.' In a growth mindset, you look for what you've learned."*
>
> Dr. Carol Dweck[13]

Imagine being dared to leap off the precipice of El Capitan without a parachute. Regardless of your mental fortitude, the sensible response would be a resounding, "No way!" This is a wise decision, as no amount of talent or determination will spontaneously sprout wings for you during your descent. Rational thinking takes precedence, overriding any irrational or perilous impulses.

On the contrary, if you were invited to deliver a keynote speech to a crowd of over several thousand people, an individual with a fixed mindset might decline the opportunity due to fear of embarrassment or failure. The mere thought of delivering the speech sends their heart racing, as they doubt their inherent abilities or talents are up to the task. Consequently, they retreat to the safety of the phrase, *I cannot do that!* or *That's not me* or *Please pick someone else.*

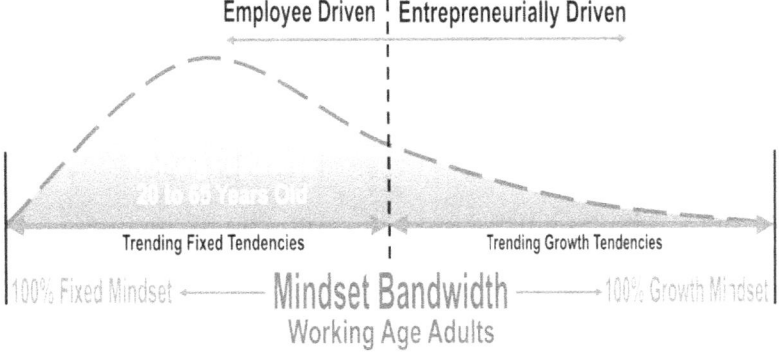

In stark contrast, an individual with a growth mindset is already formulating the speech mere moments after the invitation. They are thrilled by the prospect of the experience, viewing the challenge as a chance to broaden their skills, intellect, and influence. They are confident in their ability to succeed, believing the risk of failure to be minimal. For them, the potential reward far outweighs the perceived risk, and even if they fail, they see it as a valuable learning experience.

However, it's important to note that a growth mindset individual does not blindly accept every challenge that comes their way. They evaluate each challenge not through the lens of "limiting belief or behavior," but by considering whether the challenge or opportunity will propel their life forward.

"Your mindset matters. It affects everything, from the business and investment decisions you make, to the way you raise your children, to your stress levels and overall well-being."

Peter Diamandis[14]

Have you ever been curious about your mindset, or is this the first time you've given it thought? Don't feel left out. Most people do not think about their mindset because they benignly default to a fixed setting. You might be introspecting, trying to determine if you lean more toward a fixed or growth mindset.

Fixed Mindset Tendencies	Growth Mindset Tendencies
Avoid challenges	Challenges are opportunities
Does NOT like criticism	Likes constructive criticism
Gives up easily with obstacles	Persists in the face of obstacles
Threaten by others success	Inspired by others success
High Fear of Failure	Low Fear of Failure
Failure viewed as a setback	Failure viewed as experience
Talent & ability are static	Talent & ability evolve
Inside BOX thinking	Outside BOX thinking
Innate static Intellect	Life learning intellect
"I can't", "I'm not sure", "No"	"I can!", "Lets do this!", "Yes"
Glass half-empty attitude	Glass half-full attitude

The spectrum between a fixed and growth mindset represents the "scale of opportunity" that lies between a negative or positive action. A yes or a no response. No individual, regardless of age, possesses a 100 percent fixed or growth mindset. Instead, we all have a blend that leans more toward one end of the spectrum or the other.

Most of us approach opportunities or challenges based on our insecurities and assumptions, which is often determined by our perception of our abilities and talents. For those with a fixed mindset, it's typically a binary approach to challenge. They either believe they are good at something or not, leaving no room for ambiguity or growth.

Certain definitive beliefs that an individual might internalize could include thoughts such as, *I'm destined to mess up, so why bother trying? Or, I'm content with what I know and my skills. The situation is too far gone and beyond my control. Or, It's too late for me to learn new stuff. I'm too old to start over! Or, I don't have the smarts to accomplish that.* Or my favorite, *I am too busy. I have no time!* The last comment is a self-fulfilling prophecy. If life has you too busy on the mundane then it will be hard to find time to improve beyond the ordinary.

These are examples of fixed mindsets we often adopt to maintain our comfort zone and avoid challenge. Such absolute beliefs do not challenge the status quo and keep us on our perceived path of safety. Clint Eastwood summarized the concept of a fixed mindset in the film *Magnum Force* with the line, "A man's got to know his limitations."[15]

A more empowering mantra for those with a fixed mindset might be, "Your potential is only limited to the limits you believe you have."

> *"With a fixed mindset, you're so worried about how smart or talented you are, you don't take on challenges. You don't try new things."*
>
> Dr. Carol Dweck[16]

Conversely, an individual with an insecure intellect often perceives criticism and feedback as a personal affront, an insult reinforcing their fixed mindset. Such individuals may grapple with self-doubt about their abilities and may feel threatened or envious of others' achievements.

These insecurities and rigid beliefs are characteristic of a fixed mindset. While we all experience these thoughts to some degree, it's the frequency and intensity of these thoughts that shape our mindset between risk and reward, between challenge and opportunity.

> *"You can't just declare that you have a growth mindset. Growth mindset is hard."*
>
> Dr. Carol Dweck[17]

In a growth mindset, you hold the conviction that you can enhance your intelligence and skills by leveraging your inherent abilities and acquired talents. Individuals with a growth mindset daily prepare to invest time in studying and learning, and they are driven to act on their motivational thoughts to either succeed or fail in seizing an opportunity.

As an example, successful people read daily to support their growth mindset. In fact, on average they read fifty nonfiction books a year! They never stop learning and growing. They know reading is the greatest shortcut, the CliffsNotes for expanding growth, supporting a positive attitude and building a strong identity.

A growth mindset person views failure not as a setback, but as a valuable experience that prepares them for their next endeavor. They refuse to let the fear of failure deter them from broadening their skills, extending their influence, and fostering their personal growth. John C. Maxwell, a renowned author and international speaker, is a preeminent authority on personal development and life growth. His below quote encapsulates the self-sacrifice we accept for a greater life forward.

"Growth demands a temporary surrender of security. It may mean giving up familiar but limiting patterns, safe but unrewarding work, values no longer believed in, and relationships that have lost their meaning."

John C. Maxwell[18]

In essence, Maxwell captures the stark contrast between a fixed mindset and a growth mindset: the ability to let go of the mundane and the surety of conformity.

Can you reflect on how your formative years of education, upbringing, and social interactions have deeply influenced your thought processes, decision-making, and life choices? Because these experiences have shaped your identity and the lifestyle you lead today, this is why the early programming of your mindset is so crucial to your life journey, particularly in your pursuit of Finding JOY. It dictates how you live for a significant portion of your life, approximately sixty working years, and the value you can contribute to the world.

Recess Was Your First Lunch Break

Despite the common belief that most people consider themselves open-minded, the reality is that many of us are conditioned to live within the confines of a fixed mindset, which is often instilled in us from our early school years. For instance, we were trained to be seated at our school desks by 8:00 a.m., before the school bell rang. Then we would take a lunch break around noon, and finish our day around 3:00 p.m., often with additional homework assigned to be completed before the next day.

This routine mirrors the structure of a typical modern-day office, where rows of desks in school are replaced by rows of cubicles, and the teacher is replaced by a boss. However, the good news is, you still get your lunch break!

> *"The only limits in our life are those we impose on ourselves."*
>
> Bob Proctor[19]

We were conditioned to conform, to stay within the lines, to avoid taking risks, and to prioritize safety. In return, we were rewarded with grades in school, and as adults, with a paycheck. These early experiences have shaped us into diligent, lifelong workers.

Our society is built around this concept, from the beginning of our lives until our journey concludes. This fixed mindset, while providing structure and stability, often limits our potential for growth and exploration. If we achieve "good enough" status and get an "attaboy" or "attagirl," we stay in our place with the "award" (aka expectation) for being a good worker bee.

The moment our parents instructed us to "remain seated," "conduct yourself appropriately," "refrain from touching that," "sit quietly," and "stay safe and mind the rules," we started shaping our life's journey mindset, which further solidified our tendencies towards a fixed mindset.

> *"Train up a child in the way he should go, and when he is old, he will not depart from it."*
> Proverbs 22:6

If this Proverb does not create a fixed mindset for generations, then I don't know what would, since most parents and teachers benignly teach conformity in our childhood years. With all good intentions, we were a bit doomed from the start!

While there isn't any existing scientific research to back this up, I am deeply convinced that at the very moment of our birth, when we drew our first breath and embarked on the journey of life, we all possessed a 100 percent growth mindset. This unique instance could arguably be the only time in our existence when we were completely devoid of fear and insecurity.

From early childhood, we were subtly guided toward developing a fixed mindset, largely influenced by the cautionary "don't do that" remarks from our parents. These towering figures of authority, who seemed like giants to our young selves, inadvertently steered us away from nurturing our inherent, natural growth mindset. Thus, we embarked on a journey that seemed to predetermine our mindset, veering us toward a more rigid and less flexible way of thinking.

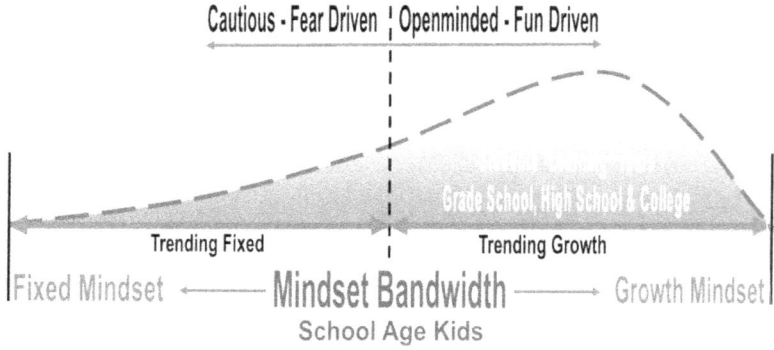

In her groundbreaking study involving school-age children, Dr. Carol Dweck discovered that excessive praise focused on outcomes, such as receiving an A or winning a race, can paradoxically diminish a child's motivation. This counterintuitive finding challenges the common parental belief that such accolades boost perseverance and drive. Dr. Dweck's research posits that "result-driven praise" sets an unsustainably high bar for success, creating immense pressure on the child to continually meet these elevated standards. Over time, this pressure can lead to a fear of failure and embarrassment.

Ultimately, causing the child to disengage and stop striving altogether.

> *"Praise your child explicitly for how capable they are of learning rather than telling them how smart they are."*
>
> Dr. Carol Dweck[20]

On the other hand, Dweck's research has demonstrated that "learning-oriented praise" significantly bolsters motivation to achieve higher levels of success by anchoring praise in the process of learning itself.[21]

This approach shifts the focus from mere outcomes to the efforts and strategies employed, thereby transforming the fear of failure into a robust confidence in our abilities. By emphasizing growth and improvement, learning-oriented praise cultivates a resilient growth mindset that embraces challenges and persists in the face of setbacks and life's obstacles.

> *"If parents want to give their children a gift, the best thing they can do is to teach their children to love challenges, be intrigued by mistakes, enjoy effort, seek new strategies, and keep on learning."*
>
> Dr. Carol Dweck[22]

In 2007, Dweck and her team conducted an insightful study on mindset among junior high school students. The objective was to ascertain the proportion of students who exhibited fixed and growth mindsets. Upon the study's completion, Dweck discovered that approximately 40 percent of the students demonstrated a fixed mindset, while an equal percentage displayed a growth mindset. The remaining 20 percent were ambiguous, exhibiting traits that fell somewhere between the two mindset categories.[23]

If we accept the premise that we are all born with a 100 percent growth mindset, it can be inferred that by the time we reach junior high, 40 percent of us have already lost a significant portion of our growth mindset tendencies. Furthermore, the remaining 20 percent appear to be on the path towards developing a fixed mindset.

Regrettably, a logical deduction is likely that many of the remaining 40 percent of students who initially exhibited a growth mindset in junior high will have lost most of their growth-oriented tendencies by the time they graduate from college and enter the working world. This transition, from school desks to corporate cubicles, often results in a shift from a growth mindset from birth to a fixed mindset in adulthood.

> *"If you don't change the direction you are going, then you're likely to end up where you're heading."*
>
> John C. Maxwell[24]

To elucidate this concept, consider that our global economy operates on a system of debt-based consumerism, where most goods and services are purchased and sold on credit. From our early education years through to college, we are groomed to acquire a profession or trade, with the aim of becoming productive and creditworthy participants in this system. In our young adulthood, we are introduced to the concept of monthly debt payments when we buy or lease our first car. This serves as our initial exposure to the world of credit and debt. Soon, we are inundated with rent, utility bills, mortgage payments, and the costs of raising children, food, clothing, fuel, and other life expenses.

Struggle Is the Loss of Freedom

Eventually, we find ourselves in a monthly struggle, realizing that our paycheck doesn't stretch far enough to cover the monthly expenses. We find ourselves needing dual incomes just to scrape by, and our jobs become a lifeline, a necessity for survival month after month.

> *"It's time to start thinking differently about money and debt and start the healing process, and the process toward wealth and freedom. Freedom from bad debt can get you started."*
> Robert Kiyosaki[25]

This quote serves as a stark reminder that without change, growth and progress are near to impossible. As individuals transition from their school years into the workforce, they become increasingly risk-averse, a tendency that grows in proportion to their debt and personal responsibilities. Any inklings of a growth mindset they may have had in their youth quickly dissipate, replaced by a fixed mindset driven by the fear of losing their assets. They remain trapped on the proverbial hamster wheel of life, too afraid to take risks or seize opportunities. They hope for better days but do little to nothing to change their circumstances. They become stuck in a cycle of working their lives away, resigned to their fate.

To prove this point, in today's economic climate, the typical sixty-four-year-old has managed to accumulate an average of $6,900 in savings after dedicating over forty years of their life to the workforce. Upon reaching the age of retirement, the average monthly social security check amounts to approximately $1,562. Given this financial scenario, a significant number of retirees find themselves donning the "Retirement Blue Vest," welcoming customers at Walmart as a means to supplement their social security income. This, of course, is contingent upon them being in good health. This lifetime state of **POOR** was embedded in a fixed mindset of *"Passing Over Opportunity Regularly"* namely due to the fear of change.

> *"If you put yourself in a position where you have to stretch outside your comfort zone, then you are forced to expand your consciousness."*
>
> Les Brown[26]

How crucial is mindset if you aspire to transform your life journey toward a higher purpose, enhance the value of your time, and attain more freedom? It is absolutely vital!

Your mindset serves as the initial step in discovering true happiness, the ultimate journey of self-discovery, expanding consciousness, and personal growth in *Finding JOY: The Journey of YOU.*

> *"You try something, it doesn't work, and maybe people even criticize you. In a fixed mindset, you say, 'I tried this, it's over.' In a growth mindset, you look for what you've learned."*
>
> Dr. Carol Dweck[27]

Journey Rest Stop 1

1) What exactly is a mindset, and why does it hold significant importance in shaping your future trajectory?

2) What main factors distinguishes a fixed mindset from a growth mindset?

3) Where do you see yourself within the bandwidth of mindset? What particular tendency characterizes your thought patterns?

Journey Thought

"It is in your moments of decision that your destiny is shaped."

Tony Robbins[28]

www.FindingJOY.us

Chapter 2

Journey of Change

Let's Change It Up!

To improve is to change,
to be perfect is to change often.

Winston Churchill[1]

You are never alone in your struggles. We all have them. Some are overwhelming, and some are manageable. But most of the time, struggle is caused by our unwillingness to change our direction, our perspective, and our associations. Change, a daunting prospect for many, is often hindered by a myriad of reasons. However, the most common obstacle for change is **FEAR**, an acronym for *False Evidence Appearing Real.*

> **"Too many of us are not living our dreams because we are living our fears. Life has no limitations, except the ones you make."**
>
> Les Brown[2]

Our fears, whether acknowledged or not, are the driving force behind every decision we make. It's challenging to abandon the familiar for the unfamiliar, or to exchange comfort for the uncomfortable. It's a mental gamble to give up what you have today for the potential thought of a setback tomorrow. Our unrealized achievements and potential successes are often buried beneath our fear of the unknown.

Consequently, we find ourselves trapped in a cycle, repeating the same behavior with the illusion that if we just work harder and longer, everything will fall into place. We opt for the safer life path. In this scenario, the only entity truly working is you, tirelessly laboring and trading your time for a mere "wholesale" paycheck.

You have the power to either take control of your life and shape your destiny, or (like most) let life dictate your path and influence your outcomes. If you allow fear to drive how you react to opportunity in your life to govern your choices and decisions, you will never discover the full potential of life or the wealth of opportunities you could have seized. It is crucial in Finding JOY to release these unfounded fears and propel your life forward.

The late Steve Jobs, the visionary co-founder of Apple, imparted a profound piece of wisdom before his untimely demise at the young age of fifty-six.

> *"For the past thirty-three years, I have looked in the mirror every morning and asked myself, 'If today were the last day of my life, would I want to do what I am about to do today?' And whenever the answer has been no for too many days in a row, I know I need to change something."*
>
> Steve Jobs[3]

When Steve Jobs crafted his first Mac computer within the confines of his parents' garage, do you suppose his mindset was static and fixed, or active and growth-oriented? The question is, of course, rhetorical. Individuals with a growth mindset are never content with the status quo or a life lived on autopilot. They are perpetually engaged in a process of transformation and education, fearlessly pushing the boundaries of their comfort zones and venturing into uncharted territories of life. They are not daunted by the uncertainty of the future; instead, they place unwavering faith in their vision.

Jobs is a testament to the power of a robust growth vision. His life serves as a compelling illustration of an individual brimming with growth mindset tendencies. The decisions he made throughout his life added immense value to the world and significantly enhanced the lives of billions of people. The legacy of Steve Jobs is a testament to the transformative power of a growth mindset.

If you find yourself believing that your life was destined for a more significant purpose, yet you feel trapped, exasperated, and in desperate need of a breakthrough, it's time to transition from the fixed mindset team to the growth mindset team. This shift necessitates change, the difficulty of which is directly proportional to how close you are to a 100 percent fixed mindset on the mindset spectrum. The closer you are to the left-hand side of mindset bandwidth, the more challenging it becomes to initiate change, and the more daunting it becomes to overcome fear.

> *"For change to happen, the pain to remain the same has to be greater than the pain of change."*
> Tony Robbins[4]

Is change challenging? Undoubtedly. Is it painful? Certainly. Is it uncomfortable? Absolutely. But is it worth it? Without a shadow of a doubt! Embrace change with a resounding yes, and you will begin to perceive the world in vibrant technicolor, teeming with boundless opportunities.

Changing Your Mindset

Aligning with Dr. Dweck's research, Dr. Jacob Towery, an adjunct clinical instructor in the department of psychiatry at Stanford University, incorporates Dweck's principles into his practice, emphasizing how adopting a growth mindset can enhance mental health and build resilience.

> *"The good news is mindsets are highly changeable, and if you are willing to learn the technology of changing your mindset and defeating your distorted thoughts, you can have significantly more happiness."*
> Dr. Jacob Towery[5]

I would add to the above quote, "you can have significantly more happiness AND JOY", a greater enhanced version of your journey, the Journey Of You.

Transitioning your mindset from fixed to growth is not as simple as flipping a light switch. It's a complex process that requires a vision, consistent effort, and dedication. There are numerous growth mindset switches that need to be activated, and an equal number of fixed mindset switches that need to be deactivated, in order to shift your mindset tendencies toward a growth perspective.

Your current mindset has been shaped over years, and altering it is akin to reprogramming your internal hard drive - your brain. This involves changing how you perceive and respond to failure, criticism, success, challenges, opportunities, and learning. It is a journey of reflection, self-discovery, and transformation that demands patience, perseverance, forgiveness and self-grace.

> *"Change is the law of life. And those who look only to the past or present are certain to miss the future."*
> John F. Kennedy[6]

Surprisingly, transitioning from a growth mindset to a fixed mindset is relatively straightforward. All it requires is to say no to every opportunity and allow fear and insecurity to guide your life decisions. However, once you've embraced a growth mindset, it's uncommon to revert back to a fixed one. The thrill of constructing a life filled with endless opportunities and boundless possibilities is simply too exhilarating to abandon.

Adopting a growth mindset involves introspection, self-assessment, and potentially changing your environment and alternating your perspective. This transformation can be daunting for many, but it is a crucial first step on your journey toward self-improvement. Many factors such as negative associations, toxic relationships, unmotivated friends, a toxic environment, and the daily information you consume can influence your mindset by inadvertently strengthening and supporting a fixed mindset, undermining your growth.

> *"We are the average of the five people we spend the most time with."*
>
> Jim Rohn[7]

Jim Rohn refers to the Law of Averages, a principle that resonates with our inherent human nature, when he talks about the power of influence. As humans, we tend to exhibit a herd mentality, conforming to societal norms and expectations due to our upbringing.

The fear of retribution, criticism, or loneliness often discourages us from breaking away from the pack and standing out. However, this conformist attitude can be costly, potentially hindering your journey toward discovering your greater purpose and true value. Consider for a moment how different the world would be if innovators like Steve Jobs, Bill Gates, Martin Luther King Jr., Elon Musk, Thomas Edison, Henry Ford, or the Wright Brothers chose to blend in with the crowd. Now imagine the unique value *you* could bring to the world if you dared to step away from the pack, from your herd.

Embarking on your transformative Journey of Change involves two crucial initial steps. The first, and often the most challenging, requires you to introspectively examine your relationships with family, friends, and associates. This introspection is necessary to discern whether these relationships are propelling you forward or hindering your progress in life.

This initial step is fundamentally about understanding the value of your time and recognizing the value of the moments you invest in others, a precious commodity that, once spent, can never be reclaimed.

> *"Align yourself with people you can learn from, people who want more out of life, people who are stretching and searching and seeking some higher ground in life."*
>
> Les Brown[8]

It is essential to ask yourself, "Who am I investing my time in? Is the value of that investment reciprocated in some form to broaden my identity and brand?"

Beware of Time Thieves!

I am not advocating for the termination of every friendship, severing all associations, or divorcing your partner - provided these relationships are not toxic, negative, or abusive. However, if they are, it is crucial to muster the courage to let go and move on. Your life is too precious to squander on individuals who are not deserving of your time and energy. Such people or groups are merely time thieves who will only steal your time and drain your dream. On the other hand, if these relationships are merely unstimulating, offer lukewarm support, or exhibit strong tendencies toward a fixed mindset, it's time to broaden your social and friendship circle, as we will discuss in chapter 5.

Seek out those who can serve as mentors, coaches, and motivators in your life, to foster a growth mindset. Surround yourself with individuals who will inspire you to grow, learn, and strive to be better. You don't need to be the smartest person in the room. And if you are, then find a smarter group!

> **"If you're the smartest person in the room, you're in the wrong room."**
>
> Jack Welsh[9]

Cherish those with a fixed mindset who genuinely value you and support you during challenging times. However, just like a favorite old shirt, you might need to diversify your friendship circle and include more individuals with a growth mindset. Begin investing more time with those in your community who can broaden your influence, enrich your life, and enhance your value and worth.

Seek inspiration from contemporary mindset mentors such as Les Brown, Grant Cardone, Brian Tracy, Tony Robbins, Gloria Mayfield Banks, Eric Worre, John C. Maxwell, and many others. While you may not know them personally, their collective wisdom and experience can help you overcome limiting beliefs, foster self-acceptance, and instill self-belief. They will remind you that in your life's journey, you are the protagonist, the LEAD actor, and everyone else plays a supporting role in the narrative you're crafting.

> *"Change will not come if we wait for some other person or some other time. We are the ones we've been waiting for. We are the change that we seek."*
> Barack Obama[10]

As the lead character, you hold the most significant role in your life's movie. How are you scripting your story? How crucial is your role? Are you merely making a cameo appearance, or are you fully committed to your role? How are you utilizing your time? Remember, it all starts with your mindset and who is in charge of directing the movie of you.

The second crucial phase in your Journey of Change involves conducting a sincere evaluation of how you utilize your leisure and free time. This refers to the moments sandwiched between your professional commitments, personal obligations, working hours, and sleep. During these intervals, what information are you feeding your cerebral hard drive? What content are you providing to nourish your conscious and subconscious mind? Is it positive, inspiring, uplifting, and educational? Or is it toxic, negative, demoralizing, and mind-numbing?

"I truly believe in positive synergy, that your positive mindset gives you a more hopeful outlook, and belief that you can do something great means you will do something great."

Russell Wilson[11]

In today's digital age, we have unprecedented access to a vast array of information and content, ranging from global news, social media, reality TV shows, the internet, webinars, movies, video games, and books. These can either broaden our mental horizons, enhance our perspective, and stimulate our intellect, or they can erode our cognitive abilities and darken our life outlook.

Every piece of content you consume directly communicates with your conscious and subconscious mind, supporting either a positive or negative attitude, and will influence your mindset. Content is the true nourishment for your thoughts, perspective, and attitude. We will dive deeper into this subject in chapter 3, Journey of Time, where we will get a more comprehensive understanding of how the content we consume impacts our mental and emotional well-being.

To initiate your journey of personal growth, Dr. Towery encourages you to challenge self-defeating emotions, thoughts, and limiting beliefs. He urges you to foster new, positive, or challenging ideas that will better serve your personal development.

Begin crafting a fresh, new narrative of the individual you aspire to be and how you wish to be perceived by others. It's time to step out of your comfort zone and reassess your strategies!

> *"The exciting news about mindsets is that they are absolutely changeable. The entire field of cognitive therapy is based on the idea that thoughts determine feelings and that you can learn powerful techniques to modify distorted thoughts and self-defeating beliefs."*
>
> Dr. Jacob Towery[12]

Consider reframing your perspective on change. Instead of adopting an "I can't because I might fail" attitude, embrace the mindset of "I can! And even if I fail, I will have a better understanding for the next challenge." This shift in thinking is the difference between an "I can" and an "I can't" mindset. Now ask yourself which mindset you believe will propel you further in life. It should be obvious.

All individuals who are successful and growth-oriented possess an "I can" mindset. Even when they are unsure of the path ahead or the steps to take, they confidently say yes and navigate their way through the process. The reality is, you can't have a growth mindset while sitting in your fixed mindset comfort zone and make excuses.

Richard Branson, the CEO of Virgin Group, a high school dropout at age sixteen, and now oversees more than four hundred companies worldwide stated.

> *"If somebody offers you an amazing opportunity*
> *but you are not sure you can do it, say yes, then*
> *learn how to do it later."*
>
> Richard Branson[13]

Abandon your hesitations, and adopt a positive, yes-oriented growth mindset, fueled by an unstoppable spirit.

Are You "Brain Change" Adaptable?

Numerous neurological studies corroborate the research of Professors Dweck and Towery, emphasizing the transformative power of shifting one's mindset from a fixed to a growth-oriented perspective. These scientific studies highlight the concept of neuroplasticity, a term that encapsulates the brain's remarkable adaptability and capacity for change. In essence, neuroplasticity refers to the brain's inherent malleability to reconfigure itself by altering the connections between its neural pathways.[14]

These neural pathways continue to evolve and expand, particularly when we engage in learning and skill development. Conversely, pathways that are not regularly activated may become inactive, or rusty for limited use. Intriguingly, when we dare to step outside our comfort zone and embrace new challenges and opportunities, our brains respond by forging fresh neural connections. This process not only enhances our intelligence but also boosts our happiness, health, resilience, and success.

As we transition from a fixed to a growth mindset, we become better equipped to tackle life's challenges. Neuroplasticity is the mechanism through which the human brain acquires and hones abilities, talents, knowledge and personal growth. It underscores the importance of learning, training, and consistency in personal development, regardless of age. In fact, neuroplasticity is fundamental in the development of a growth mindset, providing the scientific basis for our capacity to evolve and improve.

Ironically, neuroplasticity can also reinforce negative traits, behaviors, and thought patterns. Consistent negative self-talk or pessimistic thinking can strengthen neural pathways, making these thought patterns more automatic and ingrained. The perpetuation of negative thought patterns like substance abuse, addiction, aggression, envy, prejudice and even procrastination can become habitual traits in our nature and hard to change.

Further, experiencing life trauma can overstimulate neural circuits in the amygdala, which is responsible for fear and stress responses, potentially leading to increased anxiety or the development of post-traumatic stress disorder (PTSD).

The good news is that even though neuroplasticity can reinforce negative traits, it also provides the means to counteract them. By intentionally engaging in positive behaviors and thought patterns, individuals can weaken unhelpful neural pathways and strengthen healthier ones. Some techniques and methods are Cognitive

Behavioral Therapy (CBT), mindfulness and meditation, learning new skills to redirect the brains focus, and practicing positive behavior to overwrite negative habits.

Neuroplasticity underscores the importance of conscious effort and repetition in shaping the brain for better outcomes, even in the face of negative traits or experiences to change your nature and mindset.

Be careful what you think or download to your cerebral hard drive, since you will become what you consistently think. Your negative mindset shapes your reality, and you possess the power to alter this reality, regardless of the challenges life has hurled at you or the paths it has led you down. This transformation is possible if you pledge to shift the course and destination of your life. No excuses.

Go for Growth

Generally, you have the choice to either fabricate excuses or foster growth, but you cannot have both. Go for growth! It is far superior to any convenient excuse that is preventing you from truly living and discovering joy.

> *"You are the only real obstacle in your path to a fulfilling life. When your why is big enough, you will find your how."*
>
> Les Brown[15]

As the architect of your own life, how are you crafting your narrative? Are you the protagonist, the star everyone has come to see? Or are you merely a supporting character with a fleeting cameo? This is a crucial question to ponder, as your role in your life story is far more significant than a mere cameo. Each of us harbors a profound purpose, a seed to blossom and enrich the world if we germinate it. Our true mission is to connect the dots we've been given since birth, to uncover our inherent greatness and to assume the role of the lead actor in our life.

> *"The two most important days in your life are the day you are born and the day you find out why."*
> Mark Twain[16]

Regrettably, many people never discover their "second day" and depart this world with a sense of regret. Recognizing the finite nature of life and the inevitability of its end, it becomes paramount to find your second day in the journey of self-discovery, the Journey of You.

Embarking on your transformative journey toward a growth mindset, there are several essential tools you'll need to take on your trip to guide you to your ultimate destination, the discovery in Finding JOY.

Your Emotion Toolbox

You have a virtually life toolbox, jam packed with some amazing tools that you can use anytime as long as you open up your box and use these tools. Here are a few of the tools you will find in your toolbox:

•   **The LOVE Tool:** Embrace and cherish the individual who God has crafted you to be. You are a unique entity, a highly sophisticated being endowed with conscious thought. Elevate your self-perception, and think grandly about yourself. Remember, in the vast expanse of the universe, there exists only one version of you! You are a miraculous manifestation of life.

•   **The FORGIVENESS Tool:** Forgive those who have caused you pain, mentally or emotionally. I know it is hard to do, but in the end, those toxic feelings are holding you back. Document your feelings of hurt, then symbolically discard them. Holding onto anger is counterproductive, draining the vitality you need to progress in life. It's akin to having a flat tire; it leaves you stranded and unable to move forward.

•   **The GRACE Tool:** Give yourself the gift of grace, embracing your struggles and failures as integral components of your unique journey of experience. Remember, you are the master orchestrator of your life, the lead cheerleader rallying for your success. No one should be cheering louder for you than yourself, even amidst the stumbles and fumbles! It's perfectly fine, for in this journey you are granted unlimited opportunities to try again, unless you choose to surrender. Echoing the wisdom of Les Brown, "Forgive yourself for your faults and your mistakes and move on."[17] Embrace your imperfections, learn from your missteps, and continue to forge ahead on your unique path.

- **The GRATITUDE and APPRECIATION Tools:** Dedicate a few moments each day to express gratitude and appreciation - whether through contemplation, meditation, or prayer - for the gift of life in this extraordinary world we live in. You possess a golden ticket, a privileged front-row center seat to effect meaningful change within yourself and in the world.

- **The FAITH Tool:** Have FAITH in the potential of your innate intelligence to grow and evolve through opportunities and challenges. Take a proactive role in your learning journey, embracing every chance to expand your knowledge and skills.

Your Promotion Toolbox

- **The READING Tool:** Commit to reading and immersing yourself in the wisdom of your chosen mentor for at least twenty minutes, or ten pages, daily. This could be from the works of renowned thought leaders such as Jim Rohn, Napoleon Hill, John C. Maxwell, Simon Sinek, Grant Cardone, Tony Robbins, Brian Tracy, or Les Brown many others. Just as you wouldn't embark on a road trip without a GPS map to guide you to your destination, make reading a daily habit. This will serve as your compass, shielding you from the daily onslaught of negativity and keeping you steadfast on your path to success.

• **The EMBRACE Tool:** Embrace new Challenges and opportunities with enthusiasm, viewing them as stepping stones on your journey of gaining invaluable experience and knowledge.

• **The INSPIRED Tool:** Be inspired by the accomplishments of others. Remove any feelings of envy or jealousy. These feelings will destroy you in your forward progress. Absorb the lessons from the triumphs of others and integrate them into your own experiences. Continually uplift and celebrate others on their journey, fostering a positive and supportive environment. You enrich yourself by enriching others.

• **The EXCITED Tool:** Be excited and marry your narrative, your story, with enthusiasm. Fuel it with your passion and steer it in your chosen direction. Let the world bear witness to your purpose and the value you possess. Get the world excited about you, this is the secret of every successful person to build an audience.

• **The ACCESSIBLE Tool:** Be accessible, open and engage in communication with others, always accompanied by a welcoming smile! Whether you're waiting in a store queue, crossing paths with a stranger, or interacting with colleagues at work, don't hesitate to extend a friendly hello. As humans, we are inherently social creatures, and forging connections is part of our nature. You never know how or where these connections might influence your life's narrative or your journey. Networking with others is essential for life growth and can be a shortcut in your journey from "here" to "there." Celebrated author Robert Kiyosaki imparted a profound piece of wisdom, by stating, "If you want to go somewhere, it is best to find someone who has already been there."[18]

• **The SETBACK Tool:** Embrace failure as an inevitable part of tackling challenges or seizing opportunities, and as a valuable learning experience in the face of setbacks. Failure should not be seen as a negative, as we have often been taught, but rather as a crucial part of the learning process. Consider the example of Thomas Edison, who discovered a thousand ways not to make a light bulb before he found the one method that worked. Similarly, Elon Musk launched over a hundred SpaceX rockets before achieving a successful flight. When NASA signed a contract with SpaceX, they viewed these one hundred failed attempts not as failures, but as essential research and development. Failure only becomes REAL when you decide to give up. Every failure is downloaded to your cerebral hard drive as experience learned for a better future outcome OR you file under loser and never try again.

• **The GROWTH Tool:** Write down your Goal Plan to develop your Growth Plan to reach your Life Plan destination. Use a daily thought journal as your personal growth diary. What actions will you undertake today to broaden and cultivate your conscious awareness and experiences? We will talk more about your life growth in chapter 11.

•   **The CRITICISM Tool:** Gain insight from the constructive criticism of others and embrace it to shape your journey. During my college years in architectural school at Cal Poly SLO, we were tasked to present our building designs after investing sleepless nights for two continuous weeks. This presentation, known as a design critique, was held in front of students and faculty members, where we showcased our passionately crafted building design solutions. This critique was essentially a competitive arena of criticism, with classmates vying to outdo each other for the best design. Reflecting on this experience, I realize it was an invaluable life lesson in learning to accept and grow from both positive and negative feedback. It honed my design skills and fortified my resilience in the face of rejection. Life is a continuous design critique, an integral part of our existence. Welcome the critique with a smile, refine your trajectory, and continue to progress toward a better life.

> *"If you set goals and go after them with all the determination you can muster, your gifts will take you places that will amaze you."*
>
> Les Brown[19]

Did You Pack the GRIT?

Before embarking on your journey, there is one final essential tool you need: GRIT! As Professor Dweck advises, it is crucial to "cultivate grit."[20] Consider it the metaphorical body armor of the successful. A tough exterior that enables you to persist and conquer the obstacles and barriers that life and others may place in your path forward.

These barriers are life's attempt to confine you within the comfort zone of a fixed mindset. Those who embody the growth mindset invariably possess grit as a defining characteristic. It's grit that will guide you through the challenging periods of your growth, providing you with the stamina to disregard the surrounding noise and stay true to your journey and vision! So make sure you pack a large can of grit in your backpack to start your journey. You will need it!

Are you prepared to transform your mindset and reset your neuro connections in Finding JOY? Let's embark on this journey together! Your life is poised on the brink of something extraordinary, even as time refuses to pause for your indecision. Make a commitment to change today, or you will inadvertently settle by default for the comfort of the status quo.

"Don't wait. The time will never be just right."
                                    Napoleon Hill[21]

Journey Rest Stop 2

1) What three FEARs have been major obstacles, preventing you from achieving breakthroughs in your life?

2) What is the narrative of your past? How do you envision your future life story unfolding? How would you like the final scene of your life's movie to play out?

3) What daily emotional tools can you apply in your life? Which one will be the hardest for you to use and why?

Journey Thought

"Make your life a masterpiece, imagine no limitations on what you can be, what you have or what you can do."

Brian Tracy[22]

www.FindingJOY.us

Chapter 3

Journey of Time

Do You Have a Minute?

All we have to decide is what to do
with the time that is given us.

J. R. R. Tolkien[1]

Time is the most crucial non-living entity that all living beings and the cosmos share. Without time, existence is null, there is no us, and space is nonexistent. We pursue it, flee from it, cherish it, and fear it. We are inextricably bound to it. Time is an inherent part of our nature, a seamless extension of our existence. It accompanies us from our inception to our conclusion, ferrying us from one life event to the next. Isn't it remarkable that we possess the conscious awareness of time, our gauge of progress and the passage of our years?

In the grand scheme of the cosmos, our existence is but a mere microscopic speck. The entire human race, in the context of eternity, is less than a nanosecond of time. The cosmic space that surrounds us is immeasurably vast and infinite.

To illustrate, consider a journey to Alpha Centauri, the star system closest to Earth. This voyage would take 4.3 light years. This might seem feasible until you translate light years into human years. To put it into perspective,

4.3 light years equates to a staggering 6,740 human life years, or approximately 270 generations of lineage if we used our current propulsion technology of 430,000 mph with the Parker Solar Probe![2] I can almost hear the echoes of my descendants, my great-great-great-grandchildren to the 200th degree aboard our interstellar spaceship, impatiently asking, "Are we there yet?"

Alpha Centauri, our nearest celestial neighbor beyond our own solar system, reigns supreme in the cosmic landscape that surrounds us. Yet unless we master the art of time travel or master a way to "Beam me up, Scotty!" teleportation and exploration of the galactic neighborhood will remain limited.

Mars, our planetary sibling, seems a more feasible destination, being significantly closer than the distant Alpha Centauri. This realization brings us back to Earth and underscores the importance of cherishing our existence and embracing the adventure of life.

> *"It suddenly struck me that that tiny pea, pretty and blue, was the Earth. I put up my thumb and shut one eye, and my thumb blotted out the planet Earth. I didn't feel like a giant. I felt very, very small."*
> Neil Armstrong[3]

It is crucial to comprehend our microscopic existence within the boundless expanse of space, yet also recognize our extraordinary significance within the cosmos of life. There exists only one entity like you, with your unique cellular and chemical composition, amidst the entire universe teeming with life beyond our realization. The sheer incredibility of this thought and the infinite specialness of your existence, sharing life with us on planet Earth, is truly awe-inspiring.

Regrettably, many of us fail to perceive life from this perspective; instead, we lead a limited existence and spend our time focused on the mundane. We often become entangled in the trivialities of life and lose sight of our unique existence, merely surviving rather than truly living. This is the reality of life as shaped by societal norms and standards getting us distracted in the mire. Yet it is essential to remember that we are more than just cogs in the machine. We are unique, irreplaceable entities in the grand tapestry of the universe.

> *"Look up at the stars and not down at your feet. Try to make sense of what you see and wonder about what makes the universe exist. Be curious."*
> Stephen Hawking[4]

We are all extraordinary miracles of life, regardless of the unique attributes we were born with - be it skin color, gender, race, or sex. Each one of us is distinctively and individually crafted as siblings in the vast family of the human race. Though uniquely designed, we are interconnected through the intricate web of our DNA.

When you pause to contemplate our existence, it is truly awe-inspiring that we inhabit a planet that is nothing short of perfection. With its azure skies, boundless oceans, and majestic mountains, Earth is a veritable

Garden of Eden amidst an otherwise uninhabitable universe teeming with stars, planets, and galaxies.

You Are Extremely Unique

Take a moment to appreciate the rarity of your existence here on Earth, and the significant impact you can make on the world through your unique presence and value. From this perspective, can you see just how incredibly special you are? By living life fearlessly to its full capacity, you can contribute immense value to the human race.

> *"We are an impossibility in an impossible universe."*
> Ray Bradbury[5]

When you perceive life through this unique perspective, all else appears to lose significance, revealing the true value of your time and presence. Apart from death, every challenge you face in life is either a hurdle to leap over, an obstacle to navigate around, or a diagnosis to overcome. Death signifies the end of life as we understand it, but it does not mark the end of your existence. Much like birth, death is the gateway to our next awareness, our next journey, our next existence.

> *"I believe that God has put gifts and talents and ability on the inside of every one of us. When you develop that and you believe in yourself and you believe that you're a person of influence and a person of purpose, I believe you can rise up out of any situation."*
> Joel Osteen[6]

What are your inherent talents, and how do you employ these gifts within your allotted time to cultivate a life that is fulfilling, meaningful, purposeful, abundant, and enriched with value?

The Journey of Leslie

This is the story of the remarkable journey of Leslie, a man who transformed his life into one of significance. Born in 1945 alongside his twin brother in a dilapidated building in Liberty City, a suburb of Miami, Florida, plagued by poverty, Leslie's life was far from ordinary. When the twins were merely six weeks old, they were adopted from their biological mother.

Their new guardian, Mamie Brown, was a thirty-eight-year-old unmarried woman who worked as a cafeteria cook and maid. Despite her humble circumstances, Mamie embraced the boys with open arms, providing them with a loving family environment.

In his early years, Leslie was somewhat rebellious and faced academic challenges, often receiving poor grades. By the time he reached the fifth grade, his teachers had labeled him as "educable mentally retarded," a term used to describe his slow progress. Tragically, these labels began to shape Leslie's mindset at a tender age, leading him to believe that he was destined to fail. This story may resonate with many, as it highlights how societal labels can often become self-fulfilling prophecies in downloading a fixed mindset.

> *"The report card just told me, my teacher, my parents where my mind was at maybe three weeks before when they gave me a test. It had nothing to do with my potential."*
>
> Bob Proctor[7]

Leslie was a student at Booker T. Washington High School where he crossed paths with Leroy Washington, a speech and drama instructor at the school. Leroy saw a spark of untapped potential in the young and impressionable Leslie. During one particular class, Leroy challenged Leslie with a task. However, Leslie declined, stating he was told that he was "educable mentally retarded" and therefore could not perform the task.

Leroy, taken aback by Leslie's self-deprecating remark, responded with a profound statement that would forever alter the course of Leslie's life. He sternly told Leslie, "Never say those words again! Someone's opinion of you does not have to become your reality." This powerful message served as a turning point in Leslie's life, reshaping his self-perception and guiding his future life.

> *"Persistence is a unique mental strength; a strength that is essential to combat the fierce power of the repeated rejections and numerous other obstacles that sit in waiting and are all part of winning in a fast-moving, ever-changing world."*
>
> Bob Proctor[8]

These profound words by Leroy Washington bestowed upon Leslie a sense of liberation. As he journeyed through life, he would later reflect and assert, "The limitations you have, and the negative things that you internalize, are given to you by the world. The things that empower you, the possibilities, come from within."

This is the root difference between a fixed mindset versus a growth mindset: the "limitations" you were taught versus the "possibilities" that empower you. Upon completing high school, Leslie embarked on a career as a city sanitation worker, all the while nurturing his dream of becoming a disc jockey at the local radio station. Fortune smiled upon him when he was hired to perform miscellaneous tasks around the station, and an unexpected opportunity arose. One day, the regular on-air disc jockey arrived at work inebriated. With a shortage of staff, the station manager had no choice but to put Leslie on the air.

> **"One secret of success in life is for a man to be ready for his opportunity when it comes."**
> Benjamin Disraeli[9]

Leslie's charismatic on-air personality left a lasting impression on the station manager, who subsequently promoted him to a full-time disc jockey position. In the 1960s, Leslie relocated to Columbus, Ohio, where he established a highly popular, top-rated radio program focused on political activism. However, his controversial approach led to his dismissal.

Undeterred, Leslie used this setback as motivation to achieve even greater things. He decided to run for the Ohio State Legislature and triumphed, winning the 29th House District. Leslie went on to serve three successful terms, proving that his passion and determination were his keys to success.

Following his tenure in the Ohio State Legislature, he made the compassionate decision to return to Florida to tend to his ailing mother. Simultaneously, he dedicated his efforts toward addressing social issues and cultivating youth career development programs. It was during this period of personal growth and community service that he discovered his new passion and calling: public speaking.

In 1989, Leslie achieved a significant milestone when he was honored with the prestigious Council of Peers Award of Excellence from the National Speakers Association. This accomplishment was particularly noteworthy as he became the first African American to receive such a distinguished accolade, earning him the moniker, "The Motivator!"

This was an extraordinary achievement for Leslie, who had faced significant challenges in his early life. Despite being held back in school and labeled as "educable mentally retarded," he overcame these obstacles to become a beacon of inspiration and motivation.

In 1997, Leslie's life took a dramatic turn when he was diagnosed with stage 4 prostate cancer that had metastasized. However, Leslie refused to let this devastating disease strip him of his life's purpose, vision, and drive. Displaying remarkable resilience, Leslie triumphed over his cancer. He channeled his experiences into writing several books and has since risen to become one of America's most renowned and highest-earning global motivational speakers in the world!

> *"Sometimes adversity is what you need to face in order to become successful."*
>
> Zig Ziglar[10]

Born into poverty and subsequently abandoned as a child, Leslie, better known as Les Brown, has risen to global prominence as a speaker and educator on success and personal growth. His life narrative is a testament to the power of persistence and unwavering dedication to a higher purpose. Les Brown's vision to contribute value to the world has not only made him a valuable figure in his field, but also a beacon of hope and inspiration for many.

> *"You got to become a risk taker! If you're not willing to risk, you can't grow. If you can't grow, you can't become your best, and if you can't become your best, you can't be happy, and if you can't be happy, then what else is there?"*
>
> Les Brown[11]

In essence, maximize the use of your time and talents, irrespective of your life circumstances, and boldly step forward to announce your presence to the world! This sentiment echoes the words of Les Brown, who stated,

"Life takes on meaning when you become motivated, set goals, and charge after them in an unstoppable manner."[12]

Countless extraordinary individuals, such as Les Brown, began their lives facing significant challenges. Yet they instinctively understood the importance of their time in contributing value to the world. Icons like Oprah Winfrey, Elon Musk, Steve Jobs, Richard Branson, John C. Maxwell, Tony Robbins, and Ralph Lauren, among others, started from humble beginnings. Many of them had limited education and lacked college degrees.

However, they all shared a common denominator: They valued their time, carefully choosing how and with whom they spent it, aligning it with their purpose and vision. Their judicious use of time and the choices they made raised the value of their time, rendering their lives as valuable to many around the world.

> *"In every day, there are 1,440 minutes. That means we have 1,440 daily opportunities to make a positive impact."*
>
> Les Brown[13]

Do you have a minute to make a significant impact on the world? Are you ready to accept the challenge of viewing your time as a valuable commodity to be invested in bettering the world and enhancing your own time value?

When you start to perceive your time as highly valuable, your purpose becomes sharply focused, guiding you on your unique journey toward JOY. If, however, you treat your time as trivial, merely ticking off boxes on a daily checklist, your life may follow a similar path of indifference, blending into the vast crowd of humanity and mediocrity.

> *"Accept responsibility for your life. Know that it is you who will get you where you want to go, no one else."*
>
> Les Brown[14]

The Time Bank: Your Personal ATM

You are the custodian of your own time, possessing a virtual vault known as the "time bank." This bank account, unique to you, was endowed with a certain amount of time at your birth. Everyone has a time bank, but the mystery lies in the fact that we are unaware of the exact amount of time each of us has been granted. Consequently, some may be time-wealthy, while others may have a limited time supply. This is the enigma of life; none of us can precisely determine the balance of our time bank accounts, so spend wisely.

Each day, we approach our virtual Automated Time Machine (ATM) and withdraw another twenty-four hours from our time bank. We joyfully tuck this bundle of time into our time wallets, spending it as necessary until we require another twenty-four-hour allotment to continue living. This routine continues until one day, our ATM dispenses only a few hours. Suddenly, you realize you've run out of time. Following this compulsory withdrawal, your time bank account is depleted. You've reached the terminus of life's journey here on Earth.

Confronted with this stark realization, most of us will ponder on how we utilized our time. For many, the answer is tinged with regret, wishing they had made wiser decisions for a more fulfilling life. If you could transport yourself to that inevitable future day when your ATM is empty and look back, how would you want to have lived your life up to that moment of farewell?

What does it take to live a full eighty-plus years of life only to be filled with regret at the end? It's surprisingly simple. We often live our lives under the benign illusion that there is no tomorrow. This phrase is familiar to us all, and many of us abide by it without giving it a second thought. This is where the issue lies.

We live our lives as if we have an infinite amount of time, but the harsh reality is, we don't know how much time we have until something profoundly shakes our thoughts and beliefs. Unlike money, we don't have a credit card of time to extend our lifespan. Our lives are consumed by one pervasive word: *busy*. How often have you found yourself uttering phrases like, "I have no time," "I'm too busy," or "I'll deal with it tomorrow"? Most likely, more times than you or I can count!

> **"Time is what we want most, but what we use worst."**
>
> William Penn[15]

Our adult existence is often consumed by the relentless demands of a 24/7 lifestyle, until we reach a point where we become reliant on others. By then, it's often too late, and regret looms ominously in the background.

The missed opportunities, the unfulfilled desires, the tasks we planned but never accomplished due to lack of time or resources, or the challenges we never dared to face all contribute to a profound sense of regret. Many individuals spend their lives in a constant struggle, never truly realizing their full potential or the value they could bring to the world, as each day is consumed by the battle to survive another month paying bills. It's a safe bet that no physician attending to a person in their final life moments has ever heard them utter, "If only I could have worked one more day!"

This reminds me of an old fable, penned by an anonymous scribe, which goes as follows:

> One person worked long and hard toward making a great career. One day he decided to rest from the work and to live in luxury for his pleasure, which he could afford because of his wealth.
>
> Just when he made this decision, an angel of death came to him. Being a very wealthy person, he decided to buy some more time from the angel of death at any cost. He bargained for a long time, but the angel was unmoved.
>
> Desperate, the rich man made the last proposal to the angel. He said, "Give me just one hour of my life so

that I can admire the beauty of this earth for the last time and spend some time with my family and friends, whom I haven't seen for a long time, and I will give you all of my wealth."

But the angel refused again. Finally, the man asked if the angel could give him at least one minute so that he could write a goodbye note. The angel granted his final wish, and the man wrote:

Spend your time, which was given to you, in the right way. I couldn't buy even an hour of life with all of my wealth. Listen to your heart, and check if the things surrounding you have true value. Cherish every minute of your life.

This fable holds profound significance for me, offering several insights that can be gleaned from it. For one, the man in this story could easily have been my father.

The Corporate Journey of My Father

My father was a man of immense dedication and integrity, who tirelessly provided for his family and harbored a deep love for golf. He devoted over four decades of his life to a company, tirelessly climbing the corporate ladder by working ten-hour days, six days a week, with Sunday serving as his only respite. I vividly recall the day he retired, the company presented him with a gold-tone watch and a 4x6 plaque, a token of appreciation for his forty-two years of unwavering commitment and service.

My father was a prudent man, meticulously saving throughout his working years for his much-anticipated golden years of retirement. He embodied the virtues we are all taught to uphold.

His retirement dream was to indulge his passion for golf, playing at any golf club or resort of his choosing. He had meticulously planned these years, eagerly looking forward to savoring every day at the metaphorical nineteenth hole of life. However, life had a cruel twist in store. Tragically, just two years into his retirement, he suffered a massive stroke, an eventuality he had not accounted for in his plans.

In the midst of the crisis, the emergency room doctor gravely informed me that my father was unlikely to survive the night. He had suffered a catastrophic brain stem stroke, a type of massive brain trauma that few people manage to survive. As he lay there on the sterile gurney of the emergency room, I held his hand, my fingers entwined with his, and whispered softly into his ear. "Dad, I love you. This is not your time. Your grandson still needs his grandpa, and there are countless golf courses waiting for you to master." Miraculously, he defied the odds that night, joining the fortunate 3 percent who survived such a devastating stroke.

My father survived for another sixteen years following that pivotal night, but sadly, he was never able to grip a golf club again. His only connection to his beloved sport was watching The Masters Golf Tournament from the confines of his living room couch, his vision and muscles compromised by the stroke. Yes, he spent quality time with his grandson, which I am extremely grateful for, but he couldn't show him how to play golf.

That single night served as a profound turning point in my life, providing me with a powerful life lesson. It was an epiphany that sparked a fundamental shift in my perspective on life and the preciousness of time.

My Life Epiphany

The concept of time crystallized in my mind when my dad had his stroke. I found myself questioning the worth of dedicating forty-two years to tirelessly climbing the corporate ladder, working six days a week for ten hours a day, only to enjoy a mere two years of healthy, active retirement. Viewed from this angle, it's a deal that most would decline. Yet, it's a reality that many of us are living right now, unknowingly agreeing to this arrangement every day without knowing the full narrative of our lives.

> *"And then there is the most dangerous risk of all... the risk of spending your life not doing what you want on the bet you can buy yourself the freedom to do it later."*
>
> Randy Kosimar[16]

Like my father and countless individuals immersed in the hustle and bustle of daily life in the work world or the corporate world, it's easy to lose track of time. It's a common phenomenon we all experience. We just keep going to our personalized ATM every day and repeat the same day over and over, spending our time. As we age, time seems to accelerate, swiftly transitioning from one month to the next, or one holiday to another.

Our work life is a constant struggle to stay afloat amidst one or two jobs, is sandwiched between fleeting moments of personal living. Managing life's complexities such as family, friends, relationships, and even mundane tasks like car repairs, shopping, and cleaning the house becomes a relentless pursuit of daily living.

The moment we open our eyes each morning, we are thrust into the whirlwind of life. This is the persistent undertow of life, anchoring us in place while time ceaselessly marches forward. This forms the crux of our frustration until we eventually surrender and accept our work life destiny until we die. However, it often takes a significant life event to jolt us awake, prompting us to question, *Is this all there is?*

> **"Most people will choose unhappiness over uncertainty."**
>
> Tim Ferriss[17]

What we're truly contemplating is if we were merely born to pay bills and work away our lives, punctuated only by the occasional Sunday barbecue and perhaps a two-week staycation.

At this precise juncture, we are given the opportunity to redefine our concept of happiness. We have two choices:

1) accept our current existence as it is and continue living in the same manner, or 2) challenge our future with the aim of actively creating a new pathway for our lives. We must remember that our time is a precious resource, finite in nature, and it is within this limited span that we must seek and discover our journey in Finding JOY.

> **"Life isn't about finding yourself. Life is about creating yourself."**
>
> George Bernard Shaw[18]

Time is the intricate tapestry of existence, defined by how we choose to spend it and with whom we share it, in our pursuit of an ultimate life. This ultimate life may be characterized by providing for one's family, resolving life's challenges, or savoring a Sunday barbecue after a six-day work week.

In the case of motherhood, it could mean working seven days a week for the most adorable boss! If you perceive your life in these terms, then understand your influence may be limited to a small group of individuals within your immediate circle. While this lifestyle is commendable and common, it is usually marked later in life by the question, "What if . . . ?"

The decisions you make today shape the life you lead tomorrow. There is a delicate balance to maintain - from your work life to home life to friendship life to sleep life - only to find there is no time left for your growth life. This is where life wants you, absorbing your time so you have no time left over, stuck in the same routine. The routine will not broaden your influence or increase your time value.

This is not to suggest that you should neglect your primary responsibilities, but rather to emphasize the importance of allocating time for personal growth and self-development. Indeed, family and friends play a crucial role in your personal journey, but your time is an essential resource in discovering the unique value and potential you can offer the world.

> *"Any time you sincerely want to make a change, the first thing you must do is to raise your standards."*
> Tony Robbins[19]

Within the vast expanse of the universe, our existence is but a fleeting nanosecond. Yet, in the realm of life, time is the very essence of our being. The manner in which we utilize it shapes our purpose and dictates the influence we exert on the world. Our life's journey is a quest to unearth the greatness that lies within us with the time that has been given to us from God.

Journey Rest Stop 3

1) What unique skills and talents do you possess that define your individuality?

2) What obstacles are standing in your way, hindering your progress? Which individuals in your life do you need to distance yourself from in order to propel your life forward? What fears are preventing you from realizing your true purpose and worth?

3) What amount of time are you prepared to dedicate each day toward your personal development and growth?

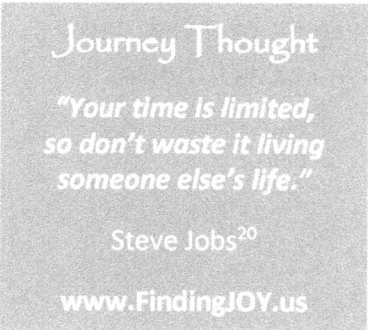

Journey Thought

"Your time is limited, so don't waste it living someone else's life."

Steve Jobs[20]

www.FindingJOY.us

Chapter 4

Journey of Value

What's the Value of Your Time?

Until you value yourself, you won't value your time.
Until you value your time, you will not do anything
with it.

M. Scott Peck[1]

The quality of life is significantly shaped by how you manage and distribute your time, as well as the importance you assign to it: your value. The genuine core of life's happiness stems from the time you selflessly offer your value in helping others achieve their dreams and life ambitions. The JOY of existence is embodied in the value you impart to the world.

Let's have a little fun. Just like our virtual time bank, we can apply this time concept, with a bit-of-a-twist, to our new virtual Time-R-Us store! Yep! Now stay with me on this one. The only product that your store sells is the highly valuable, and sought-after commodity of time. We all possess this unique virtual time store.

We sell our time in a variety of quantities, ranging from quick fifteen-minute "grab-n-go" time boxes to comprehensive eight-hour workday packages. Some buyers even have the opportunity to acquire years of our time, most likely at a significantly discounted price. Imagine that: a life box of time!

You're a Time Vendor

The thrill of cutting through the grand opening red ribbon, swinging open the doors to our store, and revealing shelves brimming with vibrant boxes of time, ready for purchase, is super exciting. However, there's always a catch. We receive only one shipment of time upon opening our store, with no possibility of restocking. Just like our virtual time bank, once we exhaust our supply of time, our store is permanently out of business.

In essence, we run out of products, and our store is literally out of time. But fear not, new TIME-R-US stores are constantly springing up in competition. The only caveat is that you can only own one time store in your life. When you have sold all your time, then you are out of business and out of time.

> *"It's really clear that the most precious resource we all have is time."*
>
> Steve Jobs[2]

Our time is a highly coveted asset, yet it faces a significant challenge: the overwhelming presence of numerous Time-R-Us stores on every street corner, each offering time from various store owners. This intense competition inevitably drives down the price for a box of time, creating a buyer's market. However, this scenario can be turned around if your time holds a higher value than that of your competitors. Hint!

> *"Time is one of your most valuable commodities and how you spend it determines what your life will be. You can either waste it, invest it or give it away."*
>
> Wayne Dyer[3]

In the course of conducting business in our store, there comes a point when some of us become aware that our time inventory is dwindling. It is at this juncture that a chilling realization dawns upon us. We may have been undervaluing and underselling our precious time.

Some individuals surrender and persistently undervalue their time, leading to mounting frustration and daily struggle. Instead of a time store, they own a dime store! However, a select few of us choose to alter our course, invest in personal growth, and redesign our life's store to amplify the value of our time. So, what type of time store do you own? A Dollar Tree or a Louis Vuitton?

As the owner, manager, product stocker, and janitor of your time store, your main objective is to charge the maximum value for your time and, in turn, sell your time to the highest bidder. When your consignment of time arrives, you will observe that there is no pre-set price tag attached to the boxes of time. As the proprietor of your store, you have the privilege to adjust the value of your time, either marking it up or down depending on the value you set. So, in your exclusive marketplace, the question arises: "What is the value of your time?"

> *"Time is the coin of your life. It is the only coin you have, and only you can determine how it will be spent. Be careful lest you let other people spend it for you."*
>
> Carl Sandburg[4]

That is an excellent question! Many individuals fail to perceive their time as a valuable asset that can be sold, often because they are too busy selling their time for wholesale or spending their time on mundane stuff. Our time is, without a doubt, the most valuable resource we possess. Once we use, spend, or sell our time, it is irreplaceable and forever lost. It's gone!

Trading Your Time for Their Money

Most people tend to quantify their time based on their needs, such as, "I need to earn this much to cover my monthly expenses and bills." They establish the value of their time based on their monthly survival threshold - alas, a fixed mindset attitude. They're setting the bar too low and settle on average, and average is the highest bar of poor. You will never change your life's destination if you are too low to exist.

> *"Most people fail in life not because they aim too high and miss, but because they aim too low and hit."*
>
> Les Brown[5]

Consequently, many of us end up trading our time at a wholesale rate in return for a paycheck, salary, or commission. In the hustle and bustle of survival and sustenance, we often lose sight of truly living an abundant life. Then, at some juncture in life, we find ourselves waking up to the harsh reality that we have little time left to truly live to find our greatness, as time continues to race past us.

> **"Most people work just hard enough not to get fired and get paid just enough money not to quit."**
> George Carlin[6]

Carlin just described the vicious work cycle of life. We trade our limited time for money in exchange for a life of work, selling our time at a wholesale rate. Most of us sold our bulk box of time at a Costco rate. The cycle of work can easily consume our entire lifetime, obscuring our vision in discovering our life's purpose. Many individuals spend their lives laboring away, never uncovering their potential or inherent greatness because they are perpetually occupied with earning enough to sustain another month of life.

This is the paradox of employment: Most paycheck-driven jobs will never provide true freedom but merely another month of struggle, perhaps punctuated by a brief two-week staycation while paying off your Visa bill. To illustrate this reality, consider a visit to any large retail store like Walmart or Home Depot. Count the number of individuals over the age of sixty who are working as greeters or stocking shelves. The reason behind this is simple: They lack sufficient savings and need to supplement their social security income to survive.

> *"Too many people get trapped in repeating the same day over and over."*
>
> Eric Worre[7]

The average Social Security check barely covers rent or a mortgage payment, leaving essential expenses such as food, medical care, utilities, and clothing to be paid out of pocket. Consequently, we find ourselves in a cycle of ceaseless labor and selling our time on the cheap.

Regrettably, in today's world, the accepted norm is to spend the majority of our lives working, with perhaps only the weekends as a brief respite to attend to personal chores or perhaps even a second or third job. As a society, we have gradually adjusted our life perspective to accommodate this relentless work cycle, treating it like a chronic condition that we must manage until our final days.

> *"If you do what you've always done, you'll get what you've always gotten."*
>
> Tony Robbins[8]

Generally speaking, individuals with a strong leaning fixed mindset perceive their time as a commodity to be traded for a job's paycheck at a wholesale rate. On the other hand, those with a strong leaning growth mindset see their time as a valuable asset to be leveraged for opportunities at a retail rate.

People with a fixed mindset view their work as a transaction, selling their time to an employer and receiving payment for each unit of time spent. This perspective is often referred to by Eric Worre, a renowned global speaker and marketing expert, as a "coin-operated" mentality.[9]

This lifestyle mentality is a simple input-output equation. You put something in to get something out. However, this mindset is inherently limited, focusing on the finite and trapping individuals in the NOW: No Other Way. This mindset restricts us from exploring alternative paths or envisioning different possibilities for their future.

> *"All we have to decide is what to do with the time that is given us."*
>
> J. R. R. Tolkien[10]

Our mindset is intrinsically intertwined with our work cycle lifestyle, shaping our perception of work and our value. From a young age, we are conditioned to follow a certain life path: Be responsible, secure a job, pay your bills, and establish a career or trade. This traditional route, often deemed the "sure" path, is life's security blanket for most people. However, it often lacks elements of creativity, self-discovery, entrepreneurship, and personal growth.

This conventional approach typically results in a work life spanning over forty-five years, with an average of twelve job changes. Individuals often switch jobs every four years, driven by the hope of a salary increase, a new career trajectory, or a change in management. This is the reality for many, a cycle of constant transition in pursuit of better opportunities in a work-cycle lifestyle.

However, it's important to remember that there is more to work life than just following the sure path. It's about finding your purpose, unleashing your creativity, embracing entrepreneurship, and continuously increasing your value. This mindset, which is growth-based, can lead to a more fulfilling and rewarding life journey.

Plan A: The Default Retirement Plan – "Frugality"

Say what? Frugality? No way! I've lived my life working; now I want to have fun! Unfortunately, most of us are forced to live Plan A in our golden years. Nothing golden about frugality! *Forbes* magazine highlighted a new trend in retirement planning, aptly named "Frugality." This approach suggests that after dedicating over four decades of your life to work, you should look forward to a retirement characterized by stringent budgeting and potentially taking on a part-time job or side gig. Most likely your Uber driver has grey hair! However, this perspective seems to overlook the fact that life is not meant to be spent solely on working it away, but this is the framework that society has established.

In a subsequent article, *Forbes* further emphasized in another article, "For many Americans, the dream of being able to retire at all, let alone retiring early might seem impossible. Just trying to get by on a daily basis can be a struggle, which is highlighted by the stats showing that 4 in 5 Americans live paycheck to paycheck."[11] This paints a stark picture of the financial challenges that many individuals face today.

> *"You are not your job. It does not define who you are or all that you have to offer. Your real value is based upon who you are, not what you do. The only thing you need to do is express your real self to the world. You've been conditioned to think this is unproductive or that you can't make money at it. But you'll never know true happiness and fulfillment until you find the courage to do it anyway. Learn to trust your inner wisdom, even if the whole world says you're wrong"*
>
> Bob Proctor[12]

The truth of the matter is, in our modern society, a paycheck was never designed to provide financial security. Its primary purpose was to ensure you could cover your monthly expenses, thereby compelling you to return to work the following day and repeat the process ad infinitum. Regrettably, a significant number of individuals find themselves in a predicament where they have "too much month at the end of the money." This is the reason why many are juggling at least two jobs or fervently hoping for overtime. When you exchange your precious time for a paycheck, you are essentially selling your hours wholesale, at a cut rate price to your employer.

> *"Let's face it, we're not about to earn our way to wealth. That's a mistake millions of Americans make. We think that if we work harder, smarter, longer, we'll achieve our financial dreams, but our paycheck alone, no matter how big, isn't the answer."*
>
> Tony Robbins[13]

On average, we spend about forty-five-plus years of our lives working, clocking in approximately 2,080 hours each year. Even after deducting eighty hours for vacation, we still end up with a staggering 90,000 hours of our lives dedicated to work!

But wait! There's more! If we factor in the time spent each day preparing for work and commuting, we can add another 35,000+ hours to the tally, bringing the total to over 125,000+ hours. This calculation doesn't even account for any additional hours spent on overtime, a second job, or part-time work during retirement. Our society has structured our lives in such a way that we gradually whittle away our time, day by day, until our productive work life is depleted. We sell our boxes of time until we run out of stock.

Tragically, many people spend their entire lives working without ever discovering their true purpose, leading to end-of-life regret. Interestingly, most doctors report that they've never heard a dying person's last words be, "I wish I could've worked one more day." This serves as a stark reminder to put work, your JOB as means to survive but not the means to your end in finding your value.

> **"Work harder on yourself than you do on your job."**
> Jim Rohn[14]

No, Wait! I Just Love My JOB!

Hold on a moment. "I absolutely love my job!" That's fantastic, but does your JOB (Just Over Broke) reciprocate that affection? If your job was akin to a marriage, brace yourself for up to twelve professional breakups without any job "alimony" compensation throughout your career. Most jobs have an "at will" agreement and can let you go for any reason. Your job is not obligated to you as your love may be for your job.

> **"If you don't know your own value, somebody will tell you your value, and it'll be less than you're worth."**
> Bernard Hopkins[15]

You might derive pleasure from your work, but it is crucial to comprehend that your job primarily requires you to execute a task at a wholesale rate for your time. Your job isn't designed to provide you with financial independence or wealth. Its sole purpose is to purchase your time from your time store for a specific service at a specific rate they need from you to generate a company profit.

There is nothing inherently wrong with this, but it's important to understand the dynamics of this work relationship: You are replaceable. I am sure you have seen many examples of this one-way job relationship in your life. But somehow we think that the next job, our next love will be different. It won't be. The game has indefinitely changed with our new job competitor who does not get sick, asks for raises, or need time off. AI robotics will affect every job from uber drivers to doctors and your future pay will be based on performance only and not a per hour paycheck. Your journey needs to accept this significant shift in the value of your time.

Thanks for Your Time... But

To illustrate, a dear friend of mine was a burgeoning talent in the corporate hierarchy of a renowned national home improvement store. Her exceptional performance was recognized to such an extent that she was invited to a prestigious corporate dinner with the company's founder and CEO, a testament to her remarkable achievements. However, a mere six months later, she found herself a casualty of a corporate restructuring within the management.

To add insult to injury, she was informed of this unfortunate news during a corporate Zoom call in the presence of a hundred other high-ranking C-level executives who were also laid off. A rather abrupt farewell, wouldn't you say? "Thank you for your time. We wish you a fulfilling life ahead! Glad you enjoyed the company picnics! Thanks for your service. Wish you the best!" Yeah, RIGHT!

> *"Job security is an oxymoron because in the new economy there is no such thing as a safe, secure job. You may have a job, but it's not secure."*
> Robert Kiyosaki[16]

When your JOB discovers a superior, cost-effective, and more productive method to deliver its services, brace yourself for a potential career upheaval. This sentiment was echoed by Andy Puzder, the former CEO of the colossal restaurant chain CKE, which includes brands like Carl's Jr and Hardee's. Puzder once asserted that robots and artificial intelligence (AI) will outperform human employees. He argued that these technological advancements are consistently courteous, always upsell, never require a vacation, are never tardy, and eliminate the risk of workplace accidents or discrimination lawsuits based on age, sex, or race.

> *"Today, you expand or you are expendable."*
> Les Brown[17]

AI has emerged as a formidable competitor in the work world landscape. From Uber drivers to medical practitioners and dentists, no profession is immune to this technological revolution. It is crucial to acknowledge and adapt to this paradigm shift in the work environment. More so than ever, your JOB will only love you until it finds a cute AI program or robot to replace you. The good news is the technological advancement will force more people to search for more creative, entrepreneurial opportunities to expand their time value.

The Daily Grind and Beyond

Now don't go out and fire your boss just yet. Every job holds significance, primarily serving as a means to manage your monthly obligations in return for your time and effort. However, it is crucial to remember that your job is neither inherently benevolent, nor does it exist solely for your benefit. You are essentially a cog in a larger machine, fulfilling a specific need or service.

It's unwise to view your job as a permanent fixture in your life or have a codependency relationship with it. Your job is unlikely to significantly enhance your value over time, beyond perhaps a modest 4 percent annual pay increase. Retirement benefits may be minimal, possibly extending to a gold-plated watch and a corporate-signed thank-you card, but not much more.

If you find contentment in the daily grind, punctuated by fleeting moments of weekend joy, and are barely scraping by each month, yet you still believe you've reached your zenith, then kudos to you. The world requires diligent individuals who willingly devote their entire lives to the ceaseless "beehive" of work.

However, if you harbor a deep-seated belief that life has more to offer, that your potential is yet to be fully realized, then rest assured, there is indeed more!

> *"If you are waking up with the sensation that there has got to be more in life... then there is."*
>
> Eric Worre[18]

If you are yearning for more, do not settle. Embrace the possibility that your potential is limitless, and that life has more to offer than the daily grind. First, assume responsibility and take charge of your career work life. Be a diligent custodian of your company's resources, but remember to hold the reins of your career trajectory firmly in your hands. Your job is your primary source of income, providing just enough to keep you from resigning.

> *"We cannot become what we need by remaining what we are."*
>
> John C. Maxwell[19]

Second, understand that the worth of your time surpasses the monetary value reflected in your paycheck. Your paycheck is merely a transaction, purchasing slices of your time. It does not encapsulate your true value or potential. Third, believe in your ability to make a significant impact on the world.

> *"The day that turns your life around is the day when you say, 'Enough. I've had it. I'm not living like this anymore.'"*
>
> Eric Worre[20]

Now, let's embark on a journey to discover your passion, to enhance your value, and to become a valuable asset to the world in our quest for Finding JOY. In reflection, what is the price tag of your time in your time store?

Journey Rest Stop 4

1) What is the name of your time store? What is the value of a box of your time?

2) What does the phrase "coin-operated" signify, and how is it relevant to your life?

3) If the JOB you are passionate about unexpectedly terminates your employment, how would you respond? What strategic adjustments would you make to navigate this sudden change?

Journey Thought

"Time has more value than money. You can get more money, but you cannot get more time."

Jim Rohn[21]

www.FindingJOY.us

Chapter 5

Journey of Friendship

Are You Friend or Foe?

You are the average of the five people you spend the most time with.

Jim Rohn[1]

If the gift of your friendship is the most precious gift you can bestow upon someone, then paradoxically, it can also be the most detrimental gift you can receive from someone. Friendships form the bedrock of our human existence and our life's journey. They represent our connection to the world and to each other - a bond that is forged in honesty, trust, and love - and shares common beliefs and experiences.

> *"Align yourself with people that you can learn from, people who want more out of life, people who are stretching and searching and seeking some higher ground in life."*
>
> Les Brown[2]

Friendships have the power to shape your life and mindset, from the innocence of childhood to the wisdom of adulthood. Intriguingly, the relationships forged through friendships are the most influential forces in your life. They have the potential to either construct a path to success or pave a road to regret. So, what kind of friendships are shaping your life's trajectory? Remember, the journey of life is not traveled alone. Therefore, it's crucial to choose your travel mates wisely on your journey, for they can significantly influence your final destination.

> *"The quality of a person's life is most often a direct reflection of the expectations of their peer group."*
> Tony Robbins[3]

This narrative brings to mind an inspiring tale of two college friends whose camaraderie literally revolutionized the world.

The Friendship that Changed the World

In 1995, a young man named Larry arrived on campus, brimming with excitement to be part of such a prestigious institution as Stanford University. He was contemplating pursuing graduate studies at the university.

His campus tour guide was a fellow student named Sergey who was tasked with showing him around the school grounds and perhaps introducing him to some popular college hangouts. Larry made the decision to attend this esteemed university, a choice that not only forged a remarkable friendship but also significantly altered the course of the world.

His friendship with Sergey took about a year to solidify, but their shared interest in a burgeoning phenomenon known as the World Wide Web was the catalyst that brought them together. Pooling their talents and resources, they set out to create a platform that would assist people in finding answers to a myriad of questions. Larry would often say, "Our objective is essentially to organize the world's information and make it universally accessible and useful."[4]

This straightforward concept, conceived by a pair of Stanford grad students, proved effective in attracting investment for their innovative venture in a world just beginning to explore the internet. Larry and Sergey successfully raised the initial capital needed to bring their idea to life.

Today, we know this revolutionary internet platform as Google. The friendship between Larry Page and Sergey Brin was not only pivotal in their lives, but also had a profound impact on the world!

I am frequently awestruck by the transformative, symbiotic friendships that have shaped our world, such as those between Bill Gates and Paul Allen, the visionaries behind Microsoft; Paul McCartney and John Lennon, the creative geniuses of the Beatles; Kevin Systrom and Mike Krieger, the innovative minds behind Instagram; and Mick Jagger and Keith Richards, the dynamic duo of the Rolling Stones, among many others. These friendships have not only revolutionized the way we work but also altered the perception we hold of ourselves.

Beyond these globally influential partnerships, there exist countless powerful, yet untold friendships that may not have made a global impact but have nonetheless significantly transformed our local communities and social environments. These relationships have influenced how we live our daily lives, shaping the various products and services we use and rely on. These friendships, though less renowned, are equally important in their capacity to effect change and inspire progress.

> **"Walking with a friend in the dark is better than walking alone in the light."**
>
> Helen Keller[5]

Friendship holds the potential to either ascend to extraordinary heights or descend into destructive depths, with the power to alter the course of world history. However, for the majority of us, friendships are woven into the fabric of our daily lives; collectively, they possess the capacity to shift societal consciousness.

Three Magic Words: Know, Like, and Trust

The bedrock of every adult friendship is built on this triad: know, like, and trust. Absence of any of these elements can prevent the formation of a genuine friendship, or worse, lead to the development of a false or deceptive friendship.

For instance, you might be acquainted with someone but not necessarily fond of them. Alternatively, you could trust someone without truly knowing them, such as a news commentator. Or you might admire someone, like an actor, without personally knowing them.

These three magic words collectively construct the level of respect you hold for an individual. This respect is the foundation upon which genuine friendships and business are built, nurtured, and expanded.

> **"All things being equal, people will do business with and refer business to those people they know, like and trust."**
>
> Bob Burg[6]

During our childhood, the bonds we formed were often influenced by the contents of our lunchboxes. For me, the kid with Twinkies or a bag of Frito's was an instant friend. Indeed, my youthful alliances could be swayed by the allure of a Twinkie or a Ding-Dong! It's a shame that we all had to mature and leave such simple negotiations behind. If only the complexities of life and the world could be resolved with the exchange of a Twinkie, things would be so much simpler!

Our childhood friends marked our initial foray into the world of friendships, serving as our first taste of autonomy in making choices without the constant supervision of our parents. During our formative years, we began to shape our "know and like" preferences, gravitating toward peers who we found interesting or appealing. Perhaps it was the child who always had an extra Ding Dong in their lunchbox, or the one who excelled at dodgeball.

These simple criteria formed the foundation of our early friendships.

The *know* and *like* factors served as the gateway to childhood camaraderie. However, the *trust* factor, which is a primary prerequisite in adult relationships, was not initially as crucial in our juvenile friendships. It was only later, perhaps during our high school years, after experiencing the sting of betrayal from a friend, that we came to understand the paramount importance of trust in any close-knit relationship.

> **"The worst part about betrayal is that it never comes from your enemies."**
>
> Anonymous

After experiencing a few emotional wounds in our early adulthood, we unconsciously began to categorize our friends into concentric circles, forming what we can call a friendship circle.

Your Friendship Circle

The individuals we trust the most, those we genuinely know and like, are placed in the first circle, also known as the *inner circle*. This circle may only contain a handful of friends, but these are the ones we value the most. They are our confidants, the ones we trust with our deepest thoughts and ideas, and they reciprocate this trust by sharing their own with us.

The second tier in the friendship hierarchy is *casual friends*. These are individuals you are familiar with and have a fondness for, but your trust in them is somewhat limited. You interact with these people occasionally, but not on a consistent basis.

The third tier is acquaintances. These are individuals you recognize and perhaps have a liking for, but your trust in them is minimal or nonexistent.

The fourth tier is *public and community*. These are individuals you are aware of, but not on a personal level. You're liking for them may be superficial, based on what you've read or seen about them, but your trust in them is either very limited or completely absent.

> **"Surround yourself with only people who are going to lift you higher."**
>
> Oprah Winfrey[7]

As you transition from your inner circle toward the public and community spheres, the know, like, and trust elements become increasingly less specific and less refined. While trust is the predominant factor within the inner circle, its significance diminishes as you extend your reach toward the outer circle of public and community.

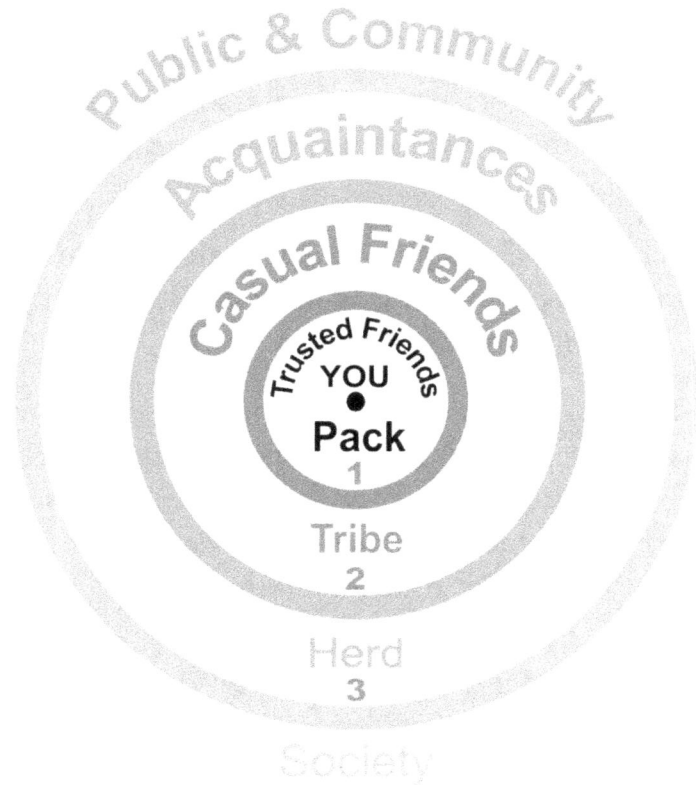

Friendship Circle

- **Inner Circle: Trusted Friends**
  Strong Know, Strong Like, Strong Trust
- **Second Circle: Casual Friends**
  Know, Like, Limited Trust
- **Third Circle: Acquaintances**
  Know, Maybe Like, Little to No Trust
- **Fourth Circle: Public & Community**
  Maybe Know, Maybe Like, No Trust

Are YOU Going Around in Circles?

The inner circle represents our intimate group of individuals with whom we interact and associate on a daily basis. Drawing parallels from the animal kingdom, this group serves as our support system, providing companionship, protection, and a sense of belonging. Rooted in our primal instincts, humans are inherently social creatures, akin to pack animals, and our inner circle comprises our most trusted confidants.

While we may engage with various social circles, including casual friends or larger groups of acquaintances, we invariably find ourselves drawn back to our inner circle, our trusted friends - our pack. This group forms the bedrock of our support network and fosters a deep sense of connectivity.

How crucial is your *pack* and your second circle of friends? As the renowned Jim Rohn stated, "You are the average of the five people you spend the most time with."[8] Are these two inner friendship circles nurturing the best version of you? If not, it might be time to reassess these relationships.

> *"My best friend is the one who brings out the best in me."*
>
> Henry Ford[9]

It's more beneficial to let go and soar rather than clutch onto an anchor and sink. Your time is too precious to waste on individuals who don't value it and who might derail your dreams. Take the time to declutter your inner circle and your second circle, stand firm, remain resilient, and safeguard yourself from the people you let into your life. Remember, this is your life journey, and your inner circles are by invite only! Not everyone is meant to accompany you, so be discerning when choosing your pack of travel companions.

You Are the Center DOT!

At the heart of the friendship circle lies the *dot*. This little dot is *you*. You should be the most important friend you know, like, and trust in the friendship circle. Paradoxically, as adults, we often find it challenging to embrace self-love, to appreciate our unique nature, and to honor the person we were divinely created to be.

If you cannot genuinely extend grace to yourself and allow room for personal growth, it becomes a daunting task to demonstrate authentic love and friendship to others. Therefore, in the friendship circle, it is essential to recognize and celebrate your value, for it is the foundation upon which all other relationships are built.

The dot holds paramount significance in the friendship circle as it represents the foundation of your friendships, the depths of your relationships, and your outlook on life. It all begins with you.

Your persistent negative thoughts can seep into your persona, influencing your reactions to your environment, people, and various situations. To cultivate a robust friendship circle, it's essential to embrace who you are, acknowledging your strengths, talents, and weaknesses. Self-acceptance is the first step toward becoming your own best friend. I often say, "To expand your horizons, look inward to grow outward."

> *"The true measure of a man is not how he behaves in moments of comfort and convenience but how he stands at times of controversy and challenges."*
>
> Martin Luther King Jr.[10]

How do people perceive you through your personality and communication style? Are you seen as positive, inspiring, dull, or a Danny or Debi Downer? The foundation of your social circle begins with your mindset, which directly influences your energy and perceived demeanor and attitude. Transforming negative and pessimistic thoughts can be a daunting task, but it is achievable with consistent practice, patience, and self-grace. The idea is to tamp down on the negative and ramp up the positive!

Start and End Your Day with Success

As depicted in chapter 1, altering your mindset can be a challenging task. However, it is an essential first step in transforming a negative daily thought pattern or the direction for your purpose. The majority of successful people incorporate two straightforward steps into their daily routine. While not difficult, these steps require discipline and consistency to create a positive habit every day for your well-being and to cultivate your growth mindset.

This practice is as vital for your positive mental health as nourishment is for your physical health. You wouldn't eat rancid food, so don't consume toxic thoughts.

Success Step 1: Practice Gratitude

Begin your day with an attitude of gratitude! Imagine Gratitude Island as your personal virtual oasis of positive self-affirmation that you can visit every day. Before you plunge into the bustling stream of daily life, take a few minutes before getting out of bed and experience a gradual buildup of positivity by expressing gratitude for what you possess and your achievements, regardless of their size or significance.

This would be like a coach delivering an inspiring pep talk to the team before they step onto the field. Yet we often leap out of bed, turn on the coffee maker, switch on the news, and dive headfirst into life's challenges without taking a breather from the previous day's stress, expecting to conquer the day ahead. Do you idle the car before sticking it in gear, or turn it on and step on the gas and jolt the engine?

Take a moment to honor yourself, to acknowledge the grace and space you need for your divine talents and skills to truly flourish. This is your sacred sanctuary, a time to connect with your inner mentor before stepping onto the playing field of life each day.

> *"Gratitude is the healthiest of all human emotions. The more you express gratitude for what you have, the more likely you will have even more to express gratitude for."*
>
> Zig Ziglar[11]

Allow yourself to feel appreciated, to bask in the glow of your own achievements, and to nurture the unique gifts bestowed upon you. Express gratitude and thankfulness for all that you possess, no matter how small or insignificant it may be.

As an example, I give thanks when the streetlight turns green as I approach the intersection because I don't have to stop! Saying thanks to the daily small stuff keeps positivity at the forefront of your brain!

Envision waking up each day, brimming with positivity about your life, even before you step onto the battlefield. There is no life hurdle that you can't master. In essence, gear yourself up for success by nurturing and fostering your growth mindset.

Before your feet even touch the bedroom floor each morning, dedicate ten to twenty minutes to expressing gratitude for all that you have. This could be as simple as appreciating your life, your family, positive friendships, a triumph from the previous day, or your financial stability. Cultivate humility and positivity in your thoughts. Refrain from allowing any negative thoughts to intrude. This is your sacred time to express gratitude for your victories in the universe and to God.

Recognize that in the vast cosmos, there is only one unique you. How extraordinary you are! Each one of us is equally special. When you view life from this perspective, no obstacle is too great to overcome, not even death, which is simply a transition into a new existence. The first twenty minutes of your day serve as a sanctuary of appreciation, empowering you to face the day with confidence, vitality, and vigor.

In the span of twenty minutes, I express my gratitude for all the fundamental necessities of life, the triumphs of the previous day, and the talents that have been bestowed upon me. I permit myself to indulge in positive affirmations, like a coach rallying his team during a match. As the minutes wind down, I say a prayer of appreciation. For you, it could be a similar prayer or an affirmation of your distinctive role in the cosmos and gratitude for your life. Here is my daily prayer:

In my journey today, Father God, please give me wisdom to understand, fortitude to endure, and inspiration to motivate. Allow me to be with others who will not waste my time, the time you gave me to find my purpose and direction for an abundant life.

Let me raise the value of my time to become valuable to others so I may help them find their life purpose. Let me focus on today while You plan my path tomorrow.

Thank you, Father God, for my life, for the gifts in my life, and for guiding me through my day and all the days of my life. In the name of my Savior, Jesus Christ, Amen.

> **"Be true to yourself, help others, make each day your masterpiece, make friendship a fine art, drink deeply from good books, especially the Bible, build a shelter against a rainy day, give thanks for your blessings and pray for guidance every day."**
>
> John Wooden[12]

By grounding your mind at the start of each day and embracing humility through gratitude, you equip yourself to tackle life's challenges and contribute meaningfully to others. As you practice this daily habit you'll notice a significant improvement in your problem-solving skills and productivity, fueled by positive energy and diminished daily anxieties. When you concentrate on your strengths, your perceived weaknesses become less dominate.

> **"If you focus on what you lack, you lose what you have. If you focus on what you have, you gain what you lack."**
>
> Dr. Benjamin Hardy[13]

Practicing gratitude daily is a simple yet transformative habit that can significantly alter your perspective on life and improve how you handle problems and challenges. In our world today, we are constantly bombarded with negativity through daily news broadcasts, reality TV shows, global events, and associations within our social circles.

This relentless exposure to negativity makes it challenging to adopt an attitude of gratitude and positivity. It's all too easy to succumb to the pervasive gloom and doom, which is precisely why dedicating the first few minutes of each day to acknowledge and appreciate your blessings is essential.

Whether through prayer or silent contemplation, these few minutes of gratitude are crucial for cultivating a growth mindset, boosting self-confidence, and fostering an unstoppable, positive outlook on life. By making this practice a daily morning habit, you arm yourself with the resilience and confidence needed to navigate a world often filled with negativity, ultimately transforming your life perspective to a positive force.

> *"Give yourself a gift of five minutes of contemplation in awe of everything you see around you. Go outside and turn your attention to the many miracles around you. This five-minute-a-day regimen of appreciation and gratitude will help you to focus your life in awe."*
>
> Wayne Dyer[14]

By cultivating a daily habit of gratitude, appreciating not only your life's achievements but also the simple, everyday occurrences, like the green light at the intersection, you will unlock a wealth of positive emotions.

This practice can significantly reduce emotional stress, improve your sleep quality, and bolster your immune system. The advantages of practicing self-gratitude every day surpass any supplement or vitamin you could possibly consume. The best part? It's absolutely free!

> **"Be thankful for everything that happens in your life... it's all an experience."**
>
> Roy T. Bennett[15]

Success Step 2: Read, Read, Read!

Conclude your day with personal development reading. As you wind down your day and prepare for sleep, immerse yourself in ten to fifteen pages of a nonfiction book focused on personal development. This simple habit, when practiced daily, equates to absorbing the wisdom of over twelve books in a year!

The world of personal development literature is vast, with renowned authors such as John Maxwell (*The 15 Invaluable Laws of Growth*), Darren Hardy (*The Compound Effect*), and Stephen Covey (*The 7 Habits of Highly Effective People*) offering invaluable insights. Reading is the shortcut to wisdom.

Every successful growth mindset person reads books to expand their knowledge, awareness, and growth. They recognize the necessity of infusing their minds with positive and empowering knowledge to expand their consciousness, to seep into their subconscious.

Simply, you are reprogramming your cerebral hard drive. Developing a reading habit from self-development authors and mentors can tap their wisdom and insights as you transition from a leaning fixed mindset to a leaning growth mindset with positivity and motivational submersion.

Making a daily habit of reading is one of the most efficient strategies to foster personal development throughout your life journey. Regrettably, a significant number of people do not read, which often results in them being stuck in life's struggles, living life informationally challenged, nurturing benign ignorance, and solving problems by assumptions.

> *"What I know for sure is that reading opens you up, it exposes you and gives you access to anything your mind can hold. What I love most about reading, it gives you the ability to reach higher ground."*
>
> Oprah Winfrey[16]

Further, limiting your knowledge base and awareness can create an autopilot, quick-fix mentality, which can be likened to a "duct-tape" approach to life. This head-in-the-sand attitude can encompass profound cultural and social voids to impede personal growth and severely curtail one's comprehension of both self and the broader world. Benign ignorance creates assumptions, and assumptions kill opportunity. This is why many remain stuck in life without clarity of purpose. You were born not just to "fit in", but to "stand-out."

Without the rich tapestry of knowledge, empathy, and perspective that books provide, people can find themselves intellectually stagnant, emotionally shallow, socially isolated, and culturally diminished. This multifaceted deprivation stifles not only personal development but also hampers one's ability to develop a significant and meaningful friendship circle to successfully network with people.

> *"The more that you read, the more things you will know. The more that you learn, the more places you'll go."*
>
> Dr. Seuss[17]

The common denominator of many successful people in expanding their knowledge base is the daily habit of reading books. Notable people like Mark Cuban, Elon Musk, Oprah Winfrey, Bill Gates, and many corporate CEOs will read two to four books a month, which is around fifty books a year! It is one of the cheapest ways to learn, build and support a growth mindset.

Self-Action Creates Traction!

If you want what success can give you, then you need to do what success does. Join a book club, and make reading more than a habit but a way of life for your personal growth and better friendships in Finding JOY!

> *"You must be willing to do things today others won't do, in order to have the things tomorrow others won't have."*
>
> Les Brown[18]

By consistently applying Success Step 1 every morning and Success Step 2 every evening, you will profoundly transform your dot perspective. This will prompt you to re-evaluate your existing relationships and friendships, as well as your overall outlook on life. As you move forward in your quest for Finding JOY, you will discover a more fulfilling and enriched life starting from day one by simply incorporating daily gratitude and consistent reading.

Combat Negative Thinking

Negative thoughts can easily affect our friendship circle and how we associate with others. Negative thinking can act as a powerful undertow, hindering your forward momentum and diminishing your happiness. They can be likened to relentless ocean waves, constantly knocking you down just as you're trying to stand while sapping your strength with each successive wave.

> *"You cannot have a positive life and a negative mind."*
>
> Dr. Joyce Meyers[19]

Negative thinking is a subtle form of self-sabotage, supporting a fixed mindset. By focusing on what could go wrong, we limit our potential and cloud our vision of what could go right.

Persistent negativity translates into internal stress, which accumulates like rust over time. This not only alters your personality but impacts your health, exacerbating disease processes and potentially shortening your lifespan. On the flip side, positive, optimistic individuals tend to live up to a decade longer! Therefore, it's worth questioning the value of harboring negative thoughts, especially when they could potentially lead to illness and a reduced lifespan.

> *"The biggest problem any of us ever face is our own negative thinking."*
>
> Robert Schuller[20]

Negativity Suffocates Creativity

Regrettably, the majority of us tend to be our own harshest critics, perpetually engaging in negative self-dialogue. If you identify with this tendency, raise your hand! The reality is, most of us should be raising our hands, as statistics reveal this is a common human trait.

National surveys indicate that 48 percent of the general population has a history of a psychiatric disorder, with anxiety disorders and depression leading the list.[21] The connection between negative thought and depressive behavior including anxieties disorders are well founded.

As example, a study published in BMC Psychiatry investigated the associations between negative cognitions, emotional regulation, and depression. The research indicated that negative thought patterns are closely linked to depressive symptoms, and that cognitive-behavioral therapy (CBT) can be effective in addressing these issues by helping individuals reframe their negative thoughts."[22]

Today our negative thought patterns are omnipresent due to our personal situations, associations, news events, social media and what we mentally allow our brains to absorb. It's amazing there is any room left for positive thought. For instance, a 2019 Psychology Today article mentions, *"80 percent of our thoughts are negative, and 95 percent repetitive"*[23] is alarming.

If this is true, and there is active conjecture on the exact percentage, this could be a big clue as to why Finding JOY is elusive for many people. A positive mental outlook is imperative to develop in your journey and associations to find your creativity, purpose, value and ultimately your freedom.

A 2020 study from Queen's University revealed that an average individual experiences approximately 6,200 thoughts on a daily basis.[24] These thoughts from the study seem to represent a final thought from "thought worms" that form the process to a final thought and does not include repetitive thoughts for an approximate total of 6,200 thoughts per day.

As the Psychology Today article suggests if you apply 80 percent of daily thoughts to negativity then the average individual will experience approximately 4,960 negative thoughts per day! Most of these thoughts are benign such as, *I don't like peas* versus a negative life self-identity thought such as, *I'm not good enough*. These types of negative thoughts are life-changing, stall our direction and influence our associations. It does not take many negative thoughts to form your life journey.

Understand these are theoretical numbers and percentages and there is much research and debate on the number of daily thoughts a person may experience, negative or positive. Suffice to say, with all this research we have countless thoughts every day, and most of them seem tend to lean negative. This may be the answer to why depression and mental disorders are on the rise absorbing our productive time and stealing our creativity.

We've all encountered individuals who constantly spew negativity, engage in gossip, and incessantly complain about various issues and circumstances. Recall the sensation you experience during such conversations. Most likely you felt an overwhelming desire to escape. You could feel your mental energy being drained away.

Negative energy operates much like an airborne disease, infecting a host and proliferating within. Your instinctive response is to distance yourself and safeguard your energy flow, your chakras, and your spirit from this toxic contagion.

Imagine if your mind is constantly bombarded with negative thoughts from within and from others, engaging in a relentless "I'm not good enough" dialogue. This "I can't" mentality will be graffitied in your consciousness until you actively clean it up.

The "I Can!" Antidote

The challenge here is that you can't escape from your own mind, but you do have the power to transform this internal dialogue into a more empowering "I can!" narrative. Further, what would your friendship circle look like if you were a negative influence? You most likely will have a very limited sphere of friends and associations.

> *"You are the only problem you will ever have, and you are the only solution."*
>
> Bob Proctor[25]

Picture this, What if you could slash your negative thoughts by half to 40 percent and fill your mind with 60 percent positive, productive, and empowering thoughts of growth and self-belief? How transformative would that be for your life? Consider the fears you could conquer, the doubts you could dispel, the blame you could relinquish and throw in your mental trash can.

Imagine the new, positive-minded friends you could attract into your life. The shift in your mindset could indeed open up a world of possibilities and a better quality of friendships.

> *"You're going to go through tough times; that's life. But I say, 'Nothing happens to you, it happens for you.' See the positive in negative events."*
>
> Joel Osteen[26]

Rather than succumbing to the limitations of your rigid thoughts, you can triumph over them by nurturing your growth mindset. By cultivating a daily habit of 60 percent positive thoughts, you can significantly transform your life journey.

This shift in mindset can boost your self-esteem, confidence, and even enhance your relationships. It all stems from the empowering "I can" antidote. Embrace this approach by reading empowering books and engaging in personal development mentorship and you'll become your own BFF!

Throughout your life's journey, companions within your social and familial circles may come and go, but the centered dot, your inner self, will remain a constant companion. As you nurture and cultivate this inner friend, fostering a mindset of positivity that exceeds 60 percent, you will naturally attract individuals who share your positive outlook and mindset. They will be drawn to your tribe.

To expand your horizons and grow, it's essential to invite introspection and strive to embody the qualities you desire in your tribe. As you evolve and transform, so will your tribe, reflecting the new you and your new direction.

If the individuals in your inner-circle pack are resistant to change as you evolve, it's perfectly acceptable to bid them farewell with good wishes. As you transition from a leaning fixed mindset to a leaning growth-oriented one, you may notice a growing disparity between you and your existing friends.

> *"You are who you are and what you are because of what has gone into your mind. You can change who you are and what you are by changing what goes into your mind."*
>
> Zig Ziglar[27]

This is a common occurrence, as many people are deeply entrenched in their present struggles and concerns, often neglecting the prospect of future growth. This is one of the reasons why reality TV shows, which often depict people in a constant state of negativity and struggle, are so popular. Change is a daunting challenge that many are reluctant to undertake because sitting on life's couch with the remote is more comfortable.

Are You Comfortably Numb?

The fear of the unknown outweighs the fear of change. While most people aspire for a better life, only a handful are willing to put in the daily effort and take the necessary actions to achieve it. It's far more convenient to let life unfold, keeping us busy and distracted, than to actively be the craftsman of our lives and build our future self.

Paradoxically, the so-called comfort zone is often not comfortable at all. However, many individuals gravitate toward it not because it offers genuine comfort, but because the familiarity of struggle is less daunting than the unknown journey of change.

> *"I want to challenge you today to get out of your comfort zone. You have so much incredible potential on the inside. God has put gifts and talents in you that you probably don't know anything about."*
>
> Joel Osteen[28]

By integrating the principles outlined in this book, you will witness a significant transformation in your friendship circle and tribe within a few years. The nature of your friendships can either tether you to a life of struggle or propel you toward a more fulfilling, joyful existence.

A wholesome friendship nurtures your growth, adds value to your life, and acts as a supportive cheerleader, celebrating your well-being and life's triumphs. A significant question to pose to your social circle and your center dot is this: "Are you a supportive ally propelling me toward success? Or are you a detractor diverting me from a life of abundance?" As Jim Rohn stated, "You are the average of the five people you spend the most time with."[29]

The friendships you cultivate significantly shape the person you evolve into. To dive deeper, if your center dot does not represent your closest confidant, your BFF, then your negative self-dialogue will mirror the type of friends you draw into your life and your identity.

> **"Because of the way your brain will unconsciously duplicate neural activity of the person you're with, anyone you spend your time with can imprint your brain with their programs. And neither of you will know it is."**
>
> Dr. Shad Helmstetter[30]

The significance of the friendships you cultivate cannot be overstated. They are absolutely crucial for a joyful and abundant life. These relationships play a pivotal role in your personal journey, aiding you in discovering true happiness and fulfillment in the Journey Of You.

> **"A man's friendships are one of the best measures of his worth."**
>
> Charles Darwin[31]

What does your friendship circle and your pack say about your identity and brand?

Journey Rest Stop 5

1) Who are the cherished companions in your circle of friends, and how do they enrich your life? What significance do you attribute to their presence in your life?

2) Provide a detailed description of your tribe and identify the shared interests that bind you together? How does your tribe distinguish itself from your herd?

3) Provide a description of your center dot companion. What are the aspects that you find appealing? What are the less attractive qualities? How does your center dot companion talk to you?

Journey Thought

"A true friend is a farmer who can cultivate the best harvest in you."

Ted Kopecko[32]

www.FindingJOY.us

Chapter 6

Journey of Identity

I'm Sorry... Who Are You?

*The privilege of a lifetime is to become
who you truly are.*

Carl Jung[1]

In this chapter, we will set sail on a captivating voyage of self-discovery and identity realization, a journey that is integral to achieving success in both personal and professional spheres. We will dive deep into the complex process of unearthing one's authentic self, emphasizing the profound impact this journey has on the quest for genuine happiness and fulfillment.

> *"You want to present yourself physically in a manner that is consistent with the new winning image that you are developing. Something as simple as how you dress, how you walk, and how you project yourself, sends a very powerful message to your subconscious mind. It also sends a strong message to everyone in your external world."*
>
> Sandra Gallagher[2]

We will traverse the psychological, social, and cultural landscapes of identity, highlighting how a profound comprehension and acceptance of one's identity can lay the foundation for a more gratifying and prosperous life.

This exploration will illuminate the intricate interplay between self-discovery and success, providing a roadmap for those seeking to navigate their own path toward self-realization, personal growth, and a winning image.

Identity is a path that leads us to the core of who we are, to the essence of our being. It is a journey that requires courage, honesty, and a willingness to explore the depths of our being. Unfortunately, many of us do not think about our identity; we simply mold into who we become based on our surroundings and the path of least resistance.

Identity is not something that we innately possess; we grow into it through our life experiences. It is not a static or an unchanging entity. Rather, it is a dynamic, evolving construct that is shaped by our experiences, our relationships, our values, and our dreams or lack of them. Identity reflects our innermost thoughts, feelings, and desires. It is the lens through which we view the world and the blueprint that guides our actions.

> *"Take the pains required to become what you want to become, or you might end up becoming something you'd rather not be."*
>
> Donald J. Trump[3]

Simply put, you either accept the identity you mold into from your environment, which most people do, or you design the identity of the person you want to become. You either wear the hand-me-down identity life gives you, or you take the effort, throw away those tattered clothes, and go to the Armani store and pick out a beautifully crafted suit - a new you to show the world.

Your identity is intrinsically linked to the magnitude of your friendship circle. Present me with an individual possessing a grand, larger-than-life identity, and I will show you a person who is at the center of an extensive network of relationships.

> *"When I let go of what I am, I become what I might be."*
>
> Lao Tzu[4]

Finding our identity is not about fitting into a pre-defined box or conforming to societal expectations. It is about discovering our unique purpose and value and embracing our individuality. It is about breaking free from the chains of conformity and daring to be ourselves in all of our glorious, messy, and beautiful complexity.

> *"God has put greatness in you. He's called you to stand out, to be a difference maker, to take your family to a new level. You're going to have to be thick-skinned and determined to not waste your time trying to win people over who are not happy when you succeed. Just stay focused on what God has called you to do."*
>
> Joel Osteen[5]

The journey of identity is not a destination; it is a continuous process of self-discovery and self-expression. It is a journey that challenges us to question, to reflect, to grow. It is a journey that invites us to shed our masks, to reveal our true selves, refine our God-given talents, and to step into our power.

In the Journey of Identity, we find not only ourselves but also our journey, our JOY. For it is in the process of discovering who we are that we uncover our deepest passions, our greatest strengths, and our most profound sense of purpose. And it's in the pursuit of these passions, the expression of these strengths, and the fulfillment of this purpose that we find our JOY as we paint the picture of our identity whether we are painting a Rembrandt or a paint-by-number. Each day in our lives represents another vibrant stroke of our paintbrush, meticulously crafting our unique identity on the canvas of our existence.

> *"If you are always trying to be normal, you will never know how amazing you can be."*
>
> Maya Angelou[6]

If your attitude is the vibrant, eye-catching graphic design that embellishes your virtual business card, then your identity is the tangible business card you hand to the world. Our identity is comparable to the attire we choose to wear each day, a visual representation of ourselves that we offer to the world. It is the physical embodiment of our unique personalities, shaping the world's perception of us. It serves as our passport, dictating how the world receives us and engages with us.

What story does your daily attire tell the world? What narrative are you broadcasting to the world? In a different perspective, the Journey of Identity is the evolving painting you are creating of yourself over time. It is the acknowledgment of the person you are or are becoming. Do people recognize you as a van Gogh, a Rembrandt, or a da Vinci? Or are you merely another paint-by-number painting in a box at a garage sale?

Your identity is a significant part of the illuminating journey of self-discovery in Finding JOY. It's not just about who you are; it's about who you aspire to be and how you choose to present your journey to the world.

> **"Identity in the form of continuity of personality is an extremely important characteristic of the individual."**
>
> Kenneth L. Pike[7]

The Journey of Serena Williams

In the world of sports, few figures have crafted an identity as distinct and recognizable as Serena Williams. From her early days on the tennis court, Serena's attitude was clear. She was a fierce competitor, unafraid to challenge the status quo and break barriers.

Her overt attitude and vibrant personality was like a graphic design on a business card, immediately catching the eye and leaving a lasting impression. But it was her identity, the business card she gave to the world, that truly set her apart.

Serena's attire on the court was a tangible manifestation of her unique personality. From her iconic catsuit at the 2002 US Open to her tutu at the 2018 French Open, Serena's outfits were more than just clothes. Her outfits were a statement, a narrative of her journey of identity. They told the world that she was not just another player on the court, but a trailblazer, a force to be reckoned with.

Over time, Serena's identity evolved, painting a picture of a person who was not only a world-class athlete, but also a devoted mother, a successful entrepreneur, and a passionate advocate for women's rights. She was no longer just a van Gogh or a Rembrandt but a masterpiece in her own right. Her journey of identity was a testament to the power of self-discovery, and it played a pivotal role in her quest in Finding JOY, both on and off the court.

> *"I've grown most not from victories, but setbacks. If winning is God's reward, then losing is how He teaches us."*
>
> Serena Williams[8]

Serena's voyage of self-discovery is intricately woven with a growth mindset that views her obstacles not as roadblocks but as stepping stones toward her triumphs, all the while recognizing her humility in the face of a greater presence.

Success often cultivates humility in individuals, fostering a sense of gratitude for their humble beginnings and the progress they've made in their journey. Just like Serena, it's essential to express gratitude for your victories as well as your setbacks. Indeed, even your setbacks are crucial as they establish the groundwork for your journey toward success.

Your Identity Journey Is Waiting

Let's define the concept of identity. It's a very amalgamous word, a multifaceted term of YOU. It encapsulates every aspect of your being, ranging from your choice of attire to your manner of speech, how you talk and what you hold deep in your heart.

An individual's identity is a intricate tapestry woven from a person's unique characteristics, deeply held beliefs, cherished values, life experiences, affiliations (your friendship circle), and characteristics that collectively shape your persona.

It is a multifaceted concept that not only encapsulates the distinctive traits that set us apart from the crowd but also includes the social connections that tie us to larger groups or communities, our circle of friends that define our tribe and herds. This intricate blend of personal uniqueness and social "belongingness" forms the essence of who we are as individuals and defines the persona we project to the world.

Identity is a composition of three basic interwoven human components. One is your *brand*, which is your presentation and how the world perceives you. Two is your value, which is your unique set of skills and what you contribute to the world. Three is your quality, which is the trust you inspire and the reliability of your word. These three elements of brand, value, and quality form the basis on which we instinctively evaluate an individual's identity, 1) who they are within our friendship circles, 2) determining who we gravitate toward and 3) who we maintain a distance from.

> *"Your identity is like a fingerprint; it is unique to you, and it leaves an impression on everything you do."*
>
> Oscar Auliq-Ice[9]

As humans, we naturally form perceptions about individuals who step into our physical surroundings or come within our line of sight. Yes, we all profile; it's human nature, and this trait is deeply rooted in many animals.

In a study completed by the Social Cognition Center Cologne at the University of Cologne, researchers said, "In summary, we believe that it is worthwhile to explore the mechanisms supporting social comparison processes further, as there is evidence from a variety of taxa that animals are able to compare themselves to others to a certain degree."[10]

Profiling is deeply ingrained in our DNA, serving as a primal survival mechanism akin to the fight-or-flight response observed in animals. In the wild, this instinct might prompt the question, "Are you a predator that will eat me?" In the human world, this instinctual profiling translates into a more complex question: "Based on my perception of your identity, are you a threat to my safety?" Our identity is perpetually assessed each time we interact with the world, be it at our workplace, at social gatherings, through our affiliations, on social media platforms, or any instance where we are visible to others.

How vital is your outward identity? It holds supreme significance in the trajectory of your life. To encapsulate it, your identity essentially serves as your personal brand that you present to the world. So, are you akin to a box of Kellogg's Frosted Flakes, or are you more of a generic store brand? Do you project an intimidating, formidable presence, or do you exude a warm, welcoming aura to those around you? How are you cultivating and projecting your personal brand?

> *"Brand is just a perception, and perception will match reality over time. Sometimes it will be ahead, other times it will be behind. But brand is simply a collective impression some have about a product."*
> Elon Musk[11]

The Identity Impact of Michael Jordan on Nike

In the world of sports, the importance of identity or personal brand is clearly illustrated by the story of basketball legend, Michael Jordan. Jordan's identity, both on and off the court, was meticulously crafted and managed. His exceptional skills, competitive spirit, and charismatic personality made him a beloved figure in the sports world. However, it was his identity as a hardworking, dedicated, and humble individual that truly set him apart.

This identity was not only reflected in his game but also in his endorsements, public appearances, and philanthropic activities. In 1984, Nike, a then-struggling shoe company, signed a deal with Jordan, launching the Air Jordan brand. The success of this brand was largely due to Jordan's identity.

His reputation for excellence and determination resonated with consumers, making Air Jordan one of the most successful and enduring sports brands.

> *"I hope the millions of people I've touched have the optimism and desire to share their goals and hard work and persevere with a positive attitude."*
> Michael Jordan[12]

Even after his retirement, Jordan's identity continues to influence and inspire millions around the world. His story underscores the power of identity and how it can shape not only our personal journey and our value but also the world around us.

In the digital age, the importance of identity is further amplified. With the advent of social media, our identities are constantly on display and scrutinized by others. Just like Jordan, we have the opportunity to shape our personal brand. Whether it's through our work, our interactions with others, or our online presence, our identity plays a crucial role in how we are perceived and ultimately, in our success.

By the way, it takes years to build your brand identity and seconds to destroy it.

> *"It takes twenty years to build a reputation and five minutes to ruin it. If you think about that, you'll do things differently."*
>
> Warren Buffett[13]

The Journey of Lance Armstrong

Lance Armstrong is a perfect illustration of how years of brand building can be destroyed in seconds. Armstrong, a professional cyclist, built a strong brand identity over the years as a seven-time winner of the Tour de France, a cancer survivor, and the founder of the Livestrong Foundation.

His story was an inspiration to millions around the world, and his brand was synonymous with resilience, determination, and integrity. However, in 2012, the United States Anti-Doping Agency (USADA) released a report accusing Armstrong of using performance-enhancing drugs throughout his career.

Despite his initial denials, Armstrong eventually confessed to the allegations in a televised interview with Oprah Winfrey in 2013. In a matter of seconds, his confession shattered his carefully constructed brand identity. He was stripped of his Tour de France titles, lost lucrative endorsement deals, and his reputation was irreparably damaged. His Livestrong Foundation, once a beacon of hope for cancer survivors, suffered a significant blow as well.

This story serves as a stark reminder that while it takes years to build a brand identity, it can be destroyed in seconds by dishonest or questionable actions. Safeguard your asset brand. It is your unique signature on the global stage.

> *"You must expect great things of yourself before you can do them."*
>
> Michael Jordan[14]

Identity is the manifestation of your innermost self, vividly displayed on the world's stage. It is intrinsically linked to the level of respect and love you hold for yourself. If you truly honor your own value, it will be reflected in the persona you project to the world and the personal brand you advocate. This is because your identity is more than just a portrayal of you; it is a powerful testament to your self-esteem, self-love, inherent value, and the quality of you.

What is the masterpiece you are unveiling to the world? What is your unique *brand*, the *value* you possess, and the *quality* you present?

BRAND (know), VALUE (like), and QUALITY (trust)

Companies pour billions into marketing, promotional activities, and branding strategies with the primary goal of capturing your attention and convincing you to buy their products. These strategies are centered around three key elements: brand, value, and quality. The ultimate objective is to establish a potent brand image that, upon recognition of their logo or product name, instills in you a sense of trust and credibility, underpinned by perceived value and quality. These principles cultivate customer relationships, brand awareness and propels business expansion. These same principles apply to your life journey as you develop your brand, your value, and your quality.

YOUR BRAND

What You Show the World and How the World Knows You

Your brand acts as the enticing exterior of your product that you showcase to the world, while your identity's value and quality is the core substance of the product that is unveiled when the packaging is removed. Both brand and identity are intimately interwoven with your distinctive personality, mirroring your authentic self.

> *"You too are a brand. Whether you know it or not. Whether you like it or not."*
>
> Mark Ecko[15]

An individual's brand represents the physical image we project to the world. It encompasses how we are viewed by others, our unique characteristics, and introduces the values and quality we stand for. Just as corporations have brands that define their identity and reputation, individuals also have personal brands that shape their public image.

An Apple a Day

In the late 1990s, Apple Inc. was on the brink of bankruptcy. The company was struggling to compete with Microsoft, and its market share was dwindling. In 1997, Steve Jobs returned to Apple and initiated a radical change in the company's marketing strategy. He launched the "Think Different" campaign, a series of advertisements that celebrated the "crazy ones," the rebels, the troublemakers, the round pegs in the square holes. The campaign was a massive success, not only because it was different, but because it resonated with people. It made them feel special, unique, and part of a select group of individuals who dared to think differently.

Apple invested heavily in this marketing campaign, and it paid off. The company's sales skyrocketed, and its market share began to grow. The Think Different campaign was more than just a series of advertisements, it was a branding strategy that defined Apple's identity and set it apart from its competitors. It was a clear illustration of how businesses invest billions in marketing, promotion, and branding strategies to captivate your interest and persuade you to purchase their products.

Today, Apple is one of the most valuable companies in the world, and its brand is recognized and admired globally. The success of Apple's Think Different campaign underscores the power of effective marketing and branding strategies.

> *"A brand for a company is like a reputation for a person. You earn reputation by trying to do hard things well."*
>
> Jeff Bezos[16]

Regrettably, most individuals fail to apply or think about these basic marketing principles to their most valuable product: *themselves.* Have you ever considered how you present yourself to the world? What is your personal brand, and how does the identity you want to achieve align with it?

It is essential to understand and cultivate your personal brand, as it plays a crucial role in shaping your professional and personal success, which underscores the speed of your success and ultimate JOY. Just as Apple had a vested interest in promoting its products, we as individuals should also adopt a similar level of strategic marketing to project our personal brand to the world.

However, it all begins with self-awareness, introspection, and motivation in order to improve. Ask yourself, "Am I merely a generic version of the herd, or am I actively shaping my unique brand to market my identity to the world?"

Hey! Get a Haircut!

An individual's personal brand is a harmonious fusion of their physical appearance and intrinsic personality traits. If appearance is akin to the iconic cover of The Beatles' *Abbey Road* album, then the music etched into the grooves of the vinyl record within represents personality. Appearance and personality are crucial components of a person's brand that daily showcases their unique, colorful album cover to the world.

> *"All of us need to understand the importance of branding. We are CEOs of our own companies: Me Inc. To be in business today, our most important job is to be head marketer for the brand called YOU."*
>
> Tom Peters[17]

Your appearance and personality serve as the external manifestation of your unique brand, essentially acting as the album cover that you proudly present to the world. Your total physical appearance, encompassing your style and demeanor, is a crucial aspect of personal branding. It is the distinguishing factor that sets your brand of corn flakes apart from the generic version.

More specifically, it's the way you dress, the style of your hair, and whether you have tattoos or piercings. These elements collectively form the physical image you project to the world. Remember, everyone is observing your packaging and making decisions based on it - whether or not they want to purchase your brand of corn flakes.

Your external presentation, or packaging, significantly influences the world's perception of your character and attention to detail. Fair or not, human nature is inherently programmed to form judgments based on what it sees and reacts to, according to those perceptions and experiences.

> *"Everyone has a personal brand... by design or by default."*
>
> Lida Citroen[18]

If your personal appearance aligns with your professional role or lifestyle, it can significantly enhance the world's perception of your personal brand. For instance, renowned rock stars such as David Bowie, Mick Jagger, and Ozzy Osbourne are known for their trend-setting styles and flamboyant personalities, which are integral parts of their brand packaging as rock stars. On the other hand, individuals like Dr. Ben Carson, a brain surgeon, TV personality, and politician adopt a more conservative presentation to mirror their professional branding.

To put it differently, imagine a scenario where two distinct brand identities intersect. Suppose your newly appointed brain surgeon greets you, sporting a vibrant purple-spiked mohawk, a nose piercing, and a teardrop tattoo. What would your immediate internal response be? Seriously, what would your thoughts and reactions be at that moment, particularly if you don't sport a teardrop tattoo?

We all form judgments based on our perceived learned behaviors, which are influenced by our understanding of reality. Whether right or wrong, your initial presentation significantly influences another person's first impression of you. Your unique piece of art. This first impression sets the tone for their initial reaction, determining whether they choose to purchase the product you are selling or opt for another.

> *"The aim of art is to represent not the outward appearance of things, but their inward significance."*
>
> Aristotle[19]

So how important is your appearance to your package? Well, it depends if you feel your outward appearance will move you forward or create self-inflected life hurdles to get over. In the world of politics, appearance often plays a significant role in shaping public perception.

The Great Debate

A classic example of public perception is the first televised presidential debate in US history between Richard Nixon and John F. Kennedy in 1960. Nixon, who had recently been hospitalized, appeared pale, underweight, and had a five o'clock shadow, while Kennedy looked tanned, fit, and confident. Those who listened to the debate on the radio thought Nixon had won, but the majority of those who watched it on television believed Kennedy was the clear winner. The debate marked a turning point in the campaign, and Kennedy went on to win the presidential election.

The Growth Journey of John C. Maxwell

Another great example of the importance of identity is found in John C. Maxwell, a distinguished authority on leadership, an acclaimed author, and a captivating speaker. Maxwell has consistently underscored the significance of cultivating a successful identity. He asserts that our identity transcends our actions and is fundamentally about our essence, our unique brand. This tenet is vividly exemplified in Maxwell's own life journey and professional trajectory.

Born in 1947 in Garden City, Michigan, Maxwell did not hail from a lineage of authors or global speakers. However, he was deeply passionate about personal growth and the tenets of leadership. With unwavering determination, he pursued this passion, securing a master's degree in divinity and a doctorate in ministry. He served as a pastor for several years before transitioning into a career as a leadership consultant, expert, and speaker.

Despite his remarkable achievements, Maxwell never lost sight of his authentic identity, his value, his appearance, and his brand. He understood that he was more than just a pastor, author, and speaker. He was a leader, fervently committed to fostering growth, value, and success in others. This identity as a leader has been the bedrock of his success, steering his career decisions, molding his message, and impacting his relationships.

Maxwell's larger-than-life identity has also been his compass in navigating challenges and setbacks. For instance, when his debut book was rejected by publishers, he didn't give up. Instead, he leveraged the rejection as a catalyst to refine his message and fortify his identity as a leader. This is a great example of a growth mindset, turning failure into success!

> *"You cannot separate your identity from your perspective. All that you are and every experience you've had color how you see things. It is your lens."*
>
> John C. Maxwell[20]

Today, Maxwell's prolific writing has resulted in over seventy books, with many achieving bestseller status. He has also mentored millions of entrepreneurial leaders globally. His success stands as a powerful testament to the transformative potential of a robust, successful identity based on a strong brand.

Both these stories underscore the point that appearance, brand and identity can significantly impact one's progress and success. However, it's also crucial to remember that while appearance can influence perception, it's the substance and talent that ultimately determine success. When you open your mouth, you remove all doubt. You validate the person you are inside.

"The person we believe ourselves to be will always act in a manner consistent with our self-image."

Brian Tracy[21]

What Does Your Album Cover Say About Your Music?

Your personality through your voice and message is the music of your album cover... your appearance. While the initial allure often lies in the physical facade, it is the personality that holds the power to create enduring impressions and foster profound connections. The charm of your personality can significantly amplify your attractiveness, particularly when it harmoniously aligns with your outward appearance.

Attributes such as self-assuredness, compassion, wit, intellect, and genuineness can positively sway others' perceptions, even when one's physical appearance doesn't adhere to conventional standards of physical attractiveness. Just like an album, you may not be drawn to the cover, but you could end up falling in love with the music.

When your personality and appearance harmoniously blend, it culminates as your attitude. Attitude is the amalgamation of your words and body language, which crafts a perception of you and evokes emotions in another person during your interaction. So how are you greeting the world? Are you downtrodden or upbeat to market your brand?

> *"Your attitude, not your aptitude, will determine your altitude."*
>
> Zig Ziglar[22]

As example, Michael Jordan perfectly illustrates the point of greeting the world with an upbeat attitude to successfully market his brand. Jordan, despite facing numerous challenges and setbacks in his career, always had a positive and determined outlook. This attitude was not only reflected in his professional games, but also in his interactions with the media, fans, and even his opponents.

In 1984, when Jordan was drafted into the NBA, he was not the first pick. He was chosen third by the Chicago Bulls, a team that was struggling both on and off the court. However, Jordan didn't let this dampen his spirits. Instead, he used it as motivation to work harder, showcase his quality, and prove his value.

> *"My attitude is that if you push me towards something that you think is a weakness, then I will turn that perceived weakness into a strength."*
>
> Michael Jordan[23]

His upbeat attitude and relentless determination quickly turned the Bulls into a championship team and made him one of the most recognized athletes in the world. His growth mindset and positive image was further amplified by his successful partnership with Nike, resulting in the creation of the Air Jordan brand. As stated earlier in this chapter, Air Jordan is more than just a brand; it's a symbol of excellence, perseverance, and positivity, much like Jordan himself. As Nike says, "Just Do It!"

Marketing Your Brand

So whether you're an athlete, an entrepreneur, or someone trying to make your mark on the world, remember to greet everyone with an upbeat attitude to market your personal brand. In doing so, remember that the main goal is to inspire others with positivity and determination. Just like Michael Jordan, you never know where a determined, positive attitude might take you. Surely it will take you much further in your journey than a bad attitude, especially when combined with a challenging or questionable appearance. As the age-old adage wisely advises, "You attract more bees with honey than with vinegar."

> *"A bad attitude is like a flat tire, you won't get nowhere until you change it."*
>
> Joyce Meyer[24]

Every day as you prepare to face the world, your appearance and personality are inseparable allies, working together to imprint your brand to shape your interactions and experiences. Your appearance serves as the sleek, polished exterior of a Lamborghini, while your personality fuels it like a powerful engine. When these two elements align harmoniously, you're destined to triumph in the journey of life!

Branding is the distinctive fusion of your innate abilities, life experiences, appearance, and personality that distinguishes you from the crowd. Your personal brand is a direct manifestation of your value, your pledge to the world about your principles and your potential contributions. It is the manner in which you portray yourself to others, on social media and in the physical world around you. It is the image you radiate, the reputation you cultivate, and the legacy you aspire to leave behind.

Your personal brand is not a creation of a single moment. It is an ongoing journey of self-exploration, self-enhancement, and self-expression. It necessitates authenticity, consistency, and dedication. It calls for bravery, resilience, and tenacity.

> *"Life isn't about finding yourself. Life is about creating yourself."*
>
> George Bernard Shaw[25]

You are a virtuoso portrait artist, meticulously crafting a masterpiece of yourself with each stroke of your brush. Unleash your inner Van Gogh, and create something truly awe-inspiring!

YOUR VALUE

What You Offer the World and How the World Likes You

Value can profoundly shape your identity and strengthen your branding. Values, defined as the deeply held beliefs and principles that you deem significant, play a pivotal role in molding your identity. These values serve as a guiding compass, influencing the way you make decisions, set your priorities, and engage with others. They are the underpinning elements that shape your world view, determine your actions and reactions in various life situations, and influence how you interact with others.

Your human value is a complex tapestry crafted from two basic core values: intrinsic and extrinsic. The authentic essence of a person is a multifaceted blend of their intrinsic and extrinsic values. Simply, intrinsic value refers to the depth of your soul's essence, your core being in what makes you a good, decent person. On the other hand, extrinsic value is the unique contribution you make to the world during your time on this earthly stage, and the legacy you leave behind after your journey is completed.

> *"The major value in life is not what you get. The major value in life is what you become."*
>
> Jim Rohn[26]

Your Intrinsic Value

Intrinsic value captures your innate worth, dignity, and distinctiveness as a unique, highly-created, culture-bearing primate. Irrespective of external elements like wealth, societal standing, or accomplishments, intrinsic value is what you do and how you act when no one is watching.

Your intrinsic value includes qualities and attributes such as integrity, honesty, kindness, empathy, intellect, creativity, and moral character. These emotions and thoughts define your basic goodness, or lack thereof. These human traits are the basis of our core character that we have learned through societal observation, mentorship, education, religion, and associations.

Intrinsic value is an integral facet of human nature, and every individual inherently possesses it merely by the virtue of their existence. Unlike material possessions or superficial attributes, intrinsic value is not reliant on external approval or societal standards.

In philosophical and ethical discussions, the concept of intrinsic human value often serves as a foundational principle for moral reasoning and the development of ethical frameworks aimed at promoting justice, fairness, and the common good. Recognizing and affirming the inherent value of every individual is a cornerstone of ethical and compassionate behavior in our world, and the lack of it produces division and, at worst, war.

Your Extrinsic Value

Your extrinsic value is the worth you hold, or are perceived to hold, and is influenced by external elements. These elements can include your professional role, societal standing, financial prosperity, material possessions, or notable accomplishments.

Extrinsic value can be influenced by societal norms and expectations and can fluctuate based on changes in society's perception. As example, like in the story of Lance Armstrong, he lost considerable extrinsic value when it was determined he took performance-enhancing drugs prior to the Tour de France races he competed in. Besides losing his racing medals, he lost the value of his reputation which was irreparably harmed.

Extrinsic value can also be influenced by cultural values and norms. For instance, in some cultures, a person's extrinsic value might be heavily tied to their family's social status or wealth; in others, it might be more closely linked to their individual achievements or contributions to society. While extrinsic value can provide a sense of accomplishment and recognition, it is important not to rely solely on it for self-worth. This is because extrinsic value can be temporary and are influenced by factors outside of your control.

In contrast, intrinsic value, which is based on your character, values, and personal growth, is more stable and enduring. As I said before, first grow inward to lay the foundation to grow outward for greater value and recognition in your journey.

> *"Define your priorities, know your values and believe in your purpose. Only then can you effectively share yourself with others."*
>
> Les Brown[27]

The Journey of Steve Jobs

The story of the late Steve Jobs, co-founder of Apple Inc., is a perfect illustration of the concept of extrinsic and intrinsic value. Jobs was born to a Syrian immigrant father and an American mother, who gave him up for adoption. His adoptive parents were not wealthy, and Jobs did not come from a high social status family. However, his individual achievements and contributions to society, particularly in the field of technology, gave him immense extrinsic value.

He was recognized globally for his innovative ideas and the success of Apple. However, Jobs did not rely solely on his extrinsic value for self-worth. Despite his success, he faced numerous challenges, including being ousted from Apple, the very company he helped to create. He also battled stage 4 pancreatic cancer. These experiences, which were largely outside of his control, could have diminished his extrinsic value. Yet Jobs remained steadfast and focused on his future without noticeable fear. His determination was due to his intrinsic value and his resilience, creativity, and relentless pursuit of innovation and a greater purpose. Despite his death in 2011, Steve Jobs's legacy endures, a testament to his intrinsic value and his value to the world.

> *"Remembering that you are going to die is the best way I know to avoid the trap of thinking you have something to lose. You are already naked. There is no reason not to follow your heart."*
>
> Steve Jobs[28]

A significant element of extrinsic value that can pave the way for an ultimate life journey is your income, which represents the value of your time. While some may argue that money isn't everything, and this holds true when juxtaposed with matters of life and death, it's undeniable that money plays a crucial role in our lives. Without it, you become dependent on societal mercy or government charity, which can limit your freedom and lead to a life of scarcity and frugality.

Consider the plight of the homeless person on the street corner. It is hardly a life of joy and fulfillment but a life of struggle. Understanding the role of money in life is essential as it is the lifeblood of our global society, facilitating the exchange of services and products in exchange for our time.

> *"Money won't create success; the freedom to make it will."*
>
> Nelson Mandela[29]

Money symbolizes the fiscal worth produced through your exertion, expertise, or capital investment by the use of your time. Simply put, money serves as a measure of the value of your time based on what you contribute to the world.

> *"I think money is a wonderful thing because it enables you to do things. It enables you to invest in ideas that don't have a short-term payback."*
>
> Steve Jobs[30]

The less value your time holds, the less income you will earn throughout your life. On the other hand, the more value your time possesses, the more freedom and opportunities you will enjoy in life. Therefore, the objective should be to raise the value of your time, making yourself a valuable asset in society. This will enable you to hopefully experience time freedom without the constant monthly struggle of paying the bills and barely making it.

Steve Jobs summed it up simply, "Money... enables you to do things." Embrace this reality! It is the fundamental mechanism of our world in buying and selling products and services. Money is almost as vital as oxygen for survival in our society. The more you have of it, the more freedom you gain over your time, and the more ability you have to help others.

Income Value Is Proportionate to Freedom

Income value plays a pivotal role in shaping your financial health. Low value equals little freedom. High value equals abundant freedom. Simple! Income value not only dictates your purchasing power; it sets the benchmark for your standard of living and your capacity to fulfill financial commitments and objectives. The ripple effects of income value extend to various facets of life, encompassing housing, healthcare, education, buying power, greater recreational activities, and, most importantly, reduced life struggle.

Gaining a comprehensive understanding of income value and managing it proficiently is indispensable for effective financial planning, budgeting, saving, and investing. This, in turn, paves the way for long-term financial stability and wealth accumulation.

The greater value for your time, the greater time freedom you will experience in life. In other words, the greater income value you build, the greater time freedom you will experience. Intriguingly, when you view your money as a representation of your time, it gains a heightened significance. This is because it symbolizes a dwindling resource: your time.

Therefore, every purchase you make or every job you undertake essentially equates to selling your precious time for a set amount. You are selling your time whether its buying a product or accepting a paycheck.

What hourly wage or salary would liberate you financially? Identify this figure and then strive toward this goal by raising the value of your time via your job, career, or purpose. Unfortunately, when you have a boss, raising your value is limited to what they want to pay you.

> *"Workers work hard enough to not be fired, and owners pay just enough so that workers won't quit."*
>
> Robert T. Kiyosaki[31]

Always bear in mind that while your job can assist you in being able to pay for your monthly expenses, it may not necessarily elevate the value of your time or provide you with financial independence and freedom.

The drug of a paycheck gives a person a false sense of security and marginal comfort. The thought is, *If I repeat the same day without get fired or digitally replaced by AI, then I can live life with weekends off and pay the bills.* This life philosophy is why most people will work their life away at various jobs without any meaningful retirement and end up working for Walmart greeting customers.

The significance of value in building a personal brand is instrumental in how the world "likes" you and how others perceive and engage with you. In this context, your authenticity, your true nature, is the cornerstone of a robust personal brand. As you grow in your personal development journey, you are growing your brand, your future self.

> *"Your actions come from your identity. When your identity is rooted in current commitments, rather than your Future Self, your actions are weak and unaligned with your goal. The only way to realize your Future Self is to be your Future Self now."*
>
> Benjamin P. Hardy[32]

Your personal brand is an evolving process, a profound reflection of your authentic self, your image, and your inherent value, which is the package people see. The contents mirrors your character, your passions, your strengths, and your vulnerabilities. It is why people like and buy your personal brand.

YOUR QUALITY

What the World Sees in You and How the World Trusts You

Whenever we visit a supermarket, we typically select a product and scrutinize its ingredients before deciding to purchase it. The product's packaging, or brand, initially captures our attention; its price and value must then meet our expectations. The ingredients a brand uses signify the product's quality.

In many ways, we are akin to these store products, subtly evaluated in a similar manner as we interact with the world. What are your personal ingredients? What is your quality? Are you composed of artificial sweeteners and fillers, or are you brimming with organic, non-GMO ingredients?

> *"Quality means doing it right when no one is looking."*
>
> Henry Ford[33]

When we refer to a "person of quality," we generally mean a person who embodies commendable attributes and characteristics. Their quality ingredients are what sets them apart from the other generic products on the shelf. Although the precise qualities may fluctuate based on context and personal beliefs, a person's quality is typically commensurate with these key ingredients: integrity, humility accountability, respectfulness, empathy, reliability, courage, positivity, and adaptability.

Adding to or enhancing your brand quality entails a multifaceted journey of personal growth development, heightened self-awareness, and a steadfast adherence to ethical principles. Here are some essential quality ingredients to add to your brand.

• **Embrace Continuous Personal Growth:** Commit to lifelong learning and self-improvement. Seek out new experiences, challenges, and knowledge that push you to grow and evolve. Improvement never stops; we are all a work in progress.

• **Cultivate Self-Awareness:** Develop a deep understanding of your strengths, weaknesses, emotions, and motivations. Regular self-reflection and mindfulness practices can enhance your awareness of how your actions affect yourself and others.

• **Uphold Ethical Values:** Adhere to a strong moral code, and make decisions based on integrity and fairness. Consistently act in ways that are honest, respectful, and responsible regardless of the outcome. When honesty is your guidepost, you never need to remember what you said, only what you did.

• **Be Your Word:** Do what you say you're going to do. If you say it, then do it! Reliance to your word is key to how people trust and follow you. Leaders are dependable; losers are expendable.

• **Foster Empathy and Compassion:** Strive to understand and share the feelings of others. Show kindness and consideration. Smile in your interactions, and support those in need. Always give value to others. It never fails!

• **Enhance Emotional Intelligence:** Improve your ability to manage your emotions and navigate social complexities. Develop skills such as empathy, conflict resolution, and effective communication. If you are angered, then *stop*! Do not open your mouth. Instead, count to five backwards in your mind. Your character is judged by your reaction, and anger only adds to your stress. It's not about winning an argument; it's about winning your position. Silence is golden because it gives you time to think!

• **Set and Pursue Meaningful Goals:** Define clear, purposeful objectives that align with your values and passions. Work diligently toward achieving them and remain adaptable in the face of obstacles. Keep focused and do "the one thing" until done. Ask yourself, "Is this distraction keeping me from my goals or purpose? If so, how important is it?" Perfect your purpose so your purpose can take precedent!

> *"Life takes on meaning when you become motivated, set goals and charge after them in an unstoppable manner."*
>
> Les Brown[34]

• **Practice Gratitude and Humility:** Recognize and appreciate the positive aspects of your life and the contributions of others. Maintain a humble attitude, acknowledging that there is always room for growth and learning. Always smile and praise others while giving thanks for your gifts.

• **Build Resilience and Perseverance:** Strengthen your ability to cope with challenges and setbacks. Develop a growth mindset that views obstacles as opportunities for growth and maintains determination in the face of adversity.

• **Be Adaptable:** Be flexible and adaptable, capable of adjusting to changing circumstances and navigating uncertainty with grace and resilience. Maintain a positive outlook on life, even in difficult circumstances. When you are struggling, inspire and uplift others with optimism and enthusiasm. Be the change leader people need during uncertain times.

•   **Engage in Community and Service:** Actively participate in and contribute to your community. Volunteer your time and skills to make a positive impact on the lives of others. Engaging actively in your community is vital as it builds a sense of connection and shared purpose. By volunteering your time and skills, you not only assist those in need but also inspire a ripple effect of positivity, strengthening and uniting the community. This involvement promotes personal growth, fosters empathy, and provides a fulfilling sense of belonging, highlighting how individual efforts can contribute to meaningful collective change.

•   **Seek Balance and Well-Being:** Prioritize your physical, mental, and emotional health. Maintain a balanced lifestyle that supports your overall well-being and enables you to function at your best. Remember, your body is on loan from God.

> *"Be a yardstick of quality. Some people aren't used to an environment where excellence is expected."*
> Steve Jobs[55]

By integrating these steps into your daily life, you can steadily develop into a person of exceptional quality, positively influencing how the world trusts you. Undoubtedly, these steps raise the bar for most of us, but the alternative is simply joining the herd. Your quality is unique and serves as a direct mirror of your brand identity. Individuals who cultivate their quality traits embody attributes that not only enhance their own well-being but also positively influence those around them. They are driven by the desire to make a meaningful impact on the world through their actions, attitudes, and relationships.

The more you cultivate and enhance your quality, the more robust and distinct your identity becomes. This, in turn, fosters a profound sense of trust between you and the world around you. Trust is the cornerstone of all relationships and interactions; without it, opportunities will remain elusive.

> **"People do business with people they know, like, and trust."**
>
> Anonymous

In crafting your identity, always remember that brand equals know, value equals like, and quality equals trust. These three attributes are the foundational components to your identity and serve as golden keys along your journey. They open up the doors of know, like, and trust and can send you on an exciting life trajectory of time freedom and abundance.

These keys to your personal and professional success are the foundation of your credibility, the source of your influence, and the catalyst for your growth. They create your unique identity in the world and make you stand out. It is what makes you, you.

> *"You were designed for accomplishment, engineered for success, and endowed with the seeds of greatness."*
>
> Zig Ziglar[36]

Your life journey is to define and cultivate these three keys to elevate your identity. The sooner in life you discover your brand, value, and quality the greater your life will become.

Understand your core values, identify your unique strengths, and articulate your personal mission. Be true to yourself, be proud of who you are, and let your unique identity shine because the world is waiting for you to be empowered by your greatness.

Defining your Core Values (CV) implies personal development, self-searching, and honest recognition of the person you are and what matters most to you. Contemplate the below points to help guide, identify and define your life core values.

• **Reflect on Your Life Experiences (CV1):** Think about the times in your life when you felt deep happiness or a sense of pride in an accomplishment. What values were being honored during these times? Conversely, what life situations made you feel uncomfortable or upset. What values were being dishonored in these experiences?

• **Itemize the Things Matters were Most (CV2):** Make a list of qualities, principles, or ideals you find meaningful. As example thoughts and feelings like honesty, creativity, compassion and growth. Think about what promotes or motivates your decisions process and brings you a sense of purpose.

• **Review Your Influences (CV3):** Who is in your tribe, your herd, your associations? Who makes up your Friendship Circle. How do they shape your beliefs, priorities and values. Consider whether any of these influences have led you to adopt values that don't feel authentic to you or distract from your identity and brand.

• **What Are Your Behavior Patterns (CV4):** Chart your recurring habits, interactions and patterns in your choices and relationships. What principles and attitudes do you consistently uphold, even when it's challenging or against popular opinion? Do you back down or stand up for the beliefs you hold regardless of the current norms or situation?

• **Prioritize Your Values (CV1 - CV4):** From the list you make, identify and rank three to six of your innate values that represent the person you believe you are from the most important to least.

• **Contemplate Your Values:** Determine if these three to six values align and are in harmony with your daily behavior and actions. Do these values support your identity and your brand as you want society to perceive you?

- **Develop and Refine Your Values:** Discuss your values with your mentors and people you respect who know you well. Their perspectives may provide additional clarity and will help you evolve your values over time to become the person you imagine to be.

As you follow this process, you can develop a clear understanding of your core values, providing a foundation for meaningful decisions and a fulfilling life to define your identity and brand.

Refining your identity is crucial in Finding JOY and it starts with defining your core values. Individuals who consciously invest time in shaping their own identity and personal growth, rather than allowing life's circumstances to define them, will discover a heightened sense of independence, financial autonomy, and mastery over their own time.

A refine and clearly articulated identity cultivates influence and broadens the reach of your friendship circle, transforming it into a high-quality network. This, in turn, paves the way for a plethora of life opportunities.

"Growth is the great separator between those who succeed and those who do not. When I see a person beginning to separate themselves from the pack, it's almost always due to personal growth."
John C. Maxwell[37]

The Identity Journey of LeBron James

As an example, in the world of professional basketball, the story of LeBron James perfectly illustrates this point. LeBron, a highly successful and influential athlete, has always been clear about his identity, both on and off the court. He is not just a basketball player; he is a philanthropist, businessman, and social activist. His well-crafted identity has allowed him to cultivate influence and broaden the reach of his friendship circle, transforming it into a high-quality network. LeBron's network includes influential figures from various fields, such as business tycoon Warren Buffet and former President Barack Obama among other influential people. This network has opened up a multitude of life opportunities for him.

His friendship with Warren Buffet, for instance, has helped him make smart investment decisions, turning him into a successful businessman. His relationship with President Obama has given him a platform to voice his opinions on social issues, making him a prominent social activist. However, it all started with James' building his value from his talents and abilities to attract value of others to him over time. Value attracts value.

Thus, LeBron's story shows how a refined and clearly articulated identity can cultivate influence, broaden your friendship circle, and pave the way for unbelievable life opportunities.

"I'm going to use all my tools, my God-given ability, and make the best life I can with it."
LeBron James[38]

That's the spirit and the concept of Finding JOY. While it's true that most of us may not be able to make a free throw, we all possess the ability to shape our unique identities, built upon the special talents we've honed throughout our lives. The power lies within us to determine whether our lives are destined for a purpose greater than merely surviving each day, rather than allowing life to dictate our paths and telling us where to go.

Your identity extends far beyond superficial aspects such as your hairstyle, the clothes you adorn, or the car you drive. It is a profoundly intricate concept. The dynamics of identity summarize the entirety of your existence, reflecting a comprehensive picture of who you truly are based on your core values.

As you embark on the journey to discover your true self and outline your life's purpose, the foundational and most vital action is to nurture a profound respect and affection for the distinctive person you are. Recognize that embracing your individuality is not just about self-acceptance, but also about celebrating the qualities that set you apart: your God-given talents. Acknowledge your strengths and weaknesses with equal grace, understanding that they both play a role in shaping your authentic self. This journey is not just about finding answers, but about appreciating the ongoing process of growth and self-discovery. As you dive deep into your identity, remember to practice self-compassion and patience, allowing yourself the space to evolve naturally. Unconditionally love the person you see in the mirror.

> *"We must look for ways to be an active force in our own lives. We must take charge of our own destinies, design a life of substance and truly begin to live our dreams."*
>
> Les Brown[39]

As we define our core values and develop our identity, we need to always extend forgiveness to ourselves and embrace our failures as life experiences. This acceptance is difficult for many of us but is a crucial step in propelling ourselves forward, enabling us to evolve into the people we aspire to be and an identity we are proud to offer the world.

It all starts with you. In the next chapter we will explore attitude and how it affects the picture you are painting of yourself. So, what does your attitude say about your identity?

Journey Rest Stop 6

1) What are the three traits of identity?

2) Define the three traits of identity and how they apply to you?

3) Define your core values and how do these values affect your identity? How would you change or modify it?

Chapter 7

Journey of Attitude

Is Your Glass Half Empty or Half Full?

Ability is what you're capable of doing. Motivation determines what you do. Attitude determines how well you do it.

Lou Holtz[1]

Attitude is the unique essence you bring to the world. It serves as your personal branded billboard, broadcasting your identity to those around you. Your attitude is an immediate indicator of how the world interacts with you. A negative attitude can be likened to a flat tire, leaving you stranded on the roadside as life passes you by.

On the other hand, a positive attitude acts as your golden ticket, granting you access to a more joyful life. It attracts a more positive caliber of friends to your inner circle and expands your network, since most people tend to gravitate toward positivity.

The role of attitude in shaping your success or happiness in any given situation is paramount. Your perspective, emotions, and actions toward any circumstance, problem, or object can significantly sway the outcome toward positivity or negativity. The power to improve or deteriorate a situation lies within your attitude, making it a pivotal factor in your approach.

> *"Positive thinking will let you do everything better than negative thinking will."*
>
> Zig Ziglar[2]

Consider your facial expression. Does it bear a constant frown, or does it light up with a smile when you encounter others? Consider your voice. Does it carry a tone of melancholy and defeat, or does it ring with enthusiasm, always ready to greet with a cheerful hello? Consider your body language. Does it suggest reservation and isolation, or does it exude warmth and generosity? In essence, are you prepared to seize the day, or are you simply waiting for the day to seize you?

These subtle cues, though seemingly insignificant on their own, collectively tip the scales toward success and a richer life experience when considered in their entirety. Your attitude is reflected in how you rise from your bed each morning and face the world, recognizing that your life's journey carries a greater purpose and significance to fulfill than carrying the burden of a negative attitude.

Moreover, your attitude serves as a significant gauge of whether you possess a predominantly fixed or growth mindset. Intriguingly, a negative attitude tends to align with a strong fixed mindset, while a consistent, optimistic attitude often signifies a more pronounced growth mindset. This correlation is logical, as most successful individuals exhibit a positive, proactive, conquer-the-world attitude on their path to success, irrespective of the setbacks they encounter.

Lou Holtz, the legendary, record setting Notre Dame football coach, who was admired for his motivational speaking and leadership wisdom, would concur that while ability and motivation are crucial, without a positive attitude, you risk restricting your avenues to success, personal fulfillment, and the pinnacles you can achieve in life.

> **"Your attitude, not your aptitude, will determine your altitude."**
>
> Zig Ziglar[3]

Your attitude significantly influences your perspective on life and how the world interacts with you. If you approach life with a pessimistic, glass-half-empty attitude, your life will reflect that negativity, yielding only partially fulfilled results and successes. You will find yourself perpetually trapped in doubt, questioning why life doesn't seem to work in your favor. However, the reality is that life continues to unfold with or without your participation.

> **"Just because fate doesn't deal you the right cards, it doesn't mean you should give up. It just means you have to play the cards you get to their maximum potential."**
>
> Les Brown[4]

The issue isn't life itself, but rather your ability to positively influence your life outcomes. The world doesn't exist to serve you. Instead, you are here to fully experience and engage with the world.

Adopting a victim mentality only fosters a pessimistic attitude, providing a convenient excuse to avoid taking responsibility for your life. This mindset not only undermines your future but also keeps you stuck in the past. Unfortunately, many people fail to realize or achieve their full potential, purpose, or greatness because they remain ensnared in the clutches of their past.

> **"You would not be here today if yesterday was your defining moment. Live this day and move towards your dreams."**
>
> Steve Maraboli[5]

Let It Go!

Maintaining a negative attitude is not only costly but also diminishes your value and squanders your time and talent. Instead, adopt the daily mantra of *"Let it go!"* to *"Go live life!"* in order to foster a mindset of abundance. Do not allow yourself to be a victim of past issues or societal expectations.

Regardless of your life circumstances, past injustices, your heritage, or the unique individual that you are, none of these factors matter. What truly matters in life is your time and how you utilize it to add value to the lives of others, which then makes you more valuable.

Dwelling on the mindset and actions of your past self will never allow you to evolve into a future self that holds greater value and abundance. So whatever mental barriers are preventing you from realizing your full potential, let them go! They are not worth your stagnation! You were divinely crafted with inherent talents that make you more than enough. View your life as a glass half full and seize the world with your unique abilities and talents.

> *"The truth is, unless you let go, unless you forgive yourself, unless you forgive the situation, unless you realize that the situation is over, you cannot move forward."*
>
> Steve Maraboli[6]

Maintaining a positive attitude is like to taking your daily dose of Vitamin A-ttitude, essential for supplementing **M**otivation, **A**ssociations, **R**esiliency, **C**reativity, and **H**ealth (MARCH). This robust daily MARCH is a crucial part of your journey toward achieving life success. It paves the way to ultimate freedom in life, allowing you to navigate your path with confidence and determination.

Motivation: March

You are either moving forward, going backwards, or standing still. It's your choice.

A positive attitude serves as the high-octane fuel for motivation. When your buoyant attitude is combined with motivation, it becomes contagious, sparking a fire within to strive toward your goals and dreams. Even in the face of life's most challenging times, a growth-mindset person will maintain an optimistic perspective, always putting a positive spin on situations.

One of the most potent traits of every successful growth-minded person is their ability to self-motivate and inspire those around them to remain focused on their objectives, fueling the drive to achieve. Without a clear life goal and a positive attitude, motivation would be nonexistent. It is safe to say that a positive attitude is not just a desirable trait; it is a crucial component in the engine of success.

> **"I'd rather be optimistic and wrong than pessimistic and right."**
>
> Elon Musk[7]

The Journey of Elon Musk and SpaceX

When Elon Musk, along with his dedicated SpaceX team, launched the largest rocket ever recorded into the annals of space history, it was a testament to their years of expertise in launching SpaceX's Falcon 9 rockets. This colossal rocket, boasting 16.7 million pounds of thrust and powered by thirty-three engines, was an experimental, unmanned behemoth standing thirty stories tall.

As it detached from the launch pad, the sight was nothing short of awe-inspiring. The gargantuan structure ascended from earth, engines blaring with voluminous clouds of smoke and a thunderous roar, piercing the pristine blue Texas sky. However, eighteen miles above the earth and four minutes into the flight, the mission met an abrupt end. A spectacular explosion unfolded as the mammoth rocket tumbled end over end, disintegrating mid-flight over the Gulf of Mexico.

Despite the unfortunate end, the launch was a testament to the audacity of human ambition and the relentless pursuit of space exploration.

> *"There's a silly notion that failure's not an option at NASA. Failure is an option here. If things are not failing, you are not innovating enough."*
> Elon Musk[8]

The initial response from SpaceX's mission control was a resounding applause and an outpouring of joy! "In a test of this magnitude, the true measure of success lies in the lessons we glean," the company declared. "The insights gained from today's test will significantly enhance Starship's reliability as SpaceX continues its pursuit of making human life multi-planetary."[9] Musk, in the aftermath of the failure, congratulated his team, saying, "Congrats, SpaceX team, on an exciting test launch of Starship! Learned a lot for our next test launch in a few months!"[10]

> *"When something is important enough, you do it even if the odds are not in your favor."*
> Elon Musk[11]

Rather than being met with disheartening remarks, such as, "We really messed up this time!" or "Heads will roll for this blunder," or "That was a colossal failure!" the initial responses from Musk were filled with optimistic encouragement for future endeavors.

This was not perceived as a failure, but rather a successful demonstration of what should be avoided in subsequent launches. Musk lauded his team for the valuable learning experience, expressing eagerness to progress toward the next flight in "a few months." This serves as an excellent illustration of a leadership growth mindset—using failure as experience to move forward.

> *"Your attitude toward failure determines your altitude after failure."*
>
> John C. Maxwell[12]

As Musk demonstrated, positive motivation fuels a relentless drive toward success. It is deeply rooted in your attitude and the perspective you adopt toward your failures, setbacks, and excuses. This positive mindset propels you forward on your journey to discover your purpose and realize your value in opening the doors of opportunity. As stated in chapter 6, *value attracts value.*

Association: mArch

Choose Your Connections Carefully

Association is our innate capacity to form connections with the world around us. Remember, you are not alone in your journey. Your success in life is intertwined with others. This holds true whether you're an active social media user, an entrepreneur, or an employee.

To broaden your reach, grow your network, enhance your business, or ascend the corporate ladder, your attitude plays a crucial role in your interaction. You are always marketing a highly unique commodity: *YOU*.

> **"You cannot climb the ladder of success dressed in the costume of failure."**
>
> Zig Ziglar[13]

A positive attitude serves as the bright beacon of your personality, paving the way for a more significant influence on your path to success. Much like moths drawn to a flame, people are naturally attracted to positivity and motivation.

As we discussed in chapter 5, your closest friends are those you naturally gravitate toward. However, your associations extend beyond this inner circle. These are the individuals who are drawn to you, seeking your advice, influence, motivation, and association. The brighter your beacon of positivity, the greater influence you will possess, and the larger the network you will cultivate to bolster your life's success.

If you find yourself alone in your "lifeboat," it may be essential to evaluate the strength and clarity of your beacon. Navigating challenges solo can sometimes leave you adrift, aimlessly rowing in circles, and it hinders your ability to find your dream destination. Cultivating a positive attitude and nurturing meaningful relationships are vital components on the path to a successful and fulfilling life.

Expand your boat's manifest by building and enriching your friendships, becoming a radiant beacon of positivity and light for others. In doing so, you'll not only chart a more purposeful course; you'll also invite others to join you on your journey in building your tribe, your associations.

> **"A man only learns in two ways, one by reading, and the other by association with smarter people."**
> Will Rogers[14]

Resilience: maRch

Bring it on! That's all you got!

Resilience is the embodiment of fortitude, a dynamic force that, when bolstered by a positive outlook, transforms any setback or failure into a valuable learning experience and a stepping stone toward personal growth. Fearless resilience is a fundamental principle of a growth mindset, as we discussed in chapter 1. A robust, resilient character, coupled with a positive "I can," forward-thinking attitude, perceives life's obstacles not as insurmountable problems, but as challenges that require solutions. Every setback in life is a setup to gain knowledge and experience. Life is a culmination of setbacks for you to build wisdom, an unstoppable attitude and a strong resilience. It's all in how you perceive these bumps in life.

> *"There will always be obstacles and challenges that stand in your way. Building mental strength will help you develop resilience to those potential hazards so you can continue on your journey to success."*
>
> Amy Morin[15]

This resilience-driven perspective acknowledges that no issue you encounter will ever outweigh the significance of your life journey. Consider the analogy of a boxer stepping into the ring. You, like a confident boxer, possess the necessary strength and mental determination to conquer any challenge that comes your way. Ultimately, your resilience to overcome life's hurdles is directly proportional to your self-belief.

If your faith in yourself is superficial or you have strong limiting beliefs, your resilience in the face of adversity will be fragile. However, a positive growth mindset can fortify your resilience, equipping you with the best possible capacity to navigate life's trials and tribulations and turn them into successful solutions.

> *"Believe in yourself. You are braver than you think, more talented than you know, and capable of more than you imagine."*
>
> Roy T. Bennett[16]

Creativity: marCh

Creativity is your brain thinking out of the box.

Creativity is the key that unlocks the power of your imagination, enabling you to think beyond conventional boundaries and venture outside the proverbial "cave." It is the catalyst that sparks innovative solutions to age-old problems, paving the way for a brighter, better world.

> **"Creativity is just connecting things."**
>
> Steve Jobs[17]

You may not perceive yourself as creative, but the truth is, we all possess this innate ability. Yes, even you! When you engage creativity, you are simply connecting things! The human brain is inherently designed to solve problems, to unravel mysteries, to question the status quo, and to devise superior strategies, to build a better mousetrap. We are, by nature, creative beings. it's embedded in our DNA!

> **"Creativity is seeing what others see and thinking what no one else ever thought."**
>
> Albert Einstein[18]

Creativity can be likened to a cognitive muscle that necessitates continuous cultivation and growth over time. However, when it is eclipsed by a negative mindset or depressive state, creativity will become stagnant, mirroring the effects of a sedentary lifestyle on a mental couch.

> **"Negativity is the enemy of creativity."**
> David Lynch[19]

A pessimistic outlook seldom fosters the emergence of positive, groundbreaking ideas. As a commercial architect who needs to be actively creating all the time and pushing the creative envelope, I know how a negative attitude can easily affect your creative nature.

Creativity serves as a powerful gauge of your leaning mindset, be it growth-oriented or fixed. The more you engage in creative thinking, the more you cultivate a mindset inclined towards growth and development.

> **"Creativity is piercing the mundane to find the marvelous."**
> Bill Moyers[20]

When you undertake problems, issues, and challenges with creative solutions, you are effectively overcoming your obstacles and broadening your horizons beyond your comfort zone, beyond your cave. Your difficulties become less daunting and more manageable when you adopt an unstoppable positive attitude.

Consistently tapping into your creative nature will not only drive you forward but also open up a world brimming with endless possibilities and innovative solutions. Regularly exercising your creative muscles can enhance your problem-solving skills and provide unique perspectives that can be applied to various aspects of life and work.

In essence, nurturing your creativity is a powerful tool for personal and professional development, paving the way for a future rich with potential and innovation. Trust your creative nature in your God-given DNA, and hurdles will become nothing more than bumps in the road.

Health: marcH

Good health allows you to live with one less problem.

Good health serves as the foundation for fostering a positive mindset, perspective, and overall happiness. Without good health, one is merely a spectator in the game of life, eagerly waiting to rejoin the action.

> *"Your body hears everything your mind says."*
> Naomi Judd[21]

Numerous studies have been conducted to explore the health benefits of maintaining an optimistic and positive attitude, which has been identified as a natural deterrent against diseases. The connection between a positive outlook and wellness, which activates your body's inherent ability to prevent and suppress disease progression, is very compelling.

An article published by the American Heart Association discussed the benefits of positive attitude. It states, "There is now an increasing appreciation of how psychological health can contribute not only in a negative way to cardiovascular disease (CVD) but also in a positive way to better cardiovascular health and reduced cardiovascular risk. There is good data showing clear associations between psychological health and CVD and risk; there is increasing evidence that psychological health may be causally linked to biological processes and behaviors that contribute to and cause CVD; the preponderance of data suggests that interventions to improve psychological health can have a beneficial impact on cardiovascular health."[22]

> *"What drains your spirit, drains your body. What fuels your spirit, fuels your body."*
>
> Carolyn Myss[23]

A lesser-known research study discussed kidney disease and attitude. The study states, "Among patients with kidney failure, well-being constructs are associated with increased health-related quality of life, reduced morbidity and complications, and increased survival. Potential mechanisms mediating these associations include reduced inflammation, improved autonomic and endothelial function, and improved health behavior adherence."[24]

The significance of maintaining a positive attitude in life cannot be overstated, especially when considering its profound impact on your overall health in preventing disease. It is of paramount importance! So is it worth jeopardizing your health and longevity for a negative, toxic, bitter, greedy, or jealous attitude? Absolutely not!

Numerous studies have consistently demonstrated a direct correlation between a positive attitude and overall wellness.

However, the precise cellular mechanisms that trigger this beneficial effect remain a subject of ongoing research.

> *"Take care of your body. It's the only place you have to live in."*
>
> Jim Rohn[25]

A positive attitude and optimistic outlook serve as your innate natural drug for robust health. When combined with a balanced diet, regular exercise, and adequate sleep, they can effectively mitigate emotional stress, enhance immune function, and foster overall wellness. This is not merely a theory but a fact that has been scientifically proven!

Dr. Becca Levy, from the Yale School of Public Health found that "psychologically, a positive view can enhance belief in one's abilities, decrease perceived stress and foster healthful behaviors. Physiologically, people with positive views of aging had lower levels of C-reactive protein, a marker of stress-related inflammation associated with heart disease and other illnesses, even after accounting for possible influences like age, health status, sex, race and education than those with a negative outlook. They also lived significantly longer."[26]

> *"If you achieve all kinds of things in the material world, but you lose your health or your peace of mind, you get little or no pleasure from your other accomplishments."*
>
> Brian Tracy[27]

A positive attitude is a core element for life success because it affects everything in MARCH: Motivation, Associations, Resilience, Creativity, and Health. Cultivating a positive attitude is a daily process that involves intentional practices and transformative mindset shifts. This journey often begins with heightened self-awareness, acknowledging how positive and negative thoughts influence emotions, behaviors and lifespan.

Key steps include regularly practicing gratitude, concentrating on life's positives, and reframing negative experiences into valuable learning opportunities. Surround yourself with a supportive and optimistic friendship circle to significantly impact your outlook. Further, engage in activities that enhance your well-being. It's okay to be selfish and put yourself first when it comes to your physical and mental wellness!

Join a gym and get on an exercise program. Enroll in a yoga class, and learn breathing and meditation. Be active in a group, club, or church to expand your network and be in new environments. Doing so will realign your focus and foster a positive mindset.

Over time, daily consistent efforts to challenge negative thinking patterns, set realistic and achievable goals, and celebrate even small successes can effectively nurture and sustain a positive attitude and outlook.

> *"Wellness is the complete integration of body, mind, and spirit - the realization that everything we do, think, feel, and believe has an effect on our state of well-being."*
>
> Greg Anderson[28]

By cultivating and sustaining a positive attitude, you can actualize your dreams and objectives and flourish in every aspect of your life. So let's change your outlook and attitude to a positive force as you greet the world every day, because finding your JOY depends on it.

Power of Positive Thinking

A consistently positive mindset builds
a consistently positive lifestyle.

The foundation of a positive attitude is rooted in internal positive thoughts from external sources. Positive thinking is influenced by the information you download to your cerebral hard drive from what you see and read, the mindset you've been nurtured with, and the environment in which you currently reside.

> *"You cannot have a positive life and a negative mind."*
>
> Joyce Meyer[29]

Adopting a positive mindset is a transformative lifestyle shift that requires time and consistent practice. It's like exercising at your local gym, but instead of toning your abs, you're strengthening your mental resilience and creating a better version of yourself.

Your commitment and faith in attending this "mind gym" must surpass your dedication to physical fitness. Here are some daily positive mental exercises you can practice every day to get a "rock hard" optimistic attitude that everyone will notice!

Limit Your M&M's... Except the Blue Ones!

First, consider moderating your intake of M&M's. And no, I'm not talking about Hershey's chocolate candies. Rather, I'm talking about the daily dose of "Murder & Mayhem" that we willfully consume from various media outlets such as TV, radio, social media, podcasts, internet, daily news programs and tabloids.

To be candid, I am a self-confessed news addict, and adjusting my daily consumption was a significant challenge. While I enjoy staying informed about current events, I've realized that safeguarding my positive mindset is of much greater importance.

The relentless barrage of negative news cycles seems to pervasively dominate our lives. It's crucial to understand that world events and situations will unfold regardless of our awareness or casual involvement. In almost all cases, there is little to nothing we can do to influence these events. Therefore, inundating our minds with negative information only serves to cloud our thoughts, affect our outlook, and adds to our daily life frustration.

Minimize your engagement with sensationalized news, "shock news," and reality TV shows. This is not to suggest that you should be uninformed about global events and news narratives. Instead, moderate your exposure. It's important to be well-versed in global affairs but strive to emotionally disengage from the negative aspects of the story.

Staying informed about diverse global events is key to cultivating an insightful persona, influencing how others perceive you as either informed or uninformed. Consider world events as a theatrical drama where you are a member of the audience, listening in but with the ability to leave at any time.

> *"Accentuate the positives, attenuate the negatives!"*
> Ted Kopecko

I know focusing on the positive can be easier said than done. The first step is to identify and document all the negative thoughts, issues, and circumstances that are currently impacting your life. These could span across various aspects of your life, including your job, friendships, relationships, situations, financial status, and even minor irritations. Essentially, anything in your daily life that induces feelings of anxiety, irritation, frustration, depression, or negativity that is causing you to have a depressive or poor attitude.

Depending on the length of your negative list, focus on addressing a few negative issues at a time until their impact on your emotions is reduced. Stay flexible and creative in finding solutions and realize that it takes time and effort in resolving issues.

Identify the top three to five issues that cause you the most distress and keep them on your cerebral radar. It is important to understand that negative thoughts trigger your emotions when you allow them to be fueled by negativity. This negativity is often driven by your assumption of a perceived loss of something or someone.

When we allow negative thoughts to take a seat at our mental dinner table and unconsciously elevate their significance, we prioritize these detrimental ideas over our own mental health. In essence, we give more credence to the negative guests at our table over ourselves and end up diminishing our own value and self-worth.

> *"Let go of negative people. They only show up to share complaints, problems, disastrous stories, fear, and judgment on others. If somebody is looking for a bin to throw all their trash into, make sure it's not in your mind."*
>
> Dalai Lama[30]

Let's add to the above quote: "Let go of negative people *and* negative thoughts."

It is crucial to recognize that the energy we spend entertaining these negative thoughts could be better invested in fostering a positive and nurturing mental environment. Cultivating mindfulness and practicing self-compassion can help us create a mental space where positivity thrives, and negative guests are less likely to find a foothold.

The Negative Critic

The tiny voice in your head

It is far easier to jettison negative people in our lives than our own critical, negative thoughts. With people, we can give a one-word solution: Goodbye! You just need to be strong enough for yourself to let go. With your thoughts, though, you are battling the negative voice that's stifling the positive voice from cheering you on! Here are some daily strategies for silencing the negative critic inside your head.

•   **Identify the Negative Voice:** The first step to overcoming your inner critic is to recognize when it starts to speak. By becoming aware of its presence, you begin to take control and can actively choose not to listen. Yes, we can all hear our inner critic.

> *"Stop saying these negative things about yourself. Look in the mirror and find something about yourself that's positive & celebrate that!"*
>
> Tyra Banks[31]

•   **Confront Negative Thoughts:** Take a moment to evaluate whether your negative thoughts are rational, logical, or rooted in facts. Frequently, these thoughts are blown out of proportion or lack a solid foundation.

Counter them by presenting evidence or formulating positive counterarguments to shift your perspective. Look for the good!

•   **Activate Positive Affirmations:** Transform your negative self-talk by embracing positive affirmations. Repeating empowering statements - such as, "I am capable" or "I choose to focus on the good" - can effectively rewire your cerebral hard-drive to foster an optimistic, resilient, and growth mindset.

> *"People become really quite remarkable when they start thinking that they can do things. When they believe in themselves, they have the first secret of success."*
> Norman Vincent Peale[32]

•   **Practice Mindfulness and Meditation:** Embrace mindfulness to anchor yourself in the present moment and cultivate a sense of detachment from negative thoughts. Engaging in regular meditation by joining a yoga studio can significantly quiet the mind, foster inner peace, and diminish the voice of the inner critic.

> *"You will never have a definite purpose in life, you will never have self-confidence, you will never have initiative and leadership unless you first create these qualities in your imagination and see yourself in possession of them."*
> Napoleon Hill[33]

• **Visualize Your Future Self:** Picture successful outcomes, and see yourself triumphing over obstacles. This practice replaces negative thoughts with empowering, positive imagery, boosting your confidence and resilience. Positive visualization is a main attribute of a growth mindset.

• **Cultivate Daily Gratitude:** Transform your mindset by concentrating on the aspects of your life for which you are thankful. Give thanks or say a daily prayer for your life, health, family, possessions, and talents. Practicing gratitude can effectively neutralize negative thoughts, allowing you to recognize and appreciate the positive elements that enrich your life.

• **Celebrate Your Achievements:** Whether they are monumental milestones or small victories, take the time to acknowledge and applaud your efforts. It's intriguing how we often dwell on our setbacks, yet we rarely take a moment to revel in our successes. To keep you excited, motivated, and strong, make it a habit to reward yourself for every accomplishment, no matter the size. This could be as small as a bowl of ice cream to treating yourself to a spa day. Personally, I always go for ice cream. And yes, I said bowl! You deserve it since you are your own BFF.

> *"The more you praise and celebrate your life, the more there is in life to celebrate."*
>
> Oprah Winfrey[34]

By consistently implementing these daily strategies, you can diminish the influence of negative self-talk and foster a more positive, empowering internal dialogue to build the most important friendship of yours: the one with yourself!

The Negative Trip Wires

Watch your step!

While external negativity around us is an undeniable force of life, it directly affects our attitude and how we treat the world. The real challenge lies in how we manage and control external negativity to minimize its impact on our mindset, emotional well-being, and attitude.

External negativity can be compared to the harmful effects of smoking over time. It is not a solitary negative incident that we see or hear that proves detrimental, but rather the cumulative effect of inhaling negativity every day to undermine a positive outlook.

Our eyes and ears serve as vigilant sentinels for our minds, meticulously sifting through the world's stimuli before they are downloaded on our cognitive hard drive. This process profoundly influences our perspective and worldview.

Many individuals within society often find themselves drawn to negativity due to a complex interplay of psychological and social factors. Let's define some of these factors and determine which ones you gravitate to.

By the way, we all fall into these negativity traps. It's how we deal with them that matters.

•   **Negativity Bias:** Humans naturally tend to focus more on negative experiences than on positive ones. This bias is believed to be an evolutionary trait, stemming from a time when early humans needed heightened awareness of potential dangers, like a saber-toothed tiger beyond their caves, to ensure their survival. By being more attuned to threats, early humans could better protect themselves, thereby enhancing their chances of living longer and passing on these fear factor genes.

•   **Stress and Anxiety:** When we encounter stress or anxiety, we become more vulnerable to negative thinking patterns. Stress has the capacity to narrow our focus, often resulting in an intensified fixation on the adverse elements of a situation. This heightened sensitivity to negativity can create a vicious cycle of distress, further amplifying feelings of anxiety and stress.

> *"Be careful not to let a negative social media life attract you to a dark way of thinking."*
>
> Germany Kent[35]

•   **Social Influence:** Negativity spreads easily in social settings because we often mirror the feelings and attitudes of others. Negative news, gossip, and complaints can quickly take over conversations, pushing aside positive topics to keep us submerged in negative talk.

- **Cognitive Patterns:** Habitual negative thinking can establish deeply entrenched cognitive patterns that are difficult to overcome. When we persistently perceive situations through a pessimistic lens, this mode of thinking can become deeply ingrained, shaping our overall outlook and response to life's challenges through a fixed mindset perspective.

- **Attention and Memory:** Negative events or information tend to seize our attention more easily and are remembered with greater clarity than positive ones. This heightened focus on adverse experiences can make them appear more significant and enduring in our minds.

- **Media Influence:** News outlets, reality TV, video games, movies, and social media platforms frequently spotlight negative events, conflicts, and problems, recognizing that such content tends to capture more attention. This relentless focus on negativity can distort our perceptions and foster a pessimistic worldview. Constant exposure to adverse content not only shapes public opinion but also has the potential to impact our mental well-being, contributing to greater anxiety and despair.

- **Self-Protection:** Some of us focus on negativity to prepare for possible dangers or disappointments. By expecting the worst, we feel more in control and less surprised by setbacks. This fixed mindset perspective acts as a psychological shield, helping us manage expectations and handle unexpected challenges.

> *"The amount of negativity I hear on a daily basis is unbelievable. But that's the kind of stuff you have to tune out, focus, stick with your vision and keep plugging every day."*
>
> Dana White[36]

• **Low Self-Esteem:** Individuals with low self-esteem often find themselves drawn to negativity, mirroring their internal struggles. Engaging in negative self-talk and harboring a pessimistic outlook can perpetuate feelings of inadequacy and unworthiness, creating a harmful cycle that further undermines their time value.

Negativity can spread like a forest fire, fostering a unique form of social connection. Extricating yourself from such patterns can be as daunting as overcoming a smoking addiction, given our genetic predisposition to expect the worst.

While these negativity traps may incline us to dwell on negativity, it is entirely feasible to counteract this tendency by developing positive habits, seeking out supportive environments, and engaging in mindfulness practices.

Value In, Value Out! It's Not Complicated!

Rather than subscribing to a "garbage in, garbage out" life approach, we should strive to refine our cognitive filter, adopting a more optimistic "value in, value out" life approach. This emphasizes the critical need to carefully curate our mental intake from external sources to ensure we are absorbing inspiring and constructive content and mentorship.

> *"Nothing happens to you, it happens for you. See the positive in negative events."*
>
> Joel Osteen[37]

We must relentlessly seek the silver linings concealed within life's adversities. They remind us that, even when confronted with challenges, there exists a unique opportunity to extract valuable lessons. Taking positive actions not only fortifies optimistic thoughts; it gradually diminishes the hold of negativity, fostering the development of a resilient growth mindset.

Dark Media and the Dark Side

You become what you do, my young Padawan!

The journey to a more fulfilling, positive life and attitude starts with a deliberate choice to eliminate dark media from our daily intake. Regrettably, this negative and pervasive content is omnipresent in today's digital environment. By consciously curating what we consume, we can foster a healthier outlook and a more optimistic attitude.

> *"Do you want to know what you think about most of the time? Take a look at the results you're getting. That will tell you exactly what's going on inside."*
>
> Bob Proctor[38]

Dark media pervades our existence, seeping into our daily routines through a multitude of channels. This is content that glorifies the most dreadful aspects of humanity, ranging from the glorification of violence and chaos to the extreme depths of human cruelty, hate speech, porn and demeaning representations of our world and its experiences. It manifests in the drama of reality TV, social media, internet, radio, podcasts, fiction books, and game videos that glorify killing, stealing, and sex.

Discerning between the beneficial and detrimental, the uplifting and the guttural, is not a challenging task. We inherently know what is positive and good for our nature versus what is negative and destructive. It's your choice what you download to your brain to calibrate your mindsets and support a positive attitude *if* you want to change to a better and positive you!

The more a pessimistic mindset consumes negative media, the more it craves to hear, watch and absorb it. This regrettable reality highlights the sinister character of dark media, which entraps us in mediocrity and the mundane. It keeps us stuck in thinking worthless thoughts and, more importantly, wasting time.

> *"Once you start down the dark path, forever will it dominate your destiny. Consume you, it will."*
>
> Yoda[39]

The power to combat this detrimental dark media influence rests within your grasp. You possess the ability to switch it off. Dark media is one of the simplest negative influences to eradicate, specifically because you have the authority to regulate what infiltrates your visual awareness and what you decide to interact with. Your paramount focus should be on cultivating your own life to personify your best self so you can genuinely affect a positive change in your attitude and identity.

> *"Guard well your spare moments. They are like uncut diamonds. Discard them and their value will never be known. Improve them and they will become the brightest gems in a useful life."*
> Ralph Waldo Emerson[40]

This quote underscores the significance of being conscious about how we utilize our time. It highlights the potential for personal development and satisfaction that can be derived from making intentional decisions in our positive media engagement and daily routines. It serves as a reminder that our choices can either contribute to our growth or hinder it, emphasizing the power we hold over our own lives in Finding JOY.

Your media consumption should serve as a wellspring of positivity, creativity, and wisdom that nourishes your intellect and attitude. Your brain is a sponge, soaking up everything your eyes witness and your ears perceive, thereby molding your attitude and sculpting your identity. Be the vigilant gatekeeper of your brain from the dark side. May the force be with you!

> *"When you look at the dark side, careful you must be. For the dark side looks back."*
>
> Yoda[41]

Oh, Joy! Another Day at the Grind

At least one third of life is spent working, so hopefully it's time well spent. The influence of a negative environment at your JOB (just over broke) or career on your overall life outlook and attitude is incredibly significant. Being perpetually immersed in a negative work atmosphere or a meaningless job can seep into your personal life and illuminate through your attitude.

Coping with office politics, financial difficulties, or job insecurity can dramatically escalate your stress levels, leading to anxiety and depression. When you're grappling with feelings of uncertainty or anxiety, maintaining a positive attitude on life or fostering healthy relationships with those around you becomes a daunting task. I've been there; I've done that!

Life is too fleeting to spend one-third of it in a miserable work environment, another third making your personal life unbearable, and the remaining third enduring restless sleep, stressed about the next workday. Your personal relationships and social connections will also be strained. If you constantly find yourself on edge or distressed due to work-related stress, it becomes challenging to be the best version of yourself as a partner, friend, or family member. Disagreements, alienation, verbal withdrawal, and emotional distress can gradually infiltrate your daily life until you eventually feel like a stranger in your own surroundings with an attitude to match.

> *"Negative thinking is subtle and deceptive. It wears many faces and hides behind the mask of excuses. It is important to strip away the mask and discover the real, root emotion."*
>
> Robert H. Schuller[42]

The amplification of these negative emotions can have a profound impact on your physical and mental well-being, as stated in many peer-reviewed university studies. When subjected to relentless stress in the workplace or the home environment you compromise your immune system, thereby increasing susceptibility to various diseases, illnesses, and syndromes. So, is stress and the accompanying negativity worth risking a cancer diagnosis? The answer is unequivocally no. Ultimately, this is like scuttling your own ship in the vast ocean of life. Yet we often find ourselves doing this daily, adhering to the corporate norm and then questioning why we feel trapped.

If you find yourself in this situation, then it's time for a strategic plan to transition from that time-sucking JOB or switch career paths. Discover your passion and have faith in your talents and abilities. Summon the courage to make the necessary changes that will lead you to your ultimate life. Embark on the journey to your mountain, to your envisioned future-self, but it begins with you making the positive change happen.

> **"Negativity in business is like a dark cloud that obscures the sun of opportunity."**
> Jon Gordon[43]

Maintaining motivation to enhance your life and pursue your dreams becomes an uphill battle when your work or home environment is a perpetual source of negativity. It becomes challenging to envision a broader perspective and the multitude of opportunities that exist beyond the confines of the office walls undermining your self-esteem, identity, and attitude.

The Journey of J. K. Rowling

J. K. Rowling is a well-known example of turning a negative job experience into positive, life-changing journey. Before her global success with the Harry Potter series, she faced many challenges. She was a single mother, endured financial struggles, and worked as a secretary at Amnesty International in London. She was unhappy in this job and often got reprimanded for daydreaming. She knew in her heart there had to be a greater life ahead.

She was eventually fired for not paying better attention to her secretarial duties. Rather than being defeated, Rowling used this as motivation to follow her passion for writing. With more free time, she dedicated herself to creating the story of a young wizard named Harry Potter.

> *"You sort of start thinking anything is possible if you've got enough nerve."*
>
> J. K. Rowling[44]

Despite enduring numerous rejections from publishers, Rowling remained steadfast in her determination. Her perseverance paid off when her manuscript was finally accepted. The result was the Harry Potter series, which skyrocketed to global fame and became one of the bestselling book series in history.

> *"I would like to be remembered as someone who did the best she could with the talent she had."*
>
> J. K. Rowling[45]

This monumental success transformed Rowling into one of the most celebrated authors of all time. What began as a negative life experience, being fired from her day job, ultimately guided her to discover her true calling and achieve unparalleled literary success. From a secretary's paycheck to one of the highest earning authors in the world, Rowling's net worth in approximately 2020 has been estimated at a mere $1.1 billion per Business Insider.[46] She found her greatness, her value, and most likely a better attitude!

We can change our outlook and attitude through determination and a shift in focus from our negative circumstances to what is possible. If you find yourself in a "value limiting" job that doesn't align with your values, then make it your mission to still be a beacon of positivity while you search for your next journey.

> *"You cannot control what happens to you, but you can control your attitude toward what happens to you, and in that, you will be mastering change rather than allowing it to master you."*
>
> Brian Tracy[47]

Always strive to elevate the atmosphere around you, contributing to a more uplifting and productive space. Alternatively, consider taking a break to assess your current position and explore other passions and career paths that may offer greater fulfillment and value for your time and talents. Remember, you are the architect of your own life. Neither your job nor your paycheck defines your potential or your happiness. Believe in yourself, and carry an unstoppable attitude in Finding JOY.

A Positive Attitude Attracts Positive-Minded People

Like mindsets think alike. So, who likes you?

In the complexities of human relationships, the power of an optimistic and positive attitude cannot be overstated. The common denominator of every success personal and professional is a positive and resilient attitude. It is not a guarantee, but it sure makes it easier to achieve your goals.

A positive attitude possess a unique ability to attract individuals of similar mindset, weaving together a harmonious and supportive social network of like-minded, growth-oriented people. This is the essence of your inner circle of friends and a great support foundation for life success.

The magnetic pull of positive dialogue and thoughts fortifies the bonds of trust, shared values, and aspirations, attracting those who radiate positivity into your life's journey. This is your tribe and pack, a concept discussed in chapter 5.

Positive dialogue and optimistic thinking radiate an energy that harmoniously aligns with those who possess a similar perspective on life. The law of attraction is at play here: Like attracts like! This principle manifests itself profoundly within the sphere of human interactions. Individuals with a positive mindset are instinctively attracted to others who exude a sense of optimism and enthusiasm.

> *"You attract what you are, not what you want. If you want great, then be great."*
> Wayne Dyer[48]

The Journey of Oprah Winfrey

Oprah's early years were marked by profound adversity. Raised in the impoverished rural landscape of Mississippi, she faced a multitude of challenges, including severe abuse, discrimination, and a stark absence of opportunities.

Despite these formidable obstacles, Oprah nurtured an unyielding sense of self-worth and determination from a tender age. Fueled by the conviction that she could transcend her circumstances, she relentlessly pursued a better life, embodying a resilient attitude and a positive determination against all odds.

As Oprah built her media career, she focused on spreading positivity, empathy, and empowerment. She wasn't just after success; she wanted to raise her value by helping others. Her genuine nature and commitment to self-improvement attracted opportunities that matched her values and goals.

Oprah became one of the most influential people in the world through her roles as a talk show host, producer, and philanthropist. She lived with purpose, integrity, and passion, which attracted life opportunities and eventually her success. Her life shows that by being great and raising her value, she achieved life greatness.

Oprah's journey illustrates that greatness isn't merely a wish or a hope; it's a state of being achieved through personal transformation and a clarity of your future self. As you evolve and grow, you inherently attract people, success, and opportunities that will resonate with an unstoppable, positive attitude. It all starts with your attitude and those you surround yourself with.

> *"Surround yourself with only people who are going to lift you higher."*
>
> Oprah Winfrey[49]

From an early stage in Oprah's career, she recognized the importance of networking with individuals who could potentially enhance the value of her time. It's safe to say that she didn't attract individuals with negative, bitter attitudes or pessimistic outlooks, but rather those with a vibrant, positive vision for the future. Again, like attracts like! Transform your attitude to transform your destination.

The takeaway: If you perceive your time as having positive value, then it will be reflected in your attitude. As a result, you will attract people who are positive and value-oriented. So be proactive and selfish with your time. Give it to those who can enrich your time with increased value and added experience on the path to your future self.

> *"Time is the coin of your life. It is the only coin you have, and only you can determine how it will be spent. Be careful lest you let other people spend it for you."*
>
> Carl Sandburg[50]

The Emotional Contagion

Are you contagious with the positivity virus?

Human emotions possess a remarkable capacity to spread and influence those around us, a phenomenon known as "emotional contagion." This concept is well-supported by psychological research, which demonstrates that emotions such as happiness, excitement, and positivity can be transmitted from one person to another through social interactions, both consciously and subconsciously.[51]

Positive emotions can cultivate an uplifting atmosphere, generating a ripple effect that elevates the mood and well-being of everyone within your influence. Conversely, negative emotions can also propagate and create a detrimental effect on the whole.

Do you have a positivity virus, or are you carrying around a "negative bacteria" and infecting everyone? The good news is a person's attitude is the tell-tale sign of what type of contagion a person is carrying! Are they sniffling with criticism, or smiling with optimism? Stay away from the sniffling person; they will infect your attitude!

> *"Positivity changes how your mind works.*
> *Positivity doesn't just change the contents of your mind, trading bad thoughts for good ones, it also changes the scope or boundaries of your mind. It widens the span of possibilities that you see."*
> Barbara L. Fredrickson[52]

Barbara Fredrickson's "broaden and build" theory of positive emotions proposes that positivity broadens our cognitive horizon, stimulating the formation and strengthening of social bonds. Again, positive people, via a positive attitude, attracts other positive people.

Positive Attitude + Purpose Clarity = Life Freedom

Positivity is intrinsically intertwined with trustworthiness. When people habitually radiate positive speech and thoughts, they naturally inspire trust in others. This trust encourages people to feel more at ease, fostering open communication and deeper connections. Trust serves as the bedrock for all thriving relationships and is the cornerstone of all successful businesses.

> *"Trust is the glue of life. It's the most essential ingredient in effective communication."*
>
> Stephen Covey[53]

Did you catch the attraction secret? Know, like, and trust foundational support is positivity based on your positive attitude! You will go nowhere fast with a negative or bitter attitude if that is your calling card.

Individuals radiating a positive attitude often cultivate environments that are not only uplifting but also memorable. When others perceive that your presence fosters positivity, they are instinctively attracted to become part of your blue-sky stratosphere.

> *"People will forget what you said, people will forget what you did, but people will never forget how you made them feel."*
>
> Maya Angelou[54]

Positive communication can serve as a potent instrument for networking, enabling you to cultivate a strong inner circle of friends and associates. It facilitates the formation of bonds with individuals who resonate with your, attitude, identity, ambitions, and dreams. Such connections frequently pave the way for collaborative efforts, reciprocal support, and individual development that leads to innovation and success.

You can choose to live under a rock and struggle your time away, or you can do your best cannonball jump into the vibrant pool of life with an infectious enthusiasm, announcing your presence to the world! Is your life's journey in pursuit of joy viewed through a lens of scarcity or abundance? Do you opt for the rock or the pool? The attitude you radiate daily will shape your life's trajectory.

> *"Virtually nothing is impossible in this world if you just put your mind to it and maintain a positive attitude."*
>
> Lou Holtz[55]

In the grand symphony of life, the chords of positivity and optimism echo with universal harmony. Positive dialogue and thoughts are not just reflections of one's attitude and mindset; they serve as powerful beacons that network positive people into our lives. It all starts with the attitude you project every day to the world.

> *"You are the only real obstacle in your path to a fulfilling life."*
>
> Les Brown[56]

The universe is calling you to find your greatness, but it begins with you embracing the world with a positive, unstoppable attitude. Do you perceive your glass as half empty or half full? The Journey of Attitude is the icing on your cake, it's your sweetness, it's your radiant beacon to light up the world. What lies beneath your sweet icing is the person you truly are, your identity.

Fear deeply affects attitude and personal identity, shaping self-perception, actions, and choices. Facing your fears can lead to significant personal growth and a more authentic self. Dealing with fear can also help us discover hidden strengths, build resilience, and develop a stronger sense of self.

In the next chapter, we will explore the Journey of Fear in how to manage fear to drive self-discovery, personal growth, and a more resilent mindset for a stronger idenity and a confident attitude.

> *"Our attitudes control our lives. Attitudes are a secret power working twenty-four hours a day, for good or bad. It is of paramount importance that we know how to harness and control this great force."*
>
> Irving Berlin[57]

Journey Rest Stop 7

1) How crucial is Vitamin A-ttitude for your persona, life goals, and well-being?

2) How can you integrate the MARCH (**Motivation, Associations, Resiliency, Creativity, and Health**) method into your daily life?

3) Your job takes up approximately one third of your life, but it can feel like it engulfs your entire being. It's worth pondering how your job shapes your identity. Is it merely a stepping stone toward achieving a higher purpose, or does it hold significant value in defining who you are?

Journey Thought

"The most important thing you'll ever wear is your attitude."

Jeff Moore[58]

www.FindingJOY.us

Chapter 8

Journey of Fear

What's Got You Scared?

Of all the liars in the world, sometimes the worst are our own fears.

Rudyard Kipling[1]

In the era of pre-history, fear was hardwired into our DNA, serving as a crucial survival mechanism. This fight-or-flight response was our lifeline, enabling us to evade the lethal clutches of predators such as the saber-toothed tiger or the formidable T-Rex. Today, although these prehistoric beasts no longer pose a mortal threat, our fear response remains active. It is now constantly engaged, working overtime to navigate the perceived stresses and threats of our modern-day society.

In our intricate, contemporary society, the nature of fear has significantly evolved. It has transitioned from the primal fear of being devoured by a saber-toothed tiger or being consumed by fire to a myriad of diverse fears that we encounter in our daily lives, such as car wrecks, break-ins, road rage, poverty, job security, relationships, and so on.

Intriguingly, Yale University's Poorvu Center for Teaching and Learning notes, "It is estimated that 75% of all people suffer from fear of public speaking."[2] When juxtaposed with the primal fears of our Neanderthal ancestors, such as becoming a mid-day snack for a T-Rex, our fears seem relatively benign. Given this perspective, I would gladly embrace the opportunity to command center stage in front of an audience of five thousand people any day!

> *"Fears are nothing more than a state of mind."*
>
> Napoleon Hill[3]

Throughout the course of human evolution, a number of fears has taken root in our psyche. These fears, despite their diversity, can be divided into four fundamental categories I call The Four Ps of Fear: primal, phobia, peripheral, and preemptive.

Each of these fears elicits similar reactions of anxiety, worry, and the instinct to flee at varying intensities. However, they differ significantly in their implications and the ways they influence the trajectory of our lives.

> *"We fear things in proportion to our ignorance of them."*
>
> Christian Nestell Bovee[4]

Certain fears serve a beneficial purpose, acting as a survival instinct that prevents us from engaging in reckless behavior. Yet a significant portion of the fears we encounter are unfounded. These fears hinder us from fully embracing life, from utilizing our talents to their maximum potential, and from adopting a growth mindset in the face of challenges and change. Our fears keep us mired in a fixed mindset, limiting our ability to evolve, adapt, and change while reinforcing our limiting beliefs and behaviors.

The Four Ps of Fear

- **Primal Fear = Hard-Wired Fear**
- **Phobia Fear = Self-Induced Fear**
- **Preemptive Fear = Generalized Fear**
- **Peripheral Fear = Behavioral Fear**

Fear can be subtyped into four groups, which I refer to as the Four "Ps" of Fear. All fear is a primal human emotion and innate instinct we experience almost on a daily basis. Regrettably, many of us live a fear driven life that stalls our ability in Finding JOY. So, let's define fear to overcome it to lead a fearless fulfilling life. A good question to keep in mind as you read this chapter is:

"How fearful would you be about anything if you knew you could not fail? Is your fear greater or less than your belief in your ultimate success?"

Primal Fears

Primal fears are deeply ingrained in our DNA, a survival mechanism inherited from our prehistoric ancestors to protect us from imminent threats such as being pursued by a T-Rex. Today, these primal fears remain an integral part of our existence, manifesting as an unsettling sensation when faced with a potential threat to our lives. Such fears may be triggered in various situations, like when an airplane pilot announces an emergency landing, when you're caught in a violent storm, or when you are being pursued by an assailant. Essentially, any uncontrollable situation that poses a real or perceived threat to your life can awaken these instinctive fears.

These survival instincts serve a crucial role, provided they are activated by genuine confrontational events that pose a risk to your life or the lives of your loved ones. They are not merely remnants of our evolutionary past; they serve as vital tools for our survival in the present when we are not running from saber-tooth tigers!

Phobia Fears

Phobia fears, which are learned fears, can have a genetic predisposition to anxiety and increase the likelihood of phobia development. But these fears are rooted in life experiences, typically from an early age. Phobia fears can evolve into life-altering mental anxieties. A phobia is defined as a "persistent, excessive, and *unrealistic* fear of an object, person, animal, activity, or situation."[5]

There are countless phobias that we can develop, ranging from the fear of insects to the fear of cell phones, known as nomophobia. Glad I don't have that one! Phobia fears trigger an unhealthy fight-or-flight response to a hyper-perceived object, animal, or situation, which may or may not pose an immediate threat to our life or physical well-being. This type of fear is classified as an anxiety disorder.

If a fear significantly inhibits our life, such as the fear of venturing outdoors, it necessitates treatment from a licensed psychologist. Life is too precious and fleeting to be hindered by such debilitating, relentless, and unrealistic fears. Fortunately, these fears can be treated, allowing us to reclaim our lives and live without the constant shadow of fear.

> *"I had the feeling every time I was on a plane everyone was going to die. It was a horrible phobia. A stupid one."*
>
> Christine McVie[6]

Preemptive Fears

Preemptive fears are persistent thoughts that plague our daily lives, often leading to generalized anxiety and depression. These fears can encompass a wide array of concerns such as financial instability, domestic problems, health issues, and the challenges of everyday life. As humans, we often find ourselves ensnared in a web of worry. However, for some of us, this constant state of apprehension becomes a deeply ingrained lifestyle.

> *"Worry does not empty tomorrow of its sorrow, it empties today of its strength."*
>
> Corrie Ten Boom[7]

The key to eliminating worry lies in the understanding and mental acceptance that worry is not a solution to any problem or issue. Rather, it drains your energy and leaves you grappling with the same problem. Worry is our instinctive response to confront an issue, often leading us to obsess over potential outcomes that we perceive as negative impacts on our lives.

Worry is a form of fear that perpetuates a fixed mindset, proving to be relentless and unyielding. It's akin to scuttling your own ship while attempting to weather a violent storm. Not only does worry impede your journey toward a joyful life, but it is also scientifically linked to heightened anxiety levels and the development of health conditions, such as hypertension and heart disease.

The Bible provides profound insights about the emotion of worry, particularly in the book of Matthew. In the renowned Sermon on the Mount, Jesus delivers a powerful message, expressing His desire for us not to be encumbered by worry. This sentiment is eloquently encapsulated in Matthew 6:25 – 34 as stated below.

"Do not worry about your life." (v. 25)

"Can any one of you by worrying add a single hour to your life?" (v. 27)

"Therefore, do not worry about tomorrow, for tomorrow will worry about itself. Each day has enough trouble of its own." (v. 34)

The profound truth in verse 27 is undeniable. Worry, rather than extending our lives, ironically shortens them and diminishes our happiness. This biblical wisdom does not promise a life devoid of troubles. Instead, these words guide us to concentrate on the challenges of the present day, allowing the future to take care of itself.

This is valuable advice, considering a recent 2020 study on generalized anxiety stated that 91.4 percent of our worries often turn out to be either baseless or significantly less severe than we initially imagined.[8] Worry is not only a waste of time, but also a hindrance to our progress and active participation in life.

While worry is an inherent part of our human nature, we can consciously work to reduce unnecessary worry from our thoughts. This way, we can focus more on the present, enhancing our overall well-being and productivity.

> **"Worry does not empty tomorrow of its sorrow. It empties today of its strength."**
>
> Corrie Ten Boom[9]

Worry stemming from fear can be rechanneled. So, what strategies can we employ to diminish worry and anxiety to redirect our energy toward more productive, joyful, and fearless pursuits? Identify the root cause of your worry by pinpointing the fear that is triggering it. Essentially, you need to ask yourself, what is the underlying fear that is causing this worry? Is it a tangible fear that could potentially cause physical harm, such as standing too close to the edge of a cliff? Or is it an emotional fear related to a particular situation, issue, or person?

You need to distinguish whether the fear is a genuine threat, like being a T-Rex's lunch, or an imagined one, such as boarding an overcrowded Boeing 747. If the fear is imagined and does not pose a real threat, you have the power to manage and redirect this fear, thereby alleviating the associated anxiety and worry.

Peripheral Fears

Peripheral fears are a common part of everyday life as we interact with people and life situations. Unlike primal fears or phobias, which can evoke intense feelings of dread, peripheral fears often go unnoticed as they are not typically associated with strong emotional responses. Instead, these behavioral fears are often manifested through verbal or mental reactions. As we know, typical fear can trigger both emotional and physical responses. However, in the case of peripheral fears, they are often reflected in our verbal responses, subtly guiding our words and actions to stay within the lines to ensure our comfort and security.

In essence, peripheral fears shape your life experiences and govern your reactions and responses to daily challenges and situations. They construct the framework of your life experiences and project your life's trajectory.

> *"Too many of us are not living our dreams*
> *because we are living our fears."*
>
> Les Brown[10]

Peripheral fears originate from a fixed mindset, an over-protective way of thinking that limits growth and opportunities. When faced with a problem or a task, you might experience temporary stress, transient anxiety, or perhaps no emotional response at all. This is because your peripheral fear reaction is a learned behavioral response, a product of your past experiences.

We all harbor peripheral fears, but the silver lining is that we have the power to transform many of them. By doing so, we can enrich our life journey and experience more opportunities and a deeper sense of life fulfillment.

Peripheral fears refer to the apprehensions or benign anxieties we experience when faced with tasks or situations that push us out of our comfort zones. These could include being asked to deliver a speech, leading a group, or making a significant life change. These fears often challenge our perceived ability to obtain success or our capability to be successful. The common antidote humans resort to when we feel fear or challenged or stressed is a simple, yet powerful word called "NO". The word "No" is our comfort blanket that keeps us safe in our cave.

In today's world, the metaphorical saber-toothed tiger that we grapple with is our inherent fear of not being successful or our fear of failure. Our protective Neanderthal cave symbolizes our modern-day comfort zone, a place we retreat to when faced with challenges and fears we can't overcome.

> *"Too many people are thinking of security instead of opportunity. They seem to be more afraid of life than death."*
>
> James Byrnes[11]

Unlike our primal ancestors who lived in constant fear of being hunted, we may not experience such daily fight-or-flight reactions. However, it's no surprise that the fear trigger is deeply ingrained in our DNA, given its historical role in protecting us from being an afternoon snack.

Today, our virtual T-Rexes may not physically consume us, but they can still confine us to our virtual Neanderthal cave, our comfort zones where we tightly hold to our primal defensive spear of "No."

In prehistoric times, primal fear might have signified the end of a Neanderthal life, but in today's modern world, peripheral fear often signifies the end of living a fulfilling and abundant life for many of us today. It's a disheartening reality that this peripheral fear is a primary reason why numerous people pass away with regret wondering, *What if I would have said yes?* "What IF..." is the precursor to life regret. The antidote to "What if" is "Why not."

"Don't fear failure so much that you refuse to try new things. The saddest summary of a life contains three descriptions: could have, might have, and should have."

Louis E. Boone[12]

Peripheral fear restrains us when we should be embracing the courage to say yes, stepping out of our comfort zones, away from our virtual caves, for greater life opportunities and experiences.

"Most people think small, because most people are afraid of success, afraid of making decisions, afraid of winning."

Donald J. Trump[13]

Peripheral fear also serves as a safeguard, shielding us from confronting failure and subsequent success. Societal norms have ingrained in us the notion that failure is a bad thing, a sign of weakness, which reinforces a fixed mindset. This societal conditioning, which we will discuss later, plays a pivotal role in shaping peripheral fear, a learned behavior early in life.

Peripheral fear can be defined into two overlapping thoughts that we experience daily: limiting behaviors and limiting beliefs. These two are closely related but refer to different actions of how we may hold ourselves back from reaching our full potential of getting out of the cave.

"You begin to fly when you let go of self-limiting beliefs and allow your mind and aspirations to rise to greater heights."

Brian Tracy[14]

Limiting Behavior

This Is Holding You Back!

Limiting behaviors are actions or patterns that restrict our ability to grow, achieve goals, or live fully. These behaviors are often rooted in limiting beliefs, which manifest in ways that hold us back from taking action. Some common examples of limiting behaviors include:

- Procrastination on important tasks due to a fear of failure.

- Avoiding social situations because of a belief that one is not likable.

- Refusing to apply for a promotion because of a belief that one is unqualified.

- Fear of taking on new opportunities due to a bad past experience. *"Done that once, never again!"*

Limiting behaviors significantly impact our ability to progress and succeed. They can reinforce limiting beliefs by providing evidence that these beliefs are true, creating a vicious cycle that is difficult to break. This is a major reason why many people find themselves stuck in life.

The life story of Howard Schultz, CEO of Starbucks, exemplifies the challenges of self-doubt and limiting beliefs. Growing up in a low-income family in Brooklyn, New York, Schultz often felt that his modest origins hindered his ambitions. He frequently questioned whether someone from his background could genuinely lead a successful business or make a significant global impact.

> *"I believe life is a series of near misses. A lot of what we ascribe to luck is not luck at all. It's seizing the day and accepting responsibility for your future. It's seeing what other people don't see and pursuing that vision."*
>
> Howard Schultz[15]

Initially, Schultz was reluctant to take risks, including the decision to acquire Starbucks when it was merely a small coffee shop in Seattle. He struggled with doubts about his ability to compete against wealthier, more experienced business leaders. However, Schultz eventually transformed his perspective, viewing his background as an asset rather than a disadvantage. He recognized that his upbringing instilled in him resilience and empathy. Schultz embraced a bold vision for Starbucks, aspiring to create more than just a coffee business; he envisioned it as a "third place" for community gathering beyond home and work. Under his leadership, Starbucks evolved from a local Seattle establishment into a global coffee phenomenon tapping into a European café concept meeting place centered around coffee drinks. This is an example of a growth mindset thinking, taking an existing idea and evolving it into a new concept. Schultz frequently shares his journey as a testament to how overcoming self-doubt and limiting beliefs can pave the way to remarkable success.

My "Stage Fright" Life Experience

Here is a personal experience with limiting behavior that could have been a lifelong fear and altered my identity. When I was about ten, I was entrusted with a few lines in our school play. The thought of performing in front of an audience of two hundred grade-school parents and teachers was a little scary.

My first brush with embarrassment was a painful one, as I blanked out and forgot my lines on stage. Everyone started to laugh, which echoed in my ears felt like a failure and was completely humiliated. In reality, they found my innocent blunder endearing, but my young mind misinterpreted their laughter. This life experience instilled a deep-seated fear in me, making me vow to never speak in front of a crowd again.

A single incident early in my life had compelled me to carry a fear of speaking, convinced that I was not good enough. It was not until my junior year in high school that I had a turning point in the form of a speech coach who encouraged me to enroll in his impromptu speech class.

I told him I was not good at speaking but did not tell him how fearful fear I was. He said, "If you can talk, then you can speak!" Checkmate! He then encouraged me to enroll. Begrudgingly, I signed up for his class, harboring the hope that I wouldn't flunk. To my surprise, impromptu speaking turned out to be a fun experience. The best part was that I didn't have to memorize any lines! Impromptu speaking, you see, is the skill of speaking spontaneously on any topic, drawing from your own knowledge. It's essentially a conversational speech. This style of speaking was an ideal match for my apprehensions and personality traits!

During my high school years, conversing with friends was a breeze, but the thought of delivering a speech in front of a live audience was utterly terrifying. However, when it came to impromptu speaking, I found a unique way to overcome my fear. I began to perceive the audience as a group of my friends, and I was simply the one leading the conversation. This mental trick helped me conquer my fear! Initially, it was a rocky start, but with time, I started to excel. I began to win speech competitions, which significantly boosted my confidence. Not only did I triumph in these contests, but I also achieved an A in the class!

Today, I still experience a little flutter of nerves before I step onto a stage. However, I simply remind myself that the audience is just a group of my high school friends, and just like that, my fear dissipates.

Limiting Beliefs

Limiting beliefs are self-imposed thoughts or assumptions that restrict our perception of what is achievable. These beliefs often become deeply embedded through personal experiences, cultural influences, or lessons learned during our formative years. Examples of limiting beliefs would be:

- *I'm not good enough to succeed in this career.*
- *I will never be able to learn a new language.*
- *People like me don't achieve great things.*

Such limiting beliefs create mental barriers that inhibit us from exploring opportunities, taking risks, or even contemplating new possibilities. They shape our self-view and potential, often leading to a self-fulfilling prophecy where we unconsciously behave in ways that validate these beliefs.

Limiting beliefs frequently result in limiting behaviors. For instance, if someone believes they are not competent enough to succeed, a limiting belief, they might shy away from challenges or opportunities, a limiting behavior. Conversely, engaging in limiting behaviors can reinforce these beliefs, making it increasingly challenging to break free from them.

> *"Many people are passionate, but because of their limiting beliefs about who they are and what they can do, they never take actions that could make their dream a reality."*
>
> Tony Robbins[16]

To overcome both limiting beliefs and limiting behaviors, it is essential to identify and challenge the underlying beliefs, then consciously adopt new, more empowering thoughts. This shift from a leaning fixed mindset can lead to changes in behavior, allowing us to act and think in ways that support growth and achievement.

In chapter 1, we discussed the concept that limiting beliefs are inherently intertwined with a fixed mindset. The greater we lean toward a fixed mindset, the greater our limiting beliefs are about our capabilities, talents, and potential as we interact with the world around us.

> **"Once you replace limiting beliefs with empowering ones, your entire world changes."**
> Eric Worre[17]

Peripheral fear operates relentlessly within a fixed mindset, constraining our life experiences due to an overwhelming fear of failure, which creates an attitude that says, "Why try?" This fear is often fueled by our adherence to a misguided internal voice, our negative critic, that keeps us tethered to our Neanderthal comfort caves.

Your negative critic voice, rather than encouraging growth and exploration, promotes stagnation and complacency, thereby limiting your potential for personal development and fulfillment. This reminds me of a great entrepreneurial story of Mary Kay Ash.

The Journey of Mary Kay Ash

In 1963, Mary Kay Ash, at the age of forty-five, boldly stepped away from the conventional eight-to-five workday and embarked on a new journey. With an initial investment of $5,000, she established Mary Kay Cosmetics, a venture that would revolutionize the beauty industry. In today's dollars, her initial investment would be around $55,000, so she was committed and had strong belief in herself!

She courageously embraced her future, rejecting the constraints of her self-limiting beliefs. Today, her legacy lives on in a company that boasts annual cosmetic sales of $2.2 billion, powered by a robust sales force of over 1.6 million consultants worldwide.

Imagine if Mary Kay had allowed the fear of failure to overshadow her desire for change. If she had chosen to conform rather than challenge the status quo, the world would have been deprived of Mary Kay Cosmetics and the opportunities it has provided for millions to enhance their lives.

> *"Don't limit yourself. Many people limit themselves to what they think they can do. You can go as far as your mind lets you. What you believe, remember, you can achieve."*
>
> Mary Kay Ash[18]

Mary Kay's secret to success was her unwavering belief in her potential. She transformed her fear-driven mindset from "I can't; therefore I am" to "I can; therefore I will become." Her conviction in her abilities far outweighed any doubts she may have had. She confronted her peripheral fears and transitioned from a frustrated fixed mindset to a growth mindset, rewriting her life story in the process and created value for millions of people.

> *"Fear defeats more people than any other one thing in the world."*
>
> Ralph Waldo Emerson[19]

Are You in the "No" Crowd?

One apprehension toward seizing opportunities is fundamentally rooted in the fear of failing in our pursuit of success. This is the breeding ground for our limiting beliefs and behavior. Transforming these restrictive beliefs can be a daunting task for many of us, as the word "no" provides a sense of safety and our comfort lies in conformity of the NO crowd.

The majority of us are resistant to change and feel uneasy when faced with uprooting the status quo. We tend to prefer conformity and like being part of the herd because there is safety in numbers, you won't be killed by a T-Rex, unlikely to get fired or worse face failure. If you like the herd, then stay. But don't complain later in life of your regret for not getting uncomfortable and doing something different like tempting T-Rex.

Indeed, we find comfort in the familiarity of the crowd and the work force. If we manage to navigate through our day without any major disruptions or challenges, we consider it a successful day spent in our comfort zone, our cave without being eaten by our boss or T-Rex.

We are generally content to replicate this routine day after day, maintaining this pattern until a significant event forces us to alter our course, or we discover a more valuable way to "spend" our time.

> *"Remember, we all get what we tolerate. So stop tolerating excuses within yourself, limiting beliefs of the past, or half-assed or fearful states."*
>
> Tony Robbins[20]

The good news is that we possess the power to transform our self-limiting beliefs and behaviors through unwavering determination, steadfast dedication, and consistent daily effort. This process involves a significant shift in our mindset, altering how we perceive challenges, manage issues, and initiate action.

If your self-imposed limitations are anchoring you to the past, causing you to view your life's journey as merely another day in the sandbox, it's time to break free. If you find yourself frustrated, knowing that there's a more fulfilling life awaiting you, then it's time to step out of your comfort zone. Step out of your cave, just like Howard Schultz or Mary Kay Ash did. Go forward, embrace change, and chart your journey toward an abundant life of purpose, value, and freedom while saying goodbye to the herd.

> *"Change happens when the pain of staying the same is greater than the pain of change."*
>
> Tony Robbins[21]

Let me offer a different spin on Tony's quote: "Change happens when the fear of conformity is greater than the fear of change." Remember, conformity does not want you to leave the herd or your cave!

When we dare to question our self-imposed limiting beliefs and behaviors, we are essentially challenging our inclination to blend in with the crowd. This act of defiance often leaves us exposed to potential embarrassment, ridicule, and criticism from both our friendship circle and our other associations.

These fears, based in our egocentric nature, can trap us in the past and keep us comfortably ensconced in our metaphorical caves. It's crucial to remember that the pressure to conform doesn't want us to break away from the crowd, which is often why many individuals fail to realize their inherent potential and value.

> *"You must accept a temporary loss of social esteem from ignorant people."*
> Eric Worre[22]

Ironically, our egos can trap us in a cycle of conformity, driven by the fear of being judged. This ultimately hinders us from embracing our true potential and stepping into the future lives we are meant to lead. Yes, our egos are a costly burden to carry to direct our lives. So what are some of the self-imposed barriers you mentally create due to fear of the unknown, fear of venturing beyond your cave or deviating from the herd?

> **"You must remain focused on your journey to greatness."**
>
> Les Brown[23]

Any thought that commences with, "I can't... I don't know... I'm not... I don't have..." or any variety of excuses that prevent you from seizing an opportunity to broaden your influence, reach, and contribution to the world serves as a protective phrase, your "no" spear.

These protective excuses are not rooted in a lack of experience, contrary to the lies we often tell ourselves. Instead, these excuses reflect a lack of confidence to navigate the unknown, to progress, and to accomplish our goals. This is the key distinction between a fixed and growth mindset.

> **"If somebody offers you an amazing opportunity but you are not sure you can do it, say yes, then learn how to do it later!"**
>
> Richard Branson[24]

Imagine if entrepreneurial visionaries like Richard Branson, Elon Musk, Bill Gates, Mark Zuckerberg, Howard Schultz, Mary Kay Ash, Larry Page, Gloria Mayfield Banks, Henry Ford, Oprah Winfrey, and countless others who have revolutionized our world had simply said, "I can't." How drastically different would our world be?

Yes, these individuals are undeniably intelligent, but they were born with the same potential for intellect and creativity as you and I. The key distinction lies in their refusal to let self-imposed limitations obstruct their path to create limitless value for themselves and contribution to the world. They developed their purpose and acted on their vision - the golden keys to success.

They may not have had initial clarity of their ultimate destination, but they all shared a common understanding. If they could contribute significant value to the world, they would, in turn, become valuable in a process, in their journey. These trailblazers didn't just wish and dream; they dared to act, to challenge, to innovate. They understood that their value was not defined by their circumstances, but by their contributions and their relentless pursuit of purpose for a better tomorrow.

> *"Successful people are always looking for opportunities to help others. Unsuccessful people are always asking, 'What's in it for me?'"*
>
> Brain Tracy[25]

Change Happens When Action Happens!

Let's embark on a journey of embracing actions and opportunities that propel us beyond our comfort caves, elevate our intrinsic value, and develop our intellect. This proactive approach will empower you to distinguish yourself and make a significant impact. Let me offer you some actionable ideas you can implement:

> *"There are risks and costs to action. But they are far less than the long-range risks of comfortable inaction."*
>
> John F. Kennedy[26]

• **Set Ambitious Goals:** Identify goals that challenge your current abilities and compel you to step outside your usual routines. Break these goals into manageable steps and track your progress regularly to stay motivated and on course. Your growth journey is worth capturing. Start a journal of your progress and reflections. You can receive a personalized Growth Journal by joining our JOY Community at www.FindingJOY.us.

• **Explore New Experiences:** Dive into new activities, hobbies, or projects that have piqued your curiosity but remain uncharted. This exploration will help you acquire new skills, broaden your perspective, and increase your friendship circle.

• **Expand Your Network:** Attend networking events, join groups or clubs, and connect with people beyond your typical social circle. Engaging with diverse people can introduce you to new opportunities and fresh ideas.

• **Take Calculated Risks:** Venture out of your comfort cave by making decisions that involve a certain level of risk. Evaluate potential outcomes and make informed choices that align with your growth aspirations. Push yourself to embody a growth mindset. Find an opportunity that aligns with your purpose.

• **Invest in Learning:** Read! Expand your knowledge through seminars, mentorship programs, and trainings in areas that captivate you to fulfill your purpose. This could encompass formal coursework, online classes, or self-directed study, all of which contribute to your personal and professional development.

• **Seek Accountability:** Regularly seek accountability from peers and mentors to gain valuable insights into areas where you can enhance your performance, achieve growth and track your progress.

• **Plan, Do, and Adjust:** Periodically assess your progress and reflect on your experiences. Adjust your strategies as needed to remain aligned with your evolving goals and values.

By implementing these steps, you'll transcend limitations, amplify your personal and professional growth, and distinguish yourself in meaningful and impactful ways.

So, what are the barriers of your limiting beliefs and behaviors? It is crucial to recognize the limiting beliefs that are impeding your progress. The majority of these limiting beliefs originate from the fear of failing, both personally and publicly. These convictions can be profoundly embedded in your subconscious mind. It might require a degree of introspection to identify the underlying reasons for the limiting thoughts that weigh you down and keep you from your joy.

Challenge Your Thoughts

Challenge your limiting beliefs: Limiting beliefs are deeply ingrained within us, primarily taking root during our formative years, and are intrinsically linked to our mindset. These beliefs act as invisible barriers, hindering our journey toward a life of abundance and prosperity.

> *"Once your mindset changes, everything on the outside will change along with it."*
>
> Steve Maraboli[27]

All of us harbor limiting beliefs to varying degrees, with some struggling more than others. If you aspire to elevate your life's journey, it's crucial to pinpoint your limiting beliefs and the underlying fears associated with them. For instance, in my personal experience, the fear of public speaking was rooted in the fear of embarrassment. This fear was intrinsically linked to a past event in my life: a school play.

Spend some time identifying each of your limiting beliefs and their corresponding fears. The foundation of all limiting beliefs is the emotional apprehension of failing in a future endeavor. Now it's time to confront and challenge these fears that give rise to your limiting beliefs.

> *"Many people are passionate, but because of their limiting beliefs about who they are and what they can do, they never take actions that could make their dream a reality."*
>
> Tony Robins[28]

These fears may include feelings of embarrassment, ridicule, rejection, imperfection, vulnerability, loneliness, and fear of change, among others. More often than not, these limiting beliefs are founded on flawed assumptions, outdated information, or past experiences that have instilled these fears within you, acting as invisible chains that hold you back. Fear, in essence, is an emotional response triggered by the anticipation of potential failure resulting from a specific action.

Reframe Your Fears

Reframe your limiting-belief fears: Rather than accepting your limiting beliefs as unshakeable truths or viewing your fears as insurmountable obstacles, endeavor to reshape them into a more positive and empowering perspective.

> *"Can you imagine a life with no fear? What if faith, not fear, was your default reaction to threats?"*
>
> Max Lucado[29]

For instance, if you're convinced that you're incapable of being a leader in your workplace or organization due to feelings of inadequacy, stemming from fear of insecurity, strive to transform that belief into a positive affirmation such as, "I am fully capable of learning and growing. I may encounter hurdles, but I will emerge stronger and more competent with each step!" As you reframe your fears, understand that everyone experiences setbacks on their path to growth. It's an integral part of the journey to success. By confronting and overcoming the fears tied to your limiting beliefs and behaviors, you build confidence and self-esteem, which will propel you forward on your journey.

> *"You have to be willing to allow the person you are today to die so that you can give birth to the person you are meant to become."*
>
> Les Brown[30]

Let Go to Expand Your Life

Let go of fear to expand your life experience. Boarding a roller coaster serves as a perfect metaphor for the limiting beliefs that many of us harbor. Initially, we may be held back by the self-imposed protective phrases, such as, "I can't do this!" followed by the accompanying fear: "I'm going to die!" This fear of harm is a primal instinct that often hinders us from getting out of our caves.

> *"All too often we're filled with negative and limiting beliefs. We're filled with doubt. We're filled with guilt or with a sense of unworthiness. We have a lot of assumptions about the way the world is that are actually wrong."*
>
> Jack Canfield[31]

The Wrath of Rakshasa

As you stand in line, a little nervous, you look up to see the massive roller coaster called Wrath of Rakshasa. At this point you are doubting yourself as to why you are getting on this behemoth but then you observe the throng of people disembarking the ride, their faces lit up with laughter and joy. You realize that they've all survived the thrilling experience, and this realization eases your fear slightly. However, the moment they strapped your body in the front row of the roller coaster with your feet dangling below you, your fear escalates into sheer panic knowing you were going to die. Lucky you, you got a front row seat to your own death!

You can't get off now, you'll embarrass yourself in front of all these people you don't know. As you were contemplating this thought, the roller coaster jolts and commences its steep ascent up the trestle. When you open your eyes, you see a breathtaking, panoramic view of our beautiful planet. The fear subsides, replaced by exhilaration and awe. You are now doing The Wrath of Rakshasa like a pro, with your hands up and screaming your head off!

As the ride ends, you find yourself laughing along with everyone else, wondering why you were so afraid in the first place. Amusingly, you find yourself drawn back to the line, ready to experience the thrill once more. You truly are a courageous soul!

"Life has no limits except the ones you make"
Les Brown[32]

In this scenario, the apprehension prior to the ride was merely an unfounded emotion. If you had succumbed to it, you would have missed out on an exhilarating experience. Moreover, you would have been deprived of the opportunity to regale others with your thrilling tale of survival. Imagine the awe in their eyes as you recount how you braved the Wrath of Rakshasa not once, but twice, and lived to talk about it!

Always bear in mind that each limiting belief is intrinsically linked to a specific fear. By successfully eliminating this underlying fear, you will consequently eradicate the limiting belief and behavior. Once you've successfully restructured your limiting beliefs and eradicated the foundational fears, it's time to actively practice your newfound attitude of "I can!"

This involves frequently reciting positive affirmations to yourself and integrating them seamlessly into your everyday life. Gradually, these empowering, positive beliefs will become second nature to you. What once filled you with fear will now inspire your new found freedom.

Having lifted your internal burden of fear, you are now liberated to boldly confront the world. Your bravery in facing your fears has the potential to revolutionize every aspect of your life. You are charting a path to a new you, a new identity, a new life forward, a new journey ahead.

> *"Science and psychology have isolated the one prime cause for success or failure in life. It is the hidden self-image you have of yourself."*
>
> Bob Proctor[33]

Surround Yourself with Positive People

Ultimately, it's crucial to immerse yourself in an environment that nurtures and supports your positive self-beliefs and your inner friendship circle. This might involve joining entrepreneurial communities such as Toast Masters, BNI, or Vistage.

Alternatively, you could explore self-improvement books, podcasts, and media. Look for guidance from global mentors and thought leaders like Tony Robbins, Les Brown, John Maxwell, Gloria Mayfield Banks, Eric Worre, Oprah Winfrey, and Brian Tracy. Or seek out others who motivate you. They don't have to be of celebrity status. By learning how other people navigated challenges and took control of their journey, your perspective will be broadened. It will also inspire you to step out of your comfort zone and have confidence in leaving your cave.

Keep in mind that transforming limiting beliefs and the corresponding fears is a journey, not a destination. It requires time, effort, and dedication to break free from the deeply rooted thought patterns within your current fixed mindset. However, with unwavering persistence and patience, you can liberate yourself.

> *"Our deepest fear is not that we are inadequate. Our deepest fear is that we are powerful beyond measure. It is our light, not our darkness that most frightens us."*
>
> Marianne Williamson[34]

You will discover your true happiness and unlock your full potential, provided you possess the will to transition to your future self, the life you are destined to live. Initially, it may not be an easy path, but the value it adds to your life and the impact you can make on the world can become an amazing story.

Dare to think bigger; thinking small only keeps you confined within your comfort zone and deep inside your cave. Life is infinitely more expansive and exciting beyond these self-imposed boundaries.

There exist numerous strategies that you can employ to alleviate fear and eradicate the accompanying anxiety and worry. Confront the imagined fear, addressing it as though it were an individual attempting to undermine you. View fear as an adversary, a tangible threat to your tranquility and joy. Cast aside fear in the same manner you would expel a toxic person from your life.

The STOP Strategy

The STOP Strategy is a straightforward approach designed to help you identify and manage fear and its associated worry and anxiety. This technique encourages you to channel your thoughts toward productivity rather than letting them be consumed by fear. When you find yourself overwhelmed with worry about a non-life-threatening situation or issue, it's an indication that you're grappling with a deep-seated fear.

By employing the STOP Strategy, you can pinpoint this fear and subsequently lessen or even eliminate the related worry. The more frequently you utilize this method, the less fear and worry will dominate your life, allowing you to tap into your resilient, invincible self!

The **STOP** Strategy is an effective, simple plan that encourages you to *Sit, Think, Observe,* and *Proceed* and is designed to help you manage your worries and navigate through challenging situations with a clarity and a calm mind.

SIT: Stop

At the initial onset of fear and anxiety, immediately sit and cease all activities. Consider this your adult time-out. Be kind to yourself by allocating five minutes for solitude and relaxation. Gently close your eyes and engage in a countdown from five, taking deep, full breaths between each number. Gradually inhale and exhale, patiently waiting until the next number. Upon completion, keep your eyes closed, and clear your mind of all thoughts. Consider this your meditative mental cleanse! You are effectively rebooting your cognitive system and will soon be prepared to upload a fresh mental program.

THINK: sTop

With your eyes shut, detach your emotions from your thoughts, and disregard any external influences from others. Focus intently on the situation at hand and strive to pinpoint the underlying fear that it presents. More often than not, this fear is linked to the potential loss or change of a person or relationship, a cherished possession, or financial stability. Once you've identified this fear, challenge yourself to evaluate whether this fear could truly manifest itself into a tangible, absolute threat to your life, your loved ones, or your financial well-being.

Regardless of the whispers of doubt and fear from your internal negative critic, research conducted by Penn State University has revealed that only about 8 percent of the concerns and issues that plague our thoughts ever actually materialize.35 Astonishing, isn't it?

This implies that a staggering 92 percent of our worries, which are often rooted in fear, never come to fruition. Moreover, even when our worries do become reality, they are typically not as severe as we initially anticipated. Therefore, the actual percentage of realized fears might be even less than 8 percent if the outcome is less severe than our worst-case scenario.

Once you grasp the fact that worry is an unproductive use of your time, you can begin to manage and eventually eliminate the fear that fuels it. This requires a certain level of inner strength and self-belief to rise above fear, rather than succumbing to it and allowing worry to dictate your life. The late Bob Proctor of the Proctor Gallagher Institute who was a noted speaker, entrepreneur and life mentor asked a great question in his teachings:

> **"Faith and fear both demand you believe in something you cannot see. You choose."**
>
> Bob Proctor[36]

Greatness is not achieved through fear and worry, but in faith in yourself for a better life and accomplishment. So which one do you choose? Faith or Fear?

OBSERVE: stOp

Indeed, it is a startling reality that only about 8 percent of the things we fret and agonize over ever come to fruition. What remains are merely figments of our imagination, fueled by unfounded fears. From a logical standpoint, one must question whether the fear is worth the worry, the wasted time, and the self-imposed hindrance to our positive progression.

Worry acts as a powerful undertow, pulling us away from our forward momentum. It is crucial to perceive your life, your existence, and your human experience as being of far greater significance than any situation that might induce fear and worry.

During his tenure as president, Bill Clinton faced numerous challenges and predicaments, some of which were self-inflicted. His unique approach to managing fear and anxiety was quite intriguing. In a media interview, when queried about his problem-solving strategy, Clinton revealed his metaphorical method.

He visualized each problem or issue as being contained within a virtual box, which he would then place on a mental shelf in his mind. He would only open this box when it was necessary to address the issue at hand. Once the problem was resolved or answered, he would metaphorically close the box. Depending on the situation, he would either return the box to the shelf for future consideration or discard it entirely, thereby eliminating the associated worry.[37]

> *"Sometimes when people are under stress, they hate to think, and it's the time when they most need to think."*
>
> Bill Clinton[38]

In this particular instance, Clinton effectively managed to isolate his fears and contain his anxieties by employing a mental compartmentalization technique. This method helped to mitigate the impact on his emotional state and responses, enabling him to progress in his personal life and build his legacy. He isolated the worry and associated fear away from his daily emotions.

Envision the global challenges and personal dilemmas he confronted on the world stage, accompanied by a palpable sense of fear and anxiety. Despite these daunting circumstances, he persevered, understanding that no fear or worry was so immense that it could overshadow his life or his ability to overcome it, be it a global threat or a personal crisis.

This presented a stark dichotomy of issues. His self-assurance was so profound that it dwarfed the fear he faced. He was capable of compartmentalizing his fears and anxieties, mentally boxing them away, thereby disassociating them from his persona.

When you perceive fear and worry as mere illusions hindering your forward momentum, you will find yourself less consumed by the uncertainties and less intimidated by the concrete challenges.

PROCEED: stoP

Once you've pinpointed the source of your fear and anxiety, you'll come to understand that your time is far too precious to be squandered on worry. You are now primed and prepared to move forward and take decisive action. Indeed, action serves as the ultimate kryptonite to fear, worry, and depression.

In the biblical narrative of David and Goliath (1 Samuel 17), Goliath symbolizes David's most profound fear. Goliath, a towering figure standing approximately ten feet tall, brandished his colossal sword in the air upon sighting David, who was of average stature.

As Goliath prepared for battle, he roared a chilling threat to David, vowing to annihilate him and leave his remains as fodder for the birds and wild beasts. Upon hearing this, David boldly defied Goliath. With his sling-shot whirling above his head, he charged fearlessly toward the giant. It's important to note that David didn't cower or retreat; instead, he confronted his fear head-on.

With a single, well-aimed shot from his sling, David struck Goliath in the forehead, toppling the giant to the ground. Standing victorious over the fallen Goliath, David seized the giant's sword and ended his life. In this decisive act, David didn't just defeat his enemy; he conquered his fear through direct, courageous action.

Taking action empowers you to conquer fear and diminish anxiety, whereas inaction allows fear to manifest in you, fostering worry. The renowned Dale Carnegie, a distinguished author and speaker, conducted numerous interviews with successful individuals throughout his career. He discovered that these individuals consistently choose to "act" instead of stalling when faced with significant challenges.[39] He firmly believed that taking action is the remedy for a life guided by fear.

> *"Inaction breeds doubt and fear. Action breeds confidence and courage. If you want to conquer fear, do not sit home and think about it. Go out and get busy."*
>
> Dale Carnegie[40]

Pledge to yourself that you are mightier than any fear you encounter, and that anxiety is not deserving of your time or the risk to your health. As Bob Proctor wisely stated, "Clearly understand that the only limitations you will ever have are the limitations you impose upon yourself. You truly do have infinite potential."[41] Always remember, your life holds more significance and is bigger than any fear or any obstacle you'll encounter in your journey.

Who or What Is Driving Your Life?

At the beginning of this chapter, I posed the question, "Is fear driving your life?" It is crucial to comprehend the fear we often imagine is not grounded in reality. Instead, it is an emotional reaction to a non-threatening situation, typically triggered by the anticipation of an unfavorable outcome.

The operative term here is *anticipation*, as most of us are prone to presuming a negative result. These assumptions, however, are not rooted in fact. They are merely perceived thoughts that have been filtered through our emotional lens. Emotions, being fluid, are often unreliable and can distort our perception of reality.

> **"Assumptions are made and most assumptions are wrong."**
>
> Albert Einstein[42]

The moment you are able to confront and eliminate fear, the accompanying worry will naturally fade away. Fear and worry are great roommates! Fear feeds worry; by removing fear, then worry has nothing to feed on!

If fear presents itself as a tangible, physical threat to your life or property, a situation that doesn't frequently occur unless you're in a perilous job or environment, then it necessitates a reaction. You either confront it – fight, or escape from it - flight.

> *"Fear defeats more people than any other one thing in the world."*
>
> Ralph Waldo Emerson[43]

However, if the fear is merely a product of your imagination, which is often the case with our daily anxieties, then you possess the ability to re-channel this fear and eliminate the associated worry. It is important to remember that worry is simply a prolonged manifestation of fear.

In the voyage of life, fear is the most potent negative emotion that often diverts us from a life of abundance to one of mediocrity, a life that remains unchallenged. The path of fear is debilitating, hindering the discovery of our purpose, value, and ultimate freedom.

If not addressed, fear will evolve into worry and escalate into anxiety and depression. This can potentially manifest as a lifelong ailment, wreaking havoc on your life. The most effective remedy is to release fear and worry, take decisive action, and propel yourself forward. Your life is too precious, and the value you can contribute to others is too immense to sit on the sidelines of life.

> *"Forward progression removes depression."*
> Ted Kopecko

The primal fear that would have propelled us to flee from a saber-toothed tiger is beneficial, but the daily fears we face, particularly those associated with challenges, will not improve our lives. These fears do not exist to safeguard us; instead, they serve to hinder us from experiencing a more fulfilling life.

When you prioritize your mental well-being and perceive the broader benefits in any situation or challenge, fear becomes secondary to your success. Embrace the power of Goliath's sword, and use it to conquer your personal giants. This positions you to face failure without fear, gaining invaluable experience that enriches your life.

> *"Fear is only as deep as the mind allows."*
> Japanese proverb

Imagine the liberation of not being held captive by fear, of not living a life dictated by apprehension. Just like David, who didn't flee from his giant but instead confronted it head-on, you, too, have the authority to vanquish your own giants.

Reject fear, embrace a life free from its shackles, and don't fret over success or failure. Instead, focus on the growth and expansion that comes from each experience. Discover your purpose, and let it guide you on your life journey to value and freedom.

> **"We fear things in proportion to our ignorance of them."**
>
> Christian Nestell Bovee[43]

Journey Rest Stop 8

1) What are the four elements of the Four Ps that define fear, and how do they apply to you?

2) Who are the key people in your life that help you overcome your fears and limitations? What self-help books are you thinking of reading? Start a weekly book club centered on personal growth to encourage ongoing progress and learning.

3) How can you use the STOP Strategy to redirect fear? Or do you have another technique?

Journey Thought

"Everything you want
is on the
other side of fear."

Jack Canfield[45]

www.FindingJOY.us

Chapter 9

Journey of Failure

Why Try... Nothing Works!

Failure is success in progress.
Albert Einstein[1]

We were conditioned to fear failure, to view it as a negative reflection of our abilities and worth. To fear failure is to fear something we cannot see and only feel emotionally. Failure was painted as a mark of disgrace, a subliminal scar that indicated we had not met the expectations of others and ourselves. The lessons we were taught discouraged failure, suggesting it was a direct reflection of our intelligence and work ethic.

In essence, failure has been synonymous with a lack of intelligence and a degree of laziness, an identity that most of us would want to avoid. Instead of fostering an environment that encouraged us to strive for success through failure, the system pushed us toward mediocrity and conformity to stay within our area of comfort and avoid challenge.

This early indoctrination that failure is inherently bad only served to reinforce the development of a fixed mindset. This teaching discouraged growth and exploration, stifling our potential and limiting our ability to learn from our mistakes and failures.

It is crucial to transition our mindset from harboring a fear of failure to embracing challenges. We should redefine failure as lessons of progress. Failure should not be viewed as a setback, but rather as a step up toward success and accomplishment.

It is also essential to discard societal prejudices associated with failure and the concern about others' opinions when we fail. If these are the principles guiding your life, your personal growth will inevitably be hindered. Remember, you are the CEO of your life. Don't pay attention to the opinions of others. After all, they aren't the ones paying your bills, and they certainly are not the boss of your life.

> *"Accept responsibility for your life. Know that it is you who will get you where you want to go, no one else."*
>
> Les Brown[2]

The word *failure* is often shrouded in negative undertones, evoking feelings of disappointment, embarrassment, and inadequacy. However, beneath its intimidating facade, it hides a crucial aspect of the human experience—an element that is indispensable for personal development, resilience, and ultimately, victory. Failure represents the building of knowledge rather than a poor reflection of you. This shift in thinking can lead to a profound change in outlook and mindset, laying the groundwork for substantial personal advancement and self-discovery.

> *"There is no such thing as failure. There are only results."*
>
> Tony Robbins[3]

Fundamentally, failure is an inherent aspect of the voyage toward accomplishment and success. It acts as a powerful wake-up call to our limitations, nudging us to reevaluate our tactics, polish our methodologies, and relentlessly pursue enhancement. Failure should not be viewed as the polar opposite of success, but rather as an integral stepping stone on the journey toward it.

One of the most profound teachings that failure bestows upon us is the virtue of resilience. When confronted with obstacles, people are compelled to tackle adversity directly, fostering a mental toughness that empowers them to persist despite the challenges. This journey cultivates resilience within us, equipping us to rebound with greater strength and determination than ever before.

J. K. Rowling is a great example of resilience in action. Before her books became a global phenomenon, Rowling faced numerous rejections from publishers who could not see the magic of a young wizard named Potter from a place called Hogwarts. Living as a single mother on welfare, she continued to write, driven by her belief in the story she was creating. Eventually, Bloomsbury, a small publishing house, took a chance on her manuscript. The rest, as they say, is history. Her relentless determination illustrates that success often lies on the other side of failure and the word *no*.

Before she became a billionaire and the founder of Spanx, Sara Blakely faced her fair share of rejections and challenges. Starting out as a door-to-door fax machine salesperson, she struggled to get by. With no formal business education, she had a vision for Spanx - a comfortable alternative to traditional women's active wear that truly worked.

When Sara began pitching her idea to manufacturers, she encountered rejection after rejection, no after no. Many people brushed off her concept, convinced it wouldn't catch on. But Blakely didn't let that stop her. She persevered until she finally found a manufacturer willing to take a chance on her idea. Driven by determination and creativity, she even wrote her own patent and Spanx was launched. Sara had a stronger belief in her idea than her fear of failure.

Now, Spanx is a well-known global brand, and Sara Blakely is admired for her tenacity and innovative spirit. She often reflects on how vital it was to embrace failure, a lesson taught to her by her father, who would frequently ask, "What did you fail at today?" This perspective enabled her to see failure as a detour around an obstacle to get to success.

> *"Resiliency is the ability to spring back from and successfully adapt to adversity."*
>
> Nan Henderson[4]

My Degree in Resilience

My first real encounter with resilience occurred during my final year at the College of Architecture and Environmental Design at California Polytechnic State University, San Luis Obispo. This prestigious institution is renowned for its rigorous admission standards, a fact that held true even during my tenure. I was in the twilight of a five-year professional degree program, rounding off a decade of higher education. I was, in essence, a career student, and I suspect my parents had begun to doubt if I would ever graduate.

The fifth year of the architecture program was optional, designed for those seeking a professional degree. The theme for this additional year was independent study, a concept that resonated deeply with me. The prospect of spending another year immersed in the idyllic surroundings of the university, coupled with the opportunity to pursue independent study, was too enticing to resist.

I was always something of a nonconformist during my college years and had a strong entrepreneurial streak. The idea of independent study seemed to offer the perfect blend of freedom and opportunity. I could break free from the confines of the traditional classroom setting and kick-start my own business, all the while continuing to savor the joys of college life, the nearby sun-soaked beaches, and the college parties! It was an opportunity I seized with both hands, fully committed and ready to embrace the challenges ahead. I was all-in!

As fortune would have it, I was blessed with a good professor named Bagnell, affectionately known to us all as Bags. Although I wasn't well-acquainted with Bags during my years at Cal Poly, he always struck me as a good guy. To paint a clearer picture of myself at the time, I sported long, curly hair reminiscent of the artist Monet and possessed an ego that could rival any backup singer for Peter Frampton. Admittedly, I was a bit of a handful, but I was undeniably serious about my future and career.

The dawn of my final college school year had arrived, and I was brimming with excitement! I found myself standing on the threshold of one of the most esteemed architectural institutions in the country, on the cusp of completing my college journey. The thrill was palpable! The anticipation of embarking on this new chapter and, more significantly, launching my own business was electrifying, since this collegiate year was designated for independent study at least that is what I thought.

As I settled into my design class, Bags outlined the course for the year and directed us to team up with another student. In the flurry of activity, I found myself with a fellow student named Dan. Little did Dan know the dynamic partnership he was about to embark on!

Following the initial week at the design lab, I transitioned to my off-campus design studio, which was my apartment! However, this was not the interpretation of independent study that Bags had in mind for our fifth year. Dan and I engaged with the class as if it were the central hub of a corporate office, attending when necessary to touch base and participate in "corporate" meetings. Predominantly, we undertook our fifth-year design project outside the traditional classroom setting while the other class students continued to frequent the corporate office.

Our fifth-year project was to design a virtual building, encompassing everything from the initial concept and planning stages to pre-construction, with Bags acting as our client. We were to develop and experience a realistic design project as possible within the confines of an educational environment.

> *"You have to learn to get comfortable being uncomfortable. You have to be willing to get out of your comfort zone and push your limits."*
> Jesse Itzler[5]

As is typical for me, I took things a step beyond the usual. I am perpetually pushing boundaries, always seeking to expand and grow. This relentless pursuit of progress is a testament to my growth leaning mindset. However, I later discovered that Bags was not in favor of me pushing the boundaries of independence, even though this was *independent* study.

Dan and I decided to create a mixed-use retail and office development on the bustling main street of San Luis Obispo. The development stretched across several parcels of property and offered a picturesque view of the San Luis Creek. It was a beautiful site and one that needed a little bit of creativity!

We reached out to the property owners and the planning department, seeking their approval to conduct an academic project on their properties. This project would involve taking a fictitious development through the various stages of planning procedures. Both parties were amenable to our proposal, thus allowing Dan and I to assume the roles of quasi-architects.

On a weekly basis, we would participate in our design class, providing updates on our progress to both our classmates and Bags while working at my office—my apartment. We viewed the class setting as our client's office. When we attended, we took the opportunity to listen to the progress reports of other ongoing class projects. Everything seemed to be progressing smoothly, until one day when Bags approached me with an unexpected request. He said, "Kopecko, I'd like to see you in my office after class."

> *"It's not the situation, but whether we react negative or respond positive to the situation that is important."*
>
> Zig Ziglar[6]

Oh boy! I was heading to the boss's office! *This can't be good*, I thought. However, my initial apprehension was quickly eclipsed by my bravado. As Dan and I made our way across the picturesque campus quad toward Bags's office on a beautiful San Luis Obispo day, I recall Dan being petrified, akin to an outlaw on his way to the gallows! I told Dan on our walk to his office, "What's the worst he can do to us?" Dan without skipping a beat and white as a sheet said, "Duh, FLUNK US!"

I reassured Dan that we had nothing to fear, Bags was not going to flunk us especially with all the work we did. We were weeks ahead of the class and had meticulously documented all our work. We were precisely following the independent study model outlined in the syllabus. My only uncertainty was whether Bags had received the same memo!

> **"If you're not failing every now and again, it's a sign you're not doing anything very innovative."**
> Woody Allen[7]

I knocked on the door to Bags's office and heard his baritone voice say, "Come in!" He sat there behind his desk, poised like a spider at the center of its web, patiently awaiting our arrival. The image of Bag's was a little imposing. He was about six feet tall, supporting a 260 pound body by Budweiser stature in his mid-sixties with unruly, brownish hair. His scruffy image is still etched in my memory. He was ensconced behind an antiquated oak desk, a relic from the 1940s war era, in a dimly lit office that was far too cramped for his imposing size, let alone a couple of guest chairs.

Dan and I squeezed into Bags's office, taking our seats in the two chairs that barely fit as Bags shoveled some papers. Our knees brushed against the front of his oak desk, a testament to this closet he called an office. Despite the awkwardness of the situation, I managed to flash a smile and asked, "What's happening?" My tone was very optimistic, a stark contrast to the dark claustrophobic surroundings and the look on Bags's face.

The notion that this would be a congenial, pleasant gathering quickly evaporated as soon as Bags began to speak. I had come well-prepared, armed with our meticulously maintained project process journals. These hefty documents, spanning several hundred pages, were printed on the official letterhead of our mock company, serving as tangible proof of our progress. As these journals rested on our laps, Bags shot me a glare so fierce it would scare Darth Vader into submission.

With his gaze fixed on me, and a fleeting glance at Dan, he declared, "Kopecko, I've reached my limit with you and your sidekick! I'm fed up with your antics and your casual approach to coming to class. The class may applaud your sporadic appearances, but I won't tolerate you imposing new rules in my classroom. I'm informing you now that you will be receiving an F. Let me be clear, you're failing your fifth year, so inform your parents to come and pick you up." He then turned to Dan and warned, "If you continue to follow his lead, you'll be facing an F as well!"

Once Bags had finished his tirade, I calmly opened our process journals, intending to enlighten him about the commendable work we were doing, which he might have overlooked. I also pointed out the fifth-year syllabus, which clearly outlined the fifth-year course as independent study designed to provide hands-on experience with real-life design projects. I shared with him the details of our communication with the property owners and the San Luis Planning Department regarding our forthcoming academic development project. The enthusiasm and support we received from all parties were overwhelming. The property owners were eager to assist us in our architectural endeavor and were highly anticipating the innovative designs we could potentially bring to this downtown site.

Regrettably, Bags remained unpersuaded, regardless of our progress in the class or the quality of our project. He was resolute in his decision to fail me. Just as much as Bags was resolute in his thoughts, so was I with mine because I knew we did the work and miles ahead of the other student's progress.

> *"The greatest glory in living lies not in never falling, but in rising every time we fall."*
> Oliver Goldsmith[8]

Bags stared at me with the stern gaze of a judge delivering a verdict to a court defendant. His voice was cold and unyielding as he declared, "Kopecko, I can't say I'm fond of you, but as it stands right now, I am giving you an F.

Dan, you are close behind. Let me make this crystal clear. You're on the brink of flunking out, and all the years you've spent here will amount to nothing. But you are resilient, Kopecko, and I am sure you are going to find a way around this. Now leave my office!" I remembered thinking, "No problem, I'm getting claustrophobic anyway. I would be grumpy too, if I had a closet like this for an office!"

As Dan and I strolled back across the grassy campus quad toward the architecture building, I couldn't shake the feeling that Dan was on the brink of a nervous breakdown. His voice, shrill with panic, echoed in my ears, "Ted, what are we going to do now? I can't possibly tell my parents I'm failing!" My mind was racing, attempting to process the scolding I got from Bags.

Yet amidst this dire situation, one word resonated with me in Bag's tirade. Bags had called me *"resilient."* I was wondering what he meant. Was it a compliment? A put down? Or a hint?

I looked at Dan, trying to sound composed. "Relax! What do you think Bags meant by calling me resilient?" Dan's face contorted into a puzzled expression as he retorted, "Wait, what? Resilient? We're on the verge of flunking out of Cal Poly, and you're concerned about resilience!" I persisted, "Yes, what do you think he meant?"

Dan, visibly frustrated, halted in his tracks and replied, "What the hell? I don't know. I suppose he thinks you have the knack to bounce back from problems. So where are we headed now?"

As I began to walk away from Dan, I declared, "We're going to Dean Hasslein's office. Let's show him our project. Are you with me? If Bags thinks I'm resilient, it's time we prove him right!"

> *"You always pass failure on your way to success."*
> Mickey Rooney[9]

At that time, the impressive School of Architecture building was a relatively new addition to the campus. Rising four stories high, it was a modern marvel of concrete and steel, standing in stark contrast to the institutional 1940's government-style buildings that peppered the rest of the campus. Dean Hasslein's office was situated on the first floor, offering a picturesque view of the campus quad.

As Dan and I neared the administrative office entry, a sense of trepidation washed over me. I found myself hoping, even praying, that Dean Hasslein was in a meeting. My nerves were akin to those of a magician about to perform a new trick on stage, I definitely had to pull a rabbit out of my hat on this one, or Dan was going to kill me and I would have to explain this one to my parents!

As we approached the receptionist, burdened by our project journals, I managed to muster a shaky smile and asked, "Is Dean Hasslein available?" Her affirmative response was the last thing I wanted to hear.

Surveying the beautifully designed open office with its numerous windows offering views of the quad, I couldn't help but think about Bags. His constant irritability was understandable, given that his office was no larger than an elevator cab. Apparently, he had been overlooked for a real office in the new building, no wonder why he seemed always cranky.

Upon mentioning our desire to discuss our fifth-year study with the Dean, we found ourselves being led down an aisle lined with staff cubicles. Our journey ended at a closed office door, bearing the name Dean Hasslein. With a pounding heart threatening to burst from my chest, I gave a light knock on the door.

My past acquaintance with Dean Hasslein was limited to distant sightings on campus. His robust voice echoed from within, "Yes! Come in!" His tone sent a shiver down my spine. I glanced at Dan, our expressions mirroring the trepidation of skydivers on the brink of our first jump, and muttered, "I am resilient, right?" Dan's eyes rolled and said "I hope Bags was right" with that vote of confidence I clutched the doorknob and turn it.

Stepping into Dean Hasslein's office was like entering a sanctuary of order and space. It was impressively large and impeccably maintained, complete with a separate guest seating area. It was a sense of arrival, "You are here and there is no turning back." The Dean himself was ensconced behind his modern, expansive desk, engrossed in some papers. I thought you could comfortably seat four people behind that desk. He glanced up at us through his black-rimmed glasses and invited us to sit. With a great big smile and very positive voice he said, "What can I do for you, gentlemen?"

Dean Hasslein was more than just an impressive figure; he was the founding Dean of the School of Architecture at Cal Poly, a living legend in academics and architecture. His reputation only served to heighten my nerves, but it was a do-or-die situation for Dan and I, with failure looming ominously. The next fifteen minutes would determine our Cal Poly future. This was like pushing all your chips to the twenty-one dealer while you're holding a queen of hearts and the four of spades. Was the Dean going to believe us or one of his professors?

Following our formal introductions, Dan and I found ourselves comfortably seated in the two Eames chairs positioned before Dean Hasslein's impressive, modern desk. The legroom in front of the Dean's was reminiscent of first-class seating on a United Airlines flight.

The irony of the situation was not lost on me. Here I was, sitting before the Dean of Architecture at one of the most prestigious universities in the nation, if not the world, on the brink of being cut from the team! The stakes were high! Dean Hasslein, a man in his sixties with a hint of grey in his hair, exuded an air of likability.

As I began to speak, I felt like a young defense attorney making his case before a seasoned judge. I detailed my journey through Cal Poly and explained my decision to pursue the professional degree of fifth year. To reinforce my point, I presented the fifth-year syllabus, reminding Dean Hasslein of the emphasis on independent study, which was the primary reason for my decision to stay on an extra year.

I then addressed the issue Bags had with our approach, highlighting how Dan and I were weeks ahead of the rest of the class. Thankfully, we had our design journals to showcase the work we had accomplished. Dean Hasslein was visibly impressed. I could sense the tide turning in our favor, like pulling a proverbial rabbit out of the hat!

> *"If you're doing your best, you won't have any time to worry about failure."*
>
> H. Jackson Brown Jr.[10]

It felt like an hour had passed, but in reality, it was only about twenty minutes before we were rising from our seats and exchanging handshakes. Dean Hasslein escorted us to his door, reassuring us with a confident smile, "Don't worry, boys, I'll have a word with Bagnell, and we'll find a solution that leaves everyone satisfied. I must say, I'm quite impressed with your self-reliance and the progress you're making in your fifth-year study! My staff will be in touch with you to iron out any details."

His words were a breath of fresh air, a hidden solution to our predicament. As we retraced our steps across the quad, Dan's expression was that of a man who had just hit the jackpot. Turning to dan as we were walking, I couldn't help but remark, "I suppose Bags was right after all. I am resilient, the Dean even said it!"

A few days later, I received a call from Dean Hasslein's office. The news was thrilling! Dan and I were being transferred to another fifth-year design class, this time under the tutelage of Professor Allan Cooper. The excitement was palpable; we were both eager to embark on a fresh new journey and finish our project.

Professor Cooper was the perfect blend of mentor and guide for us, providing the ideal environment for us to complete our independent design project. More significantly, his guidance was instrumental in our graduation from Cal Poly! In a testament to our journey from failure to success, both Dan and I achieved A's in Professor Cooper's fifth-year design class. This achievement was not just a grade but a symbol of our resilience and determination in the face of failure.

Reflecting back, I learned more than just attending fifth-year study. I learned a valuable life lesson on growth. Regardless of the magnitude of the problem or the height of the obstacle you're facing, if you maintain honesty, focused attention, and dedication, no challenge can overpower your determination or resilience to succeed.

The key is to never surrender in your quest for success. In this example, if Dan and I had been unable to demonstrate the work or progress we made, as opposed to just goofing off, our efforts would have been unsuccessful. Regardless of how much fortitude or resilience you possess, if you are not dedicated and focused to your purpose or cause, overcoming failure becomes significantly more challenging.

> *"There are no secrets to success. It is the result of preparation, hard work, and learning from failure."*
> Colin Powell[11]

Failure will always win when your excuse outweighs your resolve. In the face of failure, we instinctively assess if the challenge is insurmountable, the mountain too tall, and our time is too limited. We will activate our resilience when the potential reward of overcoming a challenge is greater than the regret of defeat. Failure will always win when defeat defines you.

The Journey of Roger Bannister

In 1954, Roger Bannister faced a seemingly insurmountable challenge: breaking the four-minute-mile barrier. Many believed it was physically impossible for humans to run a mile in under four minutes. Bannister, a medical student with limited time for training, could have easily succumbed to excuses: lack of time, the pressure of his studies, or the prevailing belief that the task was beyond human capability.

Yet his resolve was unwavering. Drawing inspiration from literature and historical figures who had overcome great odds, Bannister activated his resilience. He meticulously planned his training, balancing it with his demanding academic schedule.

On May 6, 1954, at the Iffley Road track in Oxford, Bannister's determination and hard work culminated in a historic moment as he crossed the finish line in three minutes and 59.4 seconds. His achievement shattered the psychological barrier that had held runners back for years. Bannister's story illustrates that a strong resolve and determination will diminish excuses and give your best chance over failure.

His potential reward, a place in history and the knowledge that he had pushed the limits of human endurance, was far greater than the regret he would have felt had he not answered the challenge. His legacy reminds us that resilience is key to overcoming challenges, no matter how insurmountable they may seem. He answered his "What if?" moment with action.

> **"Success is due to our stretching to the challenges of life. Failure comes when we shrink from them."**
>
> John C. Maxwell[12]

Failure is a great teacher but a lousy mentor. Ironically, failure can cultivates a growth mindset, which is rooted in the belief that one's abilities and intelligence can be developed through the process of failure and success.

Rather than perceiving failure as a testament to inherent shortcomings, individuals with a growth mindset regard it as a valuable chance for growth, self-enhancement, success, and, most importantly, a teacher. This transformative perspective enables us to tackle challenges with curiosity and receptiveness, perceiving setbacks not as hindrances but as stepping stones for learning and personal development.

Moreover, failure acts as a profound instructor of humility, highlighting our intrinsic imperfections and underscoring the vital importance of humility in our pursuit of excellence. It shatters any delusions of invincibility, compelling us to acknowledge and embrace our limitations.

This introspective journey not only humbles us but also fosters a deeper sense of empathy and understanding. By recognizing that failure is a shared human experience, we become more attuned to the struggles and challenges that others face, nurturing a more compassionate and supportive community.

> *"Failure is simply the opportunity to begin again, this time more intelligently."*
>
> Henry Ford[13]

One of the most profound aspects of failure lies in its power to nurture innovation and creativity. History abounds with examples of individuals who recognized failure as an essential stepping stone to success.

Finger-Licking Good!

Consider the story of Colonel Harland Sanders, the founder of KFC. He turned repeated failures into success through determination and innovation. Born in 1890, Sanders had a tough childhood and left school early, working various jobs like farmhand and railroad fireman. His entrepreneurial journey began in his forties when he opened a service station in Corbin, Kentucky, where he started serving his now-famous fried chicken with a secret blend of eleven herbs and spices. The chicken became popular, leading him to open a restaurant.

Unfortunately, a new highway was built and diverted traffic away from his restaurant location and predictably his customers base declined. Facing potential bankruptcy, Sanders decided to travel the country, pitching his chicken recipe to other restaurant owners for a small royalty. The Colonel was resilient and innovative!

Despite many rejections, he persisted. In 1952 at age sixty-two, he successfully franchised his recipe, opening the first KFC in Salt Lake City, Utah. The franchise model thrived, turning KFC into a global fast-food giant. Sanders' story highlights the importance of resilience, determination, and innovation. Despite numerous setbacks, he never gave up and ultimately built a lasting fast-food legacy.

Similarly, Thomas Edison in his lab faced numerous setbacks before successfully inventing the practical incandescent light bulb. Edison famously remarked, "I have not failed. I've just found ten thousand ways that won't work."[14] His relentless pursuit in the face of repeated failures not only brought light to the world but also laid the groundwork for modern electrical engineering and countless other innovations.

Failure frequently serves as the spark for innovation and revelation. It is through our encounters with failure that we broaden the horizons of possibility, challenge conventional wisdom, and pave the way for meaningful progress.

> *"Success consists of going from failure to failure without loss of enthusiasm."*
>
> Winston Churchill[15]

In another example, Steve Jobs, ousted from Apple, the company he co-founded, went on to develop groundbreaking products with NeXT and Pixar. His return to Apple heralded a renaissance for the company, leading to the creation of iconic products like the iPhone and iPad, which revolutionized technology and consumer electronics.

These examples underscore the transformative potential of failure. By embracing setbacks and learning from them, we unlock new avenues for creativity and innovation, ultimately driving forward human achievement, challenging conventional wisdom and paving the way for meaningful progress.

*"**Without failure there is no achievement.**"*
John C. Maxwell[16]

At the end of the day, failure should not be feared or shunned, but rather welcomed as an indispensable part of Finding JOY. It instills resilience, nurtures a growth mindset, promotes humility, and drives innovation. By reframing our attitude toward failure, seeing it as a teacher instead of an adversary, we unlock the potential for significant personal growth and self-discovery.

As the legendary basketball coach John Wooden wisely remarked, *"Failure is not fatal, but failure to change might be."*[17] Our willingness to embrace and learn from failure is the true catalyst for achieving lasting success.

Journey Rest Stop 9

1) How were you conditioned to fear failure? What life events or situations made you fearful of failure?

2) Why is resilience a profound teaching of failure? How resilient are you?

3) How does failure support success? How do you view failure in your life? How do you bounce back from setbacks?

Journey Thought
"If something's important enough, you should try. Even IF the probable outcome is failure."

Elon Musk[18]

www.FindingJOY.us

Which Way to Success Street?

There are people who make things happen, there are people who watch things happen, and there are people who wonder what happened. To be successful, you need to be a person who makes things happen.

Jim Lovell[1]

On the other side of failure lies success. The Journey of Success remains elusive for many because it is exceptionally challenging to attain. Achieving true success demands time, persistence, dedication, and an unwavering commitment to your purpose, cause, and dreams. In response to these daunting requirements, we often redefine success to fit a more attainable, diluted version. We settle for mediocrity, or what we deem to be good enough, and aim too low.

In today's culture, participation awards are commonly handed out, where there are no winners or losers. This practice strips away the valuable experiences of both victory and defeat. It does a disservice to everyone involved, eroding the true essence of competition and teaching that average is acceptable. On life's ladder, average is the highest attainable rung of poor and the lowest level of accomplishment. This approach to success stifles personal growth and reinforces a fixed mindset and, worse, a fear of failure, ultimately hindering the development of resilience and striving for excellence.

> *"No person ever achieved worth-while success who did not, at one time or other, find themselves with at least one foot hanging well over the brink of failure."*
> Napoleon Hill[2]

Success is the culmination of learned experiences and overcoming failures. It is often constructed on a foundation of setbacks, errors, and valuable learning moments. Instead of being impeded by failure, those who achieve greatness view it as a crucial component of their journey toward reaching greater heights. Accepting failure not only builds resilience but also fuels continuous growth and improvement, paving the way towards greater value and success.

As discussed in the previous chapter, failure offers valuable lessons that compel individuals to confront their limitations, reassess their strategies, and adapt to evolving circumstances. In essence, failure acts as a powerful catalyst for growth and development, driving individuals to pursue their excellence and full potential.

Ironically, failure also develops resilience and perseverance, the crucial abilities to rebound from setbacks and persist in the face of adversity. Successful individuals recognize that failure is not indicative of weakness; instead, it is an integral part of the journey toward success. They view failure as an opportunity to learn, grow, and improve rather than allowing it to derail their goals and ambitions.

> *"Failure is success if we learn from it."*
> Malcolm Forbes[3]

In countless scenarios, the pursuit of success mirrors a winding road more than a direct, unobstructed path. This route is marked by twists and turns, peaks and valleys. Along this journey, individuals encounter a myriad of obstacles and challenges that test their resilience and determination. Failures should not be perceived as the end of the journey but as a detour, a temporary setback that carves the route to even greater achievements.

> *"Success comes from failure, not from memorizing the right answers."*
> Donald J. Trump[4]

We All Scream for Ice Cream!

Consider the inspiring journey of Ben Cohen and Jerry Greenfield, the dynamic duo behind the delicious ice cream brand, Ben & Jerry's. Their path to success in the ice cream industry is a testament to perseverance, creativity, and friendship.

Ben and Jerry were childhood pals with a mutual passion for food, yet neither had a concrete career plan. After enduring a series of unfulfilling jobs and failed business ventures, they decided to channel their energies into something new.

In 1977, they enrolled in a modest five-dollar correspondence course on ice cream making from Penn State University. Armed with their newfound knowledge, Ben and Jerry took a leap of faith. They pooled their savings and transformed a rundown gas station in Burlington, Vermont, into a charming ice cream parlor.

> *"Develop success from failures. Discouragement and failure are two of the surest stepping stones to success."*
>
> Dale Carnegie[5]

Their early days were a blend of triumphs and trials. The locals quickly fell in love with their rich, chunky ice cream flavors, causing lines to stretch out the door. However, the brutal Vermont winters brought a sharp decline in sales, posing a significant threat to their fledgling business.

Undeterred by the seasonal slump, Ben and Jerry devised a clever solution. They began packaging their delectable ice cream in pints and distributing them to local grocery stores. This innovative move not only ensured year-round sales but also marked the beginning of their expansion beyond the confines of their small ice cream shop. Their story is a poignant reminder that the road to success is rarely straight, but with determination and ingenuity, obstacles can be transformed into opportunities. You just have to look for the silver lining.

> *"Don't just do something because it's a trendy idea and will make you a lot of money. The reason I say that is because any kind of venture involves going through difficult times. If you're doing something you are passionate about and really believe in, then that will carry you through."*
>
> Jerry Greenfield[6]

Despite their creativity and growing popularity, Ben & Jerry's faced numerous challenges. One of the most significant hurdles was competing against the industry behemoth, Häagen-Dazs, owned by the corporate titan Pillsbury at the time.

In the mid-1980s, Pillsbury attempted to stifle Ben & Jerry's growth by pressuring distributors to choose between carrying Häagen-Dazs or Ben & Jerry's, but not both. This unfair and anti-competitive tactic prompted Ben & Jerry's to launch their iconic "What's the Doughboy Afraid Of?" campaign.

Through witty and engaging marketing, coupled with grassroots mobilization, Ben & Jerry's galvanized public support. The campaign not only raised awareness but also led to a federal lawsuit against Pillsbury. The legal battle ultimately resulted in a victory for Ben & Jerry's, ensuring they could compete on a level playing field and paving the way for their continued success.

> *"Patience, persistence and perspiration make an unbeatable combination for success."*
>
> Napoleon Hill[7]

As the company expanded, it encountered a series of formidable challenges, including financial hardships and the struggle to uphold its core values in the face of corporate pressures. A particularly noteworthy setback transpired in the early 1990s when their stock price nosedived due to over-expansion and management missteps. Despite these hurdles, Ben & Jerry's unwavering dedication to social and environmental causes, coupled with their innovative marketing strategies, enabled them to bounce back. They concentrated on crafting playful, socially responsible flavors and steadfastly promoted their mission of linked prosperity for their stakeholders.

In 2000, Ben & Jerry's was acquired by the multinational conglomerate Unilever, sparking concerns that the ice cream company's original mission-driven ethos might be compromised. However, the founders of Ben & Jerry's negotiated a groundbreaking acquisition deal that allowed the company to retain a separate board of directors specifically tasked with overseeing its social mission. This strategic move ensured that Ben & Jerry's could continue to uphold its core values and social initiatives while simultaneously benefiting from Unilever's extensive distribution network and resources.

Today, Ben & Jerry's stands as a global icon, celebrated not only for its delicious ice cream but also for its steadfast dedication to social justice, environmental sustainability, and active community engagement. The company's journey, fraught with numerous failures and obstacles, has culminated in a legacy that transcends the ice cream industry. The winding road they navigated, replete with detours and challenges, has paved the way for a company that epitomizes innovation, resilience, and purpose-driven business. Ben & Jerry's is more than just a brand; it is a beacon of how a business can thrive while making a positive impact on the world.

> **"A champion is afraid of losing. Everyone else is afraid of winning."**
>
> Billie Jean King[8]

Billie Jean King underscores the distinctive mindset that sets high achievers apart from the herd. Champions, driven by an unrelenting fear of failure, push themselves to extraordinary lengths, while others may be paralyzed by the fear of stepping into the limelight and claiming victory. This profound observation illuminates the psychological nuances that define the journey to success.

> **"Success is 99 percent failure."**
>
> Soichiro Honda[9]

For a champion, be it in sports, business, or any other field, the fear of losing is an ever-present companion. This fear doesn't stem from a lack of confidence but rather from a profound desire to uphold their esteemed status.

Champions are acutely aware of the immense effort and sacrifices demanded to attain the apex of success. They understand that any misstep or defeat could jeopardize their hard-earned position. Far from being a paralyzing force, this fear acts as a powerful motivator, propelling champions to push their boundaries and relentlessly pursue excellence.

Conversely, the fear of success can be just as intimidating for many of us. Achieving success introduces a fresh array of challenges and responsibilities, along with elevated expectations from both others and ourselves. This can lead to the onset of impostor syndrome, where the fear of subsequent failure undermines one's confidence and fosters a pervasive sense of insecurity. The apprehension toward change and the uncertainty of the future can prevent people from embracing opportunities for personal and professional growth.

True champions harness the fear of losing as a powerful motivator for self-improvement, whereas others may grapple with the fear of winning and the uncertainties that accompany success. By recognizing and addressing these fears, individuals can foster a growth mindset and develop the resilience necessary to achieve their goals and unlock their full potential.

> *"Success is a state of mind. If you want success, start thinking of yourself as a success."*
> Dr Joyce Brothers[10]

Success starts with your positive mindset and transcends the mere amassing of wealth, accolades, or societal recognition. Success originates from a positive mindset on how you react to challenges, issues and problems. The mindset you nurture, whether fixed or growth, profoundly influences your actions, decisions, and ultimately, the reality you experience. When you perceive yourself as successful, you exude confidence, determination, and positivity. This outlook not only shapes your behavior but also attracts opportunities and resources that drive you toward your goals and aspirations.

Viewing yourself as a success entails cultivating a positive self-image and unwavering confidence in your abilities and potential. Whether you're a student striving for graduation, an employee ascending the corporate ladder, an entrepreneur growing a business, or a parent managing a household, this mindset is crucial. It involves not only envisioning your achievements but also approaching your journey with an optimistic outlook, even when confronted with setbacks.

This mental shift can turn challenges into opportunities for growth and learning, fostering resilience and persistence, and nurturing a growth mindset. Embracing this perspective can transform your entire approach to personal and professional ventures, enabling you to thrive in any situation.

Adopting a positive growth mindset fosters proactive behavior. When you envision yourself as successful, you become more inclined to take calculated risks, seize emerging opportunities, and persevere through challenges.

Success breeds success. Your self-belief transforms into a self-fulfilling prophecy, where your confidence and determination translate into real, measurable achievements. It serves as a poignant reminder that your thoughts and attitudes form the bedrock of your reality. By envisioning yourself as successful, you create a fertile environment for turning your dreams and aspirations into tangible achievements.

> *"Success is due to our stretching to the challenges of life. Failure comes when we shrink from them."*
> John C. Maxwell[11]

The Journey of Success starts with you by allowing yourself the opportunity to expand your life, your skills, and your capabilities. Stretching to the challenges of life is a readiness to venture beyond your comfort zone, embrace risks, and pursue personal growth.

Just as muscles strengthen when stretched and exercised, individuals become more adept and resilient when they face and overcome adversities. Yes, the Journey of Success is hard, but what is harder? Living an adult life of struggle and uncertainty in the herd, or having an unstoppable attitude to conquer barriers and experience opportunities to expand your life?

> *"Facing your fears and living a life that's free is easy. Spending the rest of your days living half a life is hard."*
> Eric Worre[12]

Embracing challenges fosters both learning and personal growth. Each hurdle serves as a valuable opportunity to acquire new skills, expand knowledge, and strengthen character. Those who consistently push their boundaries are more likely to cultivate a growth mindset, the conviction that abilities and intelligence can be enhanced through dedication and hard work.

> *"There will always be a good reason to quit and there will always be a good reason to keep going. Decide what kind of person you're going to be."*
> Eric Worre[13]

Conversely, shrinking from challenges signifies a retreat or evasion. This tendency often arises from a fear of failure, a lack of confidence, or a fixed mindset - the belief that your abilities are static and unchangeable. By steering clear of challenges, you forfeit valuable opportunities for growth and learning. Such avoidance can result in stagnation, diminished self-efficacy, and, ultimately, failure by proxy.

Avoiding challenges not only means missing out on opportunities to demonstrate personal resilience but also undermines your self-confidence. Each bypassed challenge can chip away at your self-esteem and cement a negative self-perception, making it increasingly difficult to confront future issues and challenges and reinforces a fixed mindset.

> *"Success seems to be connected with action.*
> *Successful people keep moving. They make*
> *mistakes, but they don't quit."*
>
> Conrad Hilton[14]

Successful people often leave behind valuable clues to their achievements. By paying attention to their words and mimicking their actions, we can glean insights into their paths to success.

Napoleon Hill's book, *Think and Grow Rich*, is a testament to this concept. Hill compiled his insights from extensive interviews with the most successful people of his era, delving into the reasons behind their accomplishments and uncovering their guiding principles and mantras.

As example, Conrad Hilton, the founder of Hilton Hotels, whose quote above encapsulates essential elements of success, "connected with action," "keep moving," and "don't quit." Hilton's words, drawn from his own experiences as a highly successful entrepreneur, highlight the fundamental behaviors that distinguish winning from losing and determine success or failure.

These seemingly simple clues in taking action, maintaining momentum, and persevering in the face of challenges form the bedrock of achievement and ultimate success. They are the timeless principles that have propelled many people to greatness, absent of excuses.

The Journey of Conrad Hilton

Conrad Hilton's journey is a rich tapestry woven with both triumphs and setbacks, a testament to his resilience and vision. Born into a first-generation immigrant family, Hilton grew up with modest means, working at his father's general store. Far from having a silver spoon, his early experiences shaped his work ethic and determination.

Hilton served in the Army during World War I and subsequently took on a role in the New Mexico legislature. His ambition eventually led him to Texas in pursuit of fortune. It was here that he made his first foray into the hotel business by investing in a small forty-room hotel in Cisco, Texas.

This period was marked by numerous trials and complications, including the challenges posed by the Great Depression. Despite these obstacles, his hotels survived and even thrived. Hilton did not quit; his perseverance paid off handsomely as he went on to build a staggering portfolio of over 3,600 hotels worldwide. This monumental achievement culminated in the establishment of one of the world's most prestigious hotel empires, cementing his legacy as a pioneering figure in the hospitality industry.

Hilton's creation and expansion of the Hilton Hotels chain stand as a remarkable testament to his visionary leadership and unwavering resilience. Despite encoun-tering numerous failures and formidable challenges,

Hilton's capacity for innovation, adaptability, and strategic business expansion were pivotal to his success.

Today, Hilton Hotels is one of the most recognized and esteemed brands in the hospitality industry, a status largely attributable to his pioneering efforts and enduring legacy.

> *"You were designed for accomplishment, engineered for success, and endowed with the seeds of greatness."*
>
> Zig Ziglar[15]

We all come into this world with the inherent potential to shape the quality of our lives. Ironically, many of us fail to recognize this innate ability, often becoming consumed by the busyness of daily existence.

When confronted with someone else's success, we tend to default to the rationalization that they were simply lucky or had some inherent advantage. What we overlook are the countless hours of effort, the sweat, and the risks taken to achieve that success. We only see the end result of a person success because it conforms to a non-challenging narrative for our station in life or lack of progress. Success takes work to happen.

Action Makes Luck Happen!

Elon Musk is one of the wealthiest individuals in the world. He was born into a working-class family in South Africa, then migrated to the United States in 1988 with a vision that eventually evolved into PayPal. This idea, coupled with an entrepreneurial spirit and a growth mindset, became a beacon of success. While it may seem like luck played a significant role, it was actually Musk's relentless persistence and hard work that paved the way. In essence, persistence is the force that transforms luck into reality. He made luck happen!

> *"Luck is a dividend of sweat. The more you sweat, the luckier you get."*
>
> Ray Kroc[16]

Musk leveraged his PayPal success to establish ground-breaking ventures like Tesla, SpaceX, and X (Twitter). He consistently took decisive action, maintained relentless momentum, and never gave up. Successful individuals who confront their fears and consistently push beyond their comfort zones often experience deeper and more meaningful personal and professional growth.

Your Journey of Success is to push through your limiting beliefs, be receptive to failure and get beyond busy, the things that hold you in the herd, to find and develop your greatness. It will be your discipline and perspective to view your time as priceless and your life as valuable. Cultivate a growth mindset focused on contributing to and adding value to others, all while maintaining a vision that extends beyond immediate gains.

> *"Money won't create success, the freedom to make it will."*
>
> Nelson Mandela[17]

The Journey of Michael Collins

A young man named Michael seemed destined to follow the path of mediocrity, much like the rest of his peers. Raised in a modest household, he was surrounded by limiting beliefs that dictated he should aim no higher than a steady job and a simple life. But Michael had a different vision of his life.

Michael was captivated by the stars and dreamed of exploring the vast universe. He was inspired by John F. Kennedy's bold promise to land a man on the moon, a goal that seemed impossible to many at the time. Michael knew that to achieve greatness, he had to push through his limiting beliefs and be receptive to failure.

He applied to NASA's astronaut program and faced rejection multiple times. Instead of giving up, he used each failure as a learning experience, refining his skills and deepening his knowledge. He disciplined himself, viewing every moment as an opportunity to get closer to his dream. He didn't get bogged down by the daily grind or the opinions of those who doubted him. Instead, he stayed focused on his ultimate goal.

Years of relentless effort paid off when Michael Collins was finally selected for a mission to be the Command Module Pilot to go to the moon. In 1969, he was part of the historic Apollo 11 mission that landed the first humans on the moon.

His journey from a modest background to becoming an astronaut exemplifies how pushing through limiting beliefs, embracing failure, and valuing time can lead to the pinnacle of success. Michael's story is a testament to the idea that your journey of success relies on your discipline and persistence to view your life as valuable. Michael found his greatness in a capsule flying to the moon!

> *"Many of life's failures are people who did not realize how close they were to success when they gave up."*
>
> Thomas A. Edison[13]

The road to success is often a narrow, winding, and lonely journey, which is why many people abandon their dreams and ideas in frustration, opting to rejoin the safety of the herd. The road to success can be scary and intimidating! Countless individuals experience failure not due to a lack of talent or wanting, but because they gave up their efforts just moments before their breakthrough. They frequently fail to realize how close they were to achieving success when they decided to quit.

> *"The size of your success is measured by the strength of your desire, the size of your dream, and how you handle disappointment along the way."*
>
> Robert Kiyosaki[19]

However, it is precisely during these moments of doubt and challenge that perseverance emerges as the defining factor. By forging ahead despite fear and uncertainty, individuals can turn obstacles into opportunities and make incremental progress toward their goals. The true essence of success lies in resilience and an unwavering belief in one's dream, even when the path ahead is shrouded in uncertainty.

Trump's Journey of Resilience

From the moment Donald J. Trump came down the golden escalator of Trump Tower in New York on June 16, 2015, to announce his candidacy for the 2016 U.S. presidential election, he was met was a great undertow of political resistance and unprecedented media scrutiny. These external forces were determined to unseat his potential presidency and to completely destroy his reputation. Regardless of political standing, Trump's journey through his presidential years is an amazing example of fortitude in the face of failure and resilience in the face of significant opposition. This "deep state" undertow from political opponents, federal agencies, and malicious lawsuits plus two assassination attempts created a windstorm of insurmountable challenges that most people would have caved or given up early in the process. It is a bit mind-boggling how anyone could have been successful under these relentless conditions and was able to succeed through it all.

Trump's perseverance through the storm was a testimony to his unwavering confidence (unshakable belief) and laser focused clarity (strong vision). These two elements create a resilient mindset which is tantamount to a growth mindset.

As example, Trump experienced four lawsuits sitting in a court room everyday while undergoing a national presidential campaign. He took the court setting not as a setback but as a promotional opportunity to promote his campaign and capture the news cycles to his benefit. After court one day as the news pundits were chasing him, he went to a nearby Manhattan construction site where he rallied the construction workers that was televised by many major news outlets.

His resilience made positives from negatives and raised his underdog position to rally his base of supporters to win the 2024 presidential elections. His bravado resilience became his brand, his signature red tie and blue suit became his image, and his mantra message was common sense in *"Make America Great Again"*. This trifecta combination resonated with 77 million voters winning the electoral college and popular vote in 2024 leaving his political opponents defeated and shocked.

> *"What separates the winners from the losers is how a person reacts to each new twist of fate."*
>
> Donald J. Trump[20]

Your GPS Mindset

Before embarking on the journey to success, it's crucial to activate your internal **GPS**: your **G**rowth **P**otential **S**ystem. This essential mindset serves as your navigator, guiding you toward your ultimate success destination. Without it, the path to success can be challenging and obscure, and your destination unknown.

> *"Strength and growth come only through continuous effort and struggle."*
>
> Napoleon Hill[21]

Personal growth stands as a cornerstone of genuine success, without it, achievements you achieve may feel hollow and fleeting. The clarity and strength of your growth signal are directly proportional to your growth mindset. This mindset equips you with the knowledge and resilience necessary to stay on the course toward your life's aspirations.

As esteemed leadership expert John C. Maxwell aptly stated, "What is your growth plan?"[22] This question underscores the importance of a deliberate, structured approach to personal development as the foundation for lasting success. So, what is your growth plan?

> *"Growth is the great separator between those who succeed and those who do not. When I see a person beginning to separate themselves from the pack, it's almost always due to personal growth."*
>
> John C. Maxwell[23]

Journey Rest Stop 10

1) What strategy do you use to rebound from setbacks?

2) How does action make luck happen?

3) What is your internal GPS system? How strong is your signal for growth?

Journey Thought

"You can't climb the ladder of success with your hands in your pockets."

Arnold Schwarzenegger[24]

www.FindingJOY.us

Chapter 11

Journey of Growth

Are You Still Growing?

Let your addiction for growth be stronger than your addiction for comfort.

Anonymous

Imagine an oak seed nestled in fertile soil. It doesn't magically become a towering tree overnight. This metaphor for growth mirrors our personal journeys. True growth is an ongoing process, demanding consistent nourishment, ample time, and a supportive environment. Just as the seed needs sunlight, water, and the right conditions to flourish, we too, require guidance, patience, and the proper surroundings to reach our fullest potential.

Just as that seedling needs to grow to become a big, beautiful tree, the same is true with us with our life journey. Lacking the sunlight of personal growth, our life journey risks stagnation, possibly depriving us of the potential for a greater fulfilled future self.

However, for many people, growth becomes an elusive concept after their teenage years with or without formal education. The responsibilities, distractions, and busyness of adult life take over. We secure jobs, enter marriages, accumulate bills, and become engrossed in the daily grind. We get *busy*! Life is the great distractor that keeps us busy on our monthly struggles and focused on the daily routine.

> *"Our whole life is set up in the path of least resistance. We don't want to suffer. We don't want to feel discomfort. So, the whole time, we're living our lives in a very comfortable area. There's no growth in that."*
>
> David Goggins[1]

In most cases, we focus on our immediate survival, acquiring only the knowledge essential to get through another day or to maintain our jobs. Consequently, we often, by default, limit our opportunities for learning and personal development, stunting our potential to expand and grow our lives. This, it seems, is the reality of modern living.

Moving Forward Without Moving Ahead

Have you ever felt like you are going nowhere fast no matter how hard you try? Welcome to the complexities of adult life in the working world. We are consistently moving forward in time without moving ahead in our careers, value, purpose, or time freedom. A growth paradox for sure – busily working every day but never getting ahead in building life freedom or a greater life purpose. After thousands of years from our prehistoric caves, today we are still hunters and gatherers by nature, always in survival mode trying to stay ahead of our debts in the modern world. To break the cycle takes only one word – *change*. Change your perspective, your outlook, and your attitude to change your direction to new horizons and your value to greater worth.

> **"You cannot expect to achieve new goals or move beyond your present circumstances unless you change."**
>
> Les Brown[2]

Arnold Schwarzenegger's journey perfectly illustrates the idea that to achieve new goals or rise above our current situations, we have to embrace change.

Growing up in a small village in Austria, Schwarzenegger began his career as a bodybuilder, dreaming of making it big on the international stage. He excelled in the world of bodybuilding, clinching the Mr. Olympia title multiple times, and it would have been easy for him to stay there. But he didn't stop, he aimed for Hollywood - an audacious move at the time for someone with a strong accent and minimal acting experience.

Facing a barrage of rejections, critics pointed out that his accent and muscular physique could be stumbling blocks. But instead of giving up, Schwarzenegger channeled that feedback into hard work. He dedicated himself to honing his craft and establishing his unique identity in body building and physique. His relentless dedication paid off, leading him to become a global superstar with iconic roles in films like *The Terminator* and *Predator*.

"For me life is continuously being hungry. The meaning of life is not simply to exist, to survive, but to move ahead, to go up, to achieve, to conquer."
Arnold Schwarzenegger[3]

But Arnold didn't stop at Hollywood. He took yet another bold leap into the world of politics, serving as the Governor of California for two terms. Each phase of his life demanded that he release old identities and grow into new ones, showing us all that change is not just important; it is vital for reaching new heights and life goals.

"If you want to reach your potential and become the person you were created to be, you must do much more than just experience life and hope that you learn what you need along the way. You must go out of your way to seize growth opportunities as if your future depended on it."
John C. Maxwell[4]

John C. Maxwell, a distinguished author and growth expert, is known for posing a pivotal question: "What is your growth plan?" At first glance, this might seem perplexing. A growth plan? What does that even mean?

If this concept is unfamiliar to you, don't worry; you're not alone. The reality is that most people haven't contemplated their own growth, much less devised a specific plan for it. It's quite ironic that something so fundamental to leading a fulfilled life is frequently overlooked or not thought of at all. So, what exactly is growth, and what constitutes a growth plan?

Street-Smart Growth

Everyone experiences fundamental growth or let's call it street-smart growth. This should not be confused with personal development growth, which is supplemental or adds to your skill sets and, more importantly, your identity. Street-smart growth encompasses the essential learning we acquire during our formative years, enabling us to develop basic life skills such as balancing a checkbook or cooking a meal.

A high school diploma (or GED) signifies that graduating from high school should equip you with the fundamental tools necessary for society survival, including the abilities to read, write, comprehend basic concepts and get a basic job to join the work force.

According to the U.S. Census Bureau in 2022, 27.9 percent of adults from ages twenty-five years and older listed high school as their highest level of school completed while 23.5 percent had a bachelor's degree as their highest degree.5 Deducing these percentages, if accurate, then only a small percentage of GED students obtain a BS degree while many college students do not continue past their first collegiate year. Wow!

These surprising statistics suggest that many people tend to limit or entirely halt their educational learning after high school, except maybe when it comes to changing trades or switching to a new career later in life where they need to take some continuing education courses to maintain or upgrade their job.

College is not the "end-all" destination for learning or achieving a fulfilled life. In fact, many billionaires did not finish or attend higher education like Bill Gates, Mark Zuckerberg, Steve Jobs, Larry Ellison, Michael Dell, Richard Branson to name a few. However, college does serve as a valuable resource to many of us to provide additional life tools for our skill sets plus adds to our identity and ideally broadens our perspective on the world.

Most life learning begins when formal education ends. Life learning is the wisdom and practical skills we gain from real-world experiences, distinct from personal self-development and formal education. Like many others, myself included, we often plunge into the vast ocean of life after completing our education years. We become preoccupied with keeping afloat, allowing the currents of life to dictate our direction. In this hustle, many of us halt our pursuit of personal growth and development, relying instead on life's street-smart lessons to shape us. Consequently, we often conform to the role's life assigns us, blending into the crowd and never truly discovering our inner potential and greatness. We just go along with life's flow and see where life takes us.

> *"If you don't design your own life plan, chances*
> *are you'll fall into someone else's plan. And guess*
> *what they may have planned for you? Not much."*
>   Jim Rohn[6]

If you haven't yet considered a personal growth plan, and many haven't, the first crucial step is to commit daily to your personal development. Growth is your ticket out of Dodge from the mundane to an exceptional and abundant life.

A growth plan builds greater confidence, better self-esteem, deeper knowledge, and adds to your identity. The sooner you embark on your Journey of Growth, the greater the rewards you will reap.

> *To reach your potential you must grow. And to*
> *grow, you must be highly intentional about it."*
>   John C. Maxwell[7]

Think of growth like a gym membership. If you only go sporadically, when it fits into your schedule, and don't make it part of your daily routine, you won't see significant results if any. Ironically, life itself often becomes the biggest distraction, keeping us too busy in survival mode to focus on our personal development and growth. Be intentional and consistent every day with your personal growth like a weightlifter at a gym and get busy at your "growth gym"!

Join the Growth Gym

Before you sign up for the growth gym, it's important to reflect backwards in order to move forward. Assess where you have been, where you are now, and where you want to go. Take a little time to truly recognize your current place in life. Reflect deeply on the milestones you've reached, the obstacles you've overcome, and the invaluable lessons you've garnered along the way. This is your foundation for growth.

Now pause and recognize your current place in life as an exercise in appreciation and introspection. It's good to know where you have been to chart your path to where you want to go. As you reflect, think of the life milestones you have reached and achievements you have made. Whether it was graduating from school, securing your first job, or forming lasting relationships, each milestone has shaped who you are today - your identity.

Think of the obstacles that have played a crucial role in your journey. The challenges you have faced, whether personal or professional, have tested your resilience and determination. These hurdles have not only made you stronger; they provide you with valuable lessons. You have learned the importance of perseverance, the value of patience, and the necessity of resilience in the face of change or adversity.

Each lesson garnered along the way has contributed to your growth, attitude, and identity. Good and bad lessons have enriched your perspective on life - from the importance of self-care to recognizing the significance of empathy and kindness toward others. They have hopefully guided you in making better choices and have helped you build a foundation of knowledge and experience. In life we continue to grow, whether by default or by our choices. You get to pick!

> *"All of us need to grow continuously in our lives."*
> Les Brown[8]

If you are living on autopilot, then life's got a plan for you. However, if you are the master of your domain, then lets hit the growth gym! Get your shorts and Powerade, and let's do this!

Creating a growth plan begins with establishing daily growth habits that foster personal development. While this is easier said than done, it's important to recognize that as humans, we often gravitate toward activities that are enjoyable, simple, or offer immediate gratification. There's nothing inherently wrong with this tendency. After all, who doesn't appreciate fun and easy, especially when they come with sprinkles?

However, to cultivate a good life habit, it's best to start with small, manageable daily actions that gradually integrate new processes to become routine in your life. If a task or habit lacks enjoyment, simplicity, or perceived value, it's unlikely to stick.

Personal growth doesn't happen by chance or divine intervention. It requires a conscious decision and sustained effort to evolve from where you currently are to where you aspire to be. By committing to incremental steps and recognizing the value in each action, you lay the foundation for meaningful and lasting growth. You are building growth habits.

> **"Your mission is to become better today than you were yesterday."**
>
> John C. Maxwell[9]

Whether you're embarking on your personal growth journey for the first time or rekindling it, maintaining daily motivation is crucial. Our brains thrive on reminders. Without them, the busyness of life can supersede our goals to fade into distant memories, often accompanied by excuses. Right or *RIGHT*? A straightforward yet effective daily growth reminder is to write the word growth on several "Post-it" notes and strategically place them around your home and office.

Aim for four or five of these 2x2 notes in key locations. For instance, stick one on your bathroom mirror, another on your nightstand or headboard, one on your refrigerator, and another on TV monitor, office computer, or even on your car dashboard. These strategically placed sticky notes will act as continuous prompts, subtly nudging your subconscious and creating a consistent reminder for growth. Your brain needs to be fully engaged.

> *"If you want to reach your potential and become the person you were created to be, you must do much more than just experience life and hope that you learn what you need along the way. You must go out of your way to seize growth opportunities as if your future depended on it."*
>
> John C. Maxwell[10]

These persistent reminders encourage you to take at least one action each day toward your personal growth. This simple strategy can help you stay focused and committed, ensuring that growth becomes an integral part of your daily life. Simply put, you are training your brain to be intentional about growth and your development.

Your mindset in approaching your growth journey should recognize growth as a crucial asset to your identity. If you don't associate growth with intrinsic value, it will remain just another word in the dictionary. Your mental growth journey needs to be as vital as your physical growth, much like the essentials of sleeping, eating, breathing, and exercising.

Another great way to keep on your daily growth track is to journal your growth. I realize many will not journal, but when you write down your thoughts, releasing daily thoughts, you are validating your growth commitment to your subconscious. You are getting your brain to buy into the program. Journaling is very powerful, and each word you write get imprinted onto your cerebral hard drive.

Journal Your Growth

The reason for a growth journal is simply it will keep you focused on developing your thoughts and life perspective. Start your journey with intention. Join our JOY Community at www.FindingJOY.us and download your free personal Growth Journal today. So, here are a few things to help you journal your journey.

•   **Time:** Identify a time that seamlessly fits into your daily routine for consistent journaling. This could be in the morning, offering a moment to set your intentions and reflect on the day ahead. Alternatively, consider journaling in the evening to unwind, process the events of the day, and prepare your mind for rest. Do not make this like homework; make it fun! Spend around twenty minutes reflecting on your thoughts and make sure to date each entry.

•   **Start with Prompts:** If you're uncertain about what to write, prompts can serve as invaluable tools to spark your creativity. These can range from specific questions to broad topics, designed to inspire you to dive into your thoughts and emotions. For instance, you might begin with prompts such as, "Today, I am grateful for . . ." or "One thing I learned today is . . ." These starting points not only kick-start your writing process, they help you uncover deeper insights and reflections.

• **Write Freely:** Don't stress about grammar, spelling, or structure in your journal. It's your personal space, so write freely or draw about anything that comes to mind. Whether it's your thoughts, feelings, daily experiences, aspirations, dreams, or even random observations, let your ideas flow without judgment.

• **Reflect and Review:** Regularly revisit your journal entries, taking the time to reflect deeply on what you've written the day before. This practice can provide valuable insights into your emotions, thought patterns, and personal development. By doing so, you can identify areas that need improvement and recognize and celebrate your achievements, fostering continuous growth and self-awareness.

• **Experiment with Different Styles:** There are countless ways to keep a journal beyond just writing. You can enrich your entries with sketches, poems, and lists, or even integrate photos and mementos. Experiment with various styles to discover what truly resonates with you and makes your journaling experience unique and fulfilling.

• **Stay Consistent:** Much like any other habit, journaling yields the greatest rewards when practiced consistently. Strive to make journaling a daily routine, or at the very least, engage in it several times a week. By doing so, you can fully harness the power of self-reflection and mindfulness, enriching your mental clarity and emotional well-being.

•   **Goal-Setting:** Detail your short-term and long-term goals in a dedicated section of your journal. Regularly monitor your progress and utilize your journal as a powerful tool for both planning and maintaining motivation. This practice will not only help you stay organized but also provide a tangible record of your achievements and areas for improvement.

•   **Practice Self-Compassion:** Your journal is a sanctuary where you can dive into your thoughts and emotions without fear of judgment. Treat yourself with compassion as you write and embrace this practice as a powerful tool for self-discovery and personal growth.

Remember, journaling is a profoundly personal journey, so feel free to customize your approach to align with your individual style. The essential part is to start and consistently develop it into a routine that enhances your well-being. Your journal should serve as a mirror, capturing the evolution from your past to your present. Think of yourself as the ghostwriter of your life, documenting your story from an outsider's perspective and emphasizing your growth.

> *"If you put yourself in a position where you have to stretch outside your comfort zone, then you are forced to expand your consciousness."*
> Les Brown[11]

Growth does not occur in isolation. You cannot cultivate a richer existence or broaden your horizons by remaining within the safety of the herd mindset. True growth necessitates stepping beyond familiar boundaries and daring to explore new challenges and life-expanding opportunities. It requires breaking free from the gravitational pull of conformity and embracing the discomfort that comes with uncertainty. Only by venturing into the unknown, challenging conventional wisdom, and forging your own path can you create the fertile ground where authentic personal evolution thrives.

Reading IS the Shortcut to Growth & Wisdom

The most straightforward and reliable pathway to accelerate your personal growth is through a steadfast commitment to reading. Imagine dedicating yourself to reading just ten pages a day, six days a week. Over the span of a year, this habit would enable you to complete approximately eight to twelve books!

Consider the profound transformation in your mindset, perspectives, and overall growth and greater knowledge if you were to read ten books in a year. You would undoubtedly emerge as a different person with your influence, demeanor, identity, and social associations all undergoing significant personal evolution.

There is a wealth of exceptional thought-provoking and motivational books and literature that can serve as the cornerstone of your growth journey. By committing just twenty minutes a day to reading, you can set in motion a life-changing trajectory. This simple yet powerful habit can become the catalyst for remarkable personal development and success.

To sustain and nurture this growth habit, consider joining or starting a mastermind book club! This will keep you accountable while potentially expanding your friendship circle. I can already sense the growth happening!

> *"The unsuccessful person is burdened by learning and prefers to walk down familiar paths. Their distaste for learning stunts their growth and limits their influence."*
>
> John C. Maxwell[12]

So, reach out to a few of your intellectual, success-oriented friends and make it happen! For those new to book clubs, the ideal group size is between five to eight people. The guidelines are straightforward. Everyone agrees on a weekly meeting time via Zoom or a local coffee shop and determines the number of pages or chapters to read each week. The group will assign a coordinator for each new book to keep things organized and on schedule.

The primary goal of the meetings is to discuss the week's reading material, its relevance to each person's life and to maintain group accountability. Once the group completes a book, celebrate the achievement together and choose the next one! Keep it moving for growth to happen. Your mastermind book club is like going to your personalized growth gym to exercise the most important muscle you have - your brain!

> *"No one lives long enough to learn everything they need to learn starting from scratch. To be successful, we absolutely, positively have to find people who have already paid the price to learn the things that we need to learn to achieve our goals."*
>
> Brian Tracy[13]

Here are a few excellent books to get you started on your growth journey:

- *The 15 Invaluable Laws of Growth* by John C. Maxwell
- *Live Your Dreams* by Les Brown
- *Atomic Habits* by James Clear
- *Think and Grow Rich* by Napoleon Hill
- *The 7 Habits of Highly Effective People* by Stephen R. Covey
- *Awaken the Giant Within* by Tony Robbins
- *How to Win Friends and Influence People* by Dale Carnegie
- *Rich Dad, Poor Dad* by Robert T. Kiyosaki
- *Mindset: The New Psychology of Success* by Dr. Carol S. Dweck
- *The Gap and The Gain* by Benjamin Hardy and Dan Sullivan
- *People Buy YOU* by Jeb Blount
- *The 10X Rule* by Grant Cardone
- *The Leadership Gap: What Gets Between You and Your Greatness* by Lolly Daskal

> *"Formal education will make you a living, self-education will make you a fortune."*
>
> Jim Rohn[14]

Growth is an invaluable and intangible asset that requires diligent investment of both our time and financial resources to cultivate effectively. Personal development and growth are not without their costs. They demand our conscious effort, a commitment of time, and the allocation of resources.

Unfortunately, many of us fall short in making a serious personal commitment to growth, often allowing the busyness of life to dictate our actions. As a result, true change rarely occurs, we are on default! For most people, significant change only happens when they are confronted with a major life challenge. In such moments of struggle, we tend to scramble for a quick solution, often making hasty decisions that may not be the best choices. This reactive approach is far from ideal.

True growth requires proactive planning, dedicated effort, and a steadfast commitment to continuous improvement. By investing in our personal development consistently, we can navigate life's challenges more effectively and foster meaningful, lasting change.

In his insightful book, *Dig Your Well Before You're Thirsty*, Harvey Mackay emphasizes the crucial importance of proactive planning and having a strategy in place before life inevitably throws its curve-balls. As Mackay stated, "It doesn't matter whether you are pursuing success in business, sports, the arts, or life in general: The bridge between wishing and accomplishing is discipline."[15]

Building on Mackay's wisdom, I am sure he would advocate for the inclusion of a comprehensive growth plan. Such a plan ensures that when challenges arise, they are more manageable, and the obstacles less formidable. By preparing in advance, we not only mitigate potential difficulties but also set ourselves up for continued personal and professional development.

> **"Strength and growth come only through continuous effort and struggle."**
> Napoleon Hill[16]

As a great growth example in 1995 Elon Musk moved to Silicon Valley, determined to make his mark in the burgeoning tech industry. Armed with a physics degree and an unquenchable curiosity, he knew that the easiest and surest way to expand his growth journey was to commit to reading. Musk devoured books on rocket science, engineering, and even science fiction, finding inspiration in the works of Isaac Asimov and Robert Heinlein. His voracious reading habit equipped him with a breadth and depth of knowledge that would later propel him to found companies like SpaceX and Tesla. Today, Musk is arguably the richest person in the world based on his personal development growth.

> **"I was raised by books. Books, and then my parents."**
> Elon Musk[17]

Similarly, in sports, the late Kobe Bryant's dedication to reading was equally transformative. Known for his relentless work ethic, Bryant often spoke about how reading helped him gain a competitive edge. He studied everything from leadership and strategy to the biographies of great athletes and thinkers. These readings provided him with insights that enriched his game, leading the Los Angeles Lakers to five NBA championships.

Kobe Bryant's commitment to reading exemplified how knowledge could be a powerful tool for personal and professional growth. Both Musk and Bryant illustrate the profound impact that reading can have on one's growth journey. Whether in technology, sports, or any other field, the commitment to continuous learning through reading can unlock new perspectives and opportunities, paving the way for remarkable achievements and more importantly life growth.

Reading is one of the most cost-effective and enriching avenues for personal growth and knowledge acquisition. By cultivating the habit of reading and integrating it into your daily routine, much like having breakfast, you will naturally begin to seek out the authors of the books that captivate you.

> *"Watch, listen, and learn. You can't know it all yourself. Anyone who thinks they do is destined for mediocrity."*
>
> Donald J. Trump[18]

Growth Courses and Seminars

The next logical step in your growth journey is to identify and follow a few mentors who resonate with you, such as John Maxwell, Tony Robbins, Les Brown, and other esteemed life coaches. Many authors, including myself, offer a variety of personal development resources, such as courses, seminars, and webinars, to support you on your growth journey. While most of these events are paid, there are numerous free webinars featuring valuable content from various authors are also available. Embracing these opportunities can significantly enhance your personal and professional development.

> *"Invest three percent of your income in yourself (self-development) in order to guarantee your future."*
>
> Brian Tracy[19]

Life Coaching

The third step on your growth ladder is to enlist the expertise of a life coach and, over time, become part of a mastermind group. A life coach offers indispensable support in personal development by assisting individuals in clarifying their goals, aligning their actions with their aspirations, and effectively navigating challenges. They provide a structured framework for setting and achieving objectives, supplemented by accountability and regular check-ins to ensure consistent progress.

Beyond mere goal setting, a life coach offers valuable perspective and unbiased feedback, fostering heightened self-awareness and personal growth. They empower clients to surmount obstacles, acquire new skills, and make informed decisions that resonate with their core values and ambitions. Through motivation, encouragement, and skill-building exercises, a life coach facilitates the development of confidence and resilience, ultimately steering individuals toward greater clarity, fulfillment, and success in both their personal and professional lives. Your life coach is your personal life concierge as a soundboard and feedback on your journey.

By integrating the guidance of a life coach and the collective wisdom of a mastermind group, you can create a robust support system. This combination amplifies your growth potential, helping you unlock new levels of achievement and satisfaction. Congratulations! You are diving in the deep end of the pool! Submersion is the fastest way to make significant changes in life.

> *"Success is not something you chase; it's something you attract by the person you become."*
> Jim Rohn[20]

You become the person you invest in. Don't be cheap! You evolve into the person you dedicate time and effort to nurturing. Without committing to your own growth, there can be little advancement or progress in life.

Enhancing the value of your time through continuous self-improvement makes you more valuable, and success naturally follows. The foundation of this journey is utilizing the talents and intellect God gave you to mold your future, the Journey of You. Remember, growth doesn't come from making excuses. There is no tomorrow for growth, only today.

> *"Just because fate doesn't deal you the right cards, it doesn't mean you should give up. It just means you have to play the cards you get to their maximum potential."*
>
> Les Brown[21]

Investing in yourself is the cornerstone of personal growth development. The most important investment you can make that will last a lifetime and pay major dividends every day is not in stocks or real estate - it is in you!

It's important to recognize that the journey of self-investment is ongoing. There is no greater investment in life than the investment in you. There will be challenges and setbacks in your Journey of Growth, but these are opportunities in disguise. Embrace them as part of the process and use them to fuel your determination.

The more you invest of your time and money in yourself to develop your mindset, skills, knowledge, and well-being, the more you enhance your identity, self-awareness, independence and life perspective for an abundant life and the capacity to contribute value to the world. Your ROI for inward growth produces greater life opportunities and ultimate success. Ask any successful person.

> *"Perfection does not exist, you can always do better and you can always grow."*
> Les Brown[22]

The journey to become your future self is a lifelong adventure of continuous growth and self-improvement. Life is synonymous with growth, if you are not growing you are not living. When you embark on this transformative path, remember that you are not alone.

Seek wisdom and guidance from books, thought leaders, mentors, and life coaches who can support and inspire you along the way. It all begins with a conscious decision to prioritize your personal growth development. From there, it's the daily actions and habits you cultivate that will nurture your potential and drive meaningful change.

By committing to this journey, you not only elevate your own life but also become a beacon of inspiration and influence for those around you. Your growth will enrich your circle of friends, expand your network, create deeper connections, and contribute to a more positive and enlightened world. Your presence and evolution will resonate, making a lasting difference in the lives of others to have an impactful Journey of You.

> *"Change is inevitable. Growth is optional."*
> John C. Maxwell[23]

Journey Rest Stop 11

1) What does "moving forward without moving ahead" mean in your life?

2) How do you plan to journal your daily growth? (Hint: Go to www.FindingJOY.us, join our community and get your free growth plan outline.)

3) How important is reading to your growth, identity, and personal development?

Journey Thought

"Conformity is the jailer of freedom and the enemy of growth."

-John F. Kennedy[24]

www.FindingJOY.us

Chapter 12

Journey of YOU

It's a Wonderful Life!

You must remain focused on your
journey to greatness.

Les Brown[1]

The Journey of YOU is perhaps the most pivotal life adventure you can embark upon. Every life decision you make to either turn right or left, continue straight ahead, or turn off the engine shapes your path forward. The individuals you encounter, the faith you hold, and the care you invest in your "vehicle" of life profoundly influence your ultimate destination and the duration of your stay there.

> *"If you take responsibility for yourself you will*
> *develop a hunger to accomplish your dreams."*
> Les Brown[2]

Imagine it's twenty years from now and you have successfully reached your life destination. What does your life look like? Are you struggling or enjoying financial freedom? Are you enjoying great health, or are you fighting a disease? Do you have time to spend how you want? Or do you have to wholesale your time to pay the bills? What does your future lifestyle freedom look like?

What wisdom would your future-self share with your present-self to achieve your dream destination? What advice would your future-self offer to help your present self to make the necessary course corrections today to live an exciting Journey of You toward an abundant life.

> *"The worst thing one can do is not to try, to be aware of what one wants and not give in to it, to spend years in silent hurt wondering if something could have materialized... never knowing."*
>
> Jim Rohn[3]

The Journey of You begins with the essence of who you are today and evolves into the person you will become tomorrow. It's your quest to build your life skills with the innate talent tools you were given to develop your purpose for an abundant and value giving life.

We all make choices in life and then we become our choice. Every decision you make shapes your destiny. These choices are influenced by our self-respect, our health, our time value, our faith, and how we perceive our existence. It's these collective thoughts that are the algorithms of our mindset on how we respond in our journey to life choices and challenges.

Awareness of your present life situation is the first step to change, and frustration is the second step for action to happen. The fuel for action is your will that will empower you to alter your course and transform your journey. Embrace your journey with intention, consistency, and mindfulness, for it holds your key to future fulfillment, success, and abundance or lack of them.

> *"The major value in life is not what you get. The major value in life is what you become."*
>
> Jim Rohn[4]

No matter where you find yourself in life, whether on the street, stuck in a dead-end, time-consuming job or climbing the endless corporate ladder and you're frustrated in knowing there's got to be more.

Fear not! You have the power to change your direction and final destination. Society may not agree and put up resistance when you try to leave the herd but give yourself permission to grow and develop your future self now.

This life transition requires you to develop a journey dream and then an action plan, dedicated work, consistent effort with a strong will. A life course correction is often fueled by sheer frustration with your current circumstances going nowhere fast! Embrace this frustration as octane for your future self.

Channel this frustration as a reflection of your past, not a picture of your future. To help you on your journey, each chapter in *Finding JOY* provides deep introspection into various aspects of your life, ranging from mindset and embracing challenges to overcoming fears and forging a new, confident identity. This journey, if you choose to accept it, will guide you toward an abundant, purposeful life of value and meaning with little to no regrets. When you channel your frustration into fuel, it sparks action and that action can evolve into joy as it leads you toward a refined direction and renewed purpose.

> *"Life takes on meaning when you become motivated, set goals and charge after them in an unstoppable manner. We must look for ways to be an active force in our own lives. We must take charge of our own destinies, design a life of substance and truly begin to live our dreams."*
>
> Les Brown[5]

I know you are excited about getting ready for your new life journey with all the new journey tools you have learned, but before you take off there are just a few more journey snacks you need to pack in the Igloo! Without packing these journey snacks, your trip will definitely take longer as you face a few detours along the way.

Your Health Journey

Once you have made the commitment to move your life forward to a greater life destination, then you need to prepare your vehicle before your journey! Just like any road trip we make sure the car is in good working order before we put the keys in the ignition. Oil . . . check! Tires . . . check! Battery . . . check! Gas . . . check! Snacks . . . double check!

Most of us are more concerned about our car maintenance before a road trip than we are with our health as we venture in our life journey. It's easy to take for granted our health since our bodies run fairly seamlessly for years without much maintenance. However, when health issues arise, they can derail our life plans, ambitions, and shorten our lifespan, leaving us stranded on the roadside, watching life pass us by. Clearly, maintaining our health is a crucial factor in our pursuit of Finding JOY.

> **"Take care of your body. It's the only place you have to live."**
>
> Jim Rohn[6]

Health is a major component of your life's journey, encompassing your physical well-being, mental health, and emotional wellness. When you maintain good health, you gain the energy and resilience needed to pursue your goals, nurture relationships, and navigate life's challenges with greater resilience and ease.

> **"No matter what your DNA says, a good diet, regular exercise, not smoking, limiting alcohol, and some other surprising lifestyle decisions, can change that destiny."**
>
> Dr. Sanjay Gupta[7]

Optimal health fuels productivity, stimulates creativity, and enhances overall happiness, forming a foundation that influences every facet of your life. Prioritizing and maintaining your good health is essential in Finding JOY. Most people on the road to success have a daily health regimen; it's integral to their journey. Without your health you will not realize your full potential and purpose. So, as you pack for your life journey, remember to incorporate a few good health habits in your daily routine to keep your vehicle running smoothly!

Health is a vital underlying component in Finding JOY. Incorporating a daily health regimen into your routine should be regarded as sacred time, integral to your overall self-development, just as crucial as nurturing your mindset, identity, reading habits, and social connections.

Many mentors and leadership coaches emphasize that health awareness and a comprehensive wellness program are essential for personal growth and long-term success. Your well-being is an intrinsic part of your path to achievement. The most effective health plan is one that prioritizes maintaining optimal health, enabling you to fully enjoy and sustain the journey of life for as long as possible.

Regrettably, there is no assurance that you won't encounter a significant health issue, ranging from heart disease to cancer, or any of the myriad conditions in between. These health problems can arise due to a combination of lifestyle choices and the inherent risks of daily living.

Sometimes life is not fair, and you hear of a very fit and health-conscious person suffer a heart attack or diagnosed with a terminal disease. Poor health can happen to any of us, regardless of our level of fitness. However, an unfit person is two to four times more likely to develop a chronic disease than a fit person who is serious about their wellness. Many studies validate this stat for various diseases from cardiovascular to cancer.[8]

As one example, the physical activity guidelines determined by the CDC highlight that physical inactivity is a significant risk factor for chronic diseases and aligns with our stat above in developing chronic conditions compared to those who are active and fit.[9]

According to a 2018 study titled "Prevalence of Multiple Chronic Conditions Among US Adults," 51.8 percent of US adults had at least one chronic condition, and 27.2 percent suffered from multiple chronic conditions. This data underscores the prevalence of illness in our society and highlights how poor lifestyle choices can adversely impact our health.[10]

You must be your body's advocate! By adopting a few simple, healthy habits into your daily routine, you can significantly improve your health outcomes and reduce your risk of becoming an early statistic. Embracing positive lifestyle changes can help you better manage your physical and mental health and enhance your overall quality of life, allowing you to fully concentrate on your life journey.

> *"The way you think, the way you behave, the way you eat, can influence your life by thirty to fifty years."*
>
> Deepak Chopra[11]

Choose a healthy lifestyle regime that easily aligns with your new life journey. Be aware of the main cause of most illnesses and diseases so you can be as healthy as possible, giving you the best hedge in your wellness journey. Poor lifestyle choices are the trigger, and your cellular response to these choices is the bullet.

Your Body's Cellular Response

Many studies have identified the cellular response of oxidative stress as a precursor to a wide array of chronic diseases. A quick search on PubMed.gov reveals over 335,000+ studies examining the link between oxidative stress and various illnesses and diseases. So, what exactly is oxidative stress, and why is it so crucial to our health journey?

A bit of science for your beginning health research. Cellular "oxidative stress" occurs when there is an imbalance between free radicals (ROS - Reactive Oxygen Species) and antioxidants in the body. Free radicals are unstable molecules with unpaired electrons that cause damage to cells, protein genes, and DNA. Antioxidants are compounds that neutralize these free radicals, preventing them from causing harm. "When a balance between production of ROS and anti-oxidative defense is disturbed, state of oxidative stress occurs. Oxidative stress leads to many diseases."[12] Some of these diseases include cardiovascular diseases, diabetes, neuro-degenerative disorders, and cancer just to name a few. In fact, oxidative stress can initiate and contribute to over four hundred chronic diseases.[13] It's the precursor to most diseases we face in life.

Understanding cellular oxidative stress is essential for anyone committed to a health-conscious journey. By recognizing the factors that contribute to high oxidative stress and adopting lifestyle and dietary measures to manage its levels, you can potentially mitigate the risk of developing chronic diseases and increase your lifespan.

Cellular oxidative stress refers to the measurement of cell damage and apoptosis occurring in our brains, vital organs, and tissues. This form of cellular stress is minimal at birth but significantly escalates after the age of twenty, serving as a primary precursor to aging besides most chronic diseases. Beyond the essential activities of living, breathing, and eating, your lifestyle choices will contribute greatly to increasing cellular oxidative stress in your body.

Lifestyle choices such as smoking, alcohol consumption, drug use (legal and illicit), obesity, and depression all contribute to increasing cellular oxidative stress, which creates an increased risk of developing chronic diseases earlier in life. As we all know, battling a chronic disease can divert focus, disrupt life direction, stall opportunities, and change our life course.

The encouraging news is that we have the ability to actively reduce or slow down cellular oxidative stress process in our bodies. Currently, numerous studies published on PubMed.gov and many universities are focusing on cellular activation to "switch on" a variety of enzymes, hormones, genes and cell pathways to reduce cellular oxidative stress for disease control and prevention and enhance both health span and lifespan.[14] Researchers are exploring innovative biohacking techniques to support and revitalize these cellular pathways created when we were infants, thereby mitigating the harmful effects of oxidative stress.[15]

> *"Biohacking could literally change the world as we know it."*
>
> Ryan Bethencourt[16]

Daily Health Habits

Scientific evidence has shown that adopting healthier lifestyle choices and a positive attitude can prevent or alter the course of diseases linked to oxidative stress. By making informed decisions and embracing a healthier way of living, we can mitigate the impact of oxidative stress and enhance our overall well-being in Finding JOY!

Below are a few health habits you may want to incorporate in your daily routine:

- Meditate twenty minutes a day, or join a yoga studio.
- Walk at least one or three miles daily or join a gym.

- Hire a fitness coach or nutritionist for wellness knowledge and accountability.

- Study nutrition and diet. You become what you eat and what you know.

- Stop smoking and limit alcohol intake.

- Use daily self-promoting affirmations.

- Practice smiling every day to everyone you meet.

- Research scientifically based dietary supplements and drugs before taking them. Be a health advocate for your body.

- Schedule annual doctor physicals and a complete blood work panel to determine any issues and if you are lacking any nutrients.

There are thousands of supplements on the market claiming great health benefits, from weight loss to better cognitive memory. Most of these supplements are a combination of vitamins, minerals, herbs, and direct antioxidants that advertise some health benefits.

Unfortunately, many of these supplements, while maybe harmless when taken correctly, have little effect on their health claims. Yes, they may have a clinical study completed, but generally these studies were paid for by the company that makes the product and the study is based on "borrowed science". Borrowed science is where a company uses an ingredient that have been separately studied and use it in the product they are promoting. A little bit self-serving!

Other than a basic multivitamin, do your research on PubMed or Scholar Google for any supplements you might want to take. If it's on either of these scientific websites, then you can trust it's a researched product or supplement especially if the product name is in the study. Also, go to *FindingJOY.us* under the "Health Journey" tab on research we have done for your wellness. Do your health homework! It's your body, without it you are going nowhere!

Your Faith Journey

"Now faith is confidence in what we hope for and assurance about what we do not see"

Hebrews 11:1

Faith and belief in God can profoundly influence your life, enhancing your sense of purpose, resilience, and overall success. Although the impact of faith varies from individual to individual, several reasons highlight why faith and belief in God are frequently regarded as crucial elements for achieving success.

Faith is your BFF travel companion in the Journey of YOU. Faith has got your back when the path seems impossible or the mountain to tall. Faith is there to give you strength to pursue, clarity to see, and focus to maintain. Faith is there to calm your fears and to raise you up to new heights. More than just a source of resilience, faith provides a profound sense of purpose and a solid foundation upon which to build your life.

Faith gives you humility in your success and gratitude in failure. With faith as your travel companion, you can navigate life's challenges and victories with grace and confidence. Faith is your personal relationship and connection with God in your life journey. You are not alone, God wants you to be successful and enjoy the time He gave you to find your purpose and value.

> *"Take the first step in faith. You don't have to see the whole staircase, just take the first step."*
> Martin Luther King Jr.[17]

Faith has always been an integral part of my life journey. From attending church with my parents as a young boy to consciously choosing to embrace God in my adult life, faith has been a constant companion. It is a journey unto itself, shaping our understanding of what God means in our lives.

During my darkest moments and most fearful times, having God as my confidant has brought light to the shadows and strength to face challenges. I cannot imagine traversing life's path without an active relationship with God. My faith is rooted in the belief that God desires for me to live an abundant life, contingent upon the choices I make. It is up to me to harness my innate talents and acquired skills to reach my full potential.

God serves as my Coach, my Cheerleader, and my Protector, guiding me and encouraging me every step of the way. Eliminating life fear and anxiety through faith, I embrace the understanding that every result or outcome in failure or success serves a greater purpose in my life journey. You see, God does not want us in daily struggle or a "barely making it" existence. His plan is for us to live an abundant life, free from worry, strife, and hatred.

God wants us to live a life of freedom to use our time and talents to develop our purpose and build our value in the paradise He created. God is all around us and is waiting for you to open His door. You are not alone. You have never been alone. God is there just waiting for you to knock on His door.

> **"Faith is about trusting God when you have unanswered questions."**
>
> Joel Osteen[18]

The Journey of Denzel Washington

Denzel Washington, renowned for his remarkable skills as an actor, director, and producer, is equally admired for his deep-rooted faith in God. Throughout his illustrious career, Denzel has been candid about how his spiritual beliefs have been a cornerstone in his life.

A particularly life-changing event happened when Denzel was about twenty stands out in his faith journey, a miraculous experience that profoundly affirmed his faith. He was in church when the pastor asked the congregation to "let it go" and let God in their lives. Denzel took the challenge and went to the altar. That moment changed his life. As Denzel said, "You know this time, I'm just going to go down there and give it up and see what happens. I went in the prayer room and gave it up and let go and experienced something I've never experienced in my life." Denzel went on to say, "I was filled with the Holy Ghost, and it scared me. I said, 'Wait a minute, I didn't want to go this deep, I want to party.'"[19]

> *"If you don't have a spiritual anchor you'll be easily blown by the wind and you'll be led to depression."*
>
> Denzel Washington[20]

This life-changing event at his young age convinced Denzel that he was destined for a unique purpose, significantly influencing his personal and professional life. His story is a testament to how faith can serve as a guiding light, shaping one's path and providing a sense of direction and meaning. In 2020, *The New York Times* named Denzel the greatest actor of the 21st century.[21]

> *"Number one, put God first in everything you do. Everything that you think you see in me and everything you think I've accomplished and everything you think I have, everything I have is by the grace of God, understand that. It's a gift."*
>
> Denzel Washington[22]

Denzel opened the door and let his life unfold while using his God given talents to raise the value of his time to experience an abundant life and give value and influence to millions of people. Faith is and has been at the core of Denzel's life success.

Miracles Happen Through Faith

Faith in action makes miracles happen! In the summer of 2018, the world was captivated by the plight of twelve boys and their soccer coach trapped deep within the Tham Luang cave in Thailand. As torrential rains flooded the cave, the boys were stranded for over two weeks in pitch darkness, with dwindling food and no sure means of escape. The situation seemed dire, yet their faith in God and the resilience of the human spirit shone through. Ekkapol Chantawong, their coach, led the boys in daily meditation and prayer, instilling in them a sense of calm and hope. Despite their grim circumstances, they believed they would be rescued.

Their faith was mirrored by the global community, as experts from around the world, including Thai Navy SEALs and British cave divers, converged to mount a perilous rescue operation. Against daunting odds, and after days of meticulous planning and supreme effort, each boy and their coach were brought to safety. The rescue was hailed as a miracle and a testament to the power of faith, teamwork, and human ingenuity.[23] Faith is always stronger than fear when God is faith centered in your life.

> *"Without faith, nothing is possible. With it, nothing is impossible."*
>
> Mary McLeod Bethune[24]

The Thai cave rescue reminds us that, even in the darkest of times, faith in God and the collective strength of humanity can lead to miraculous outcomes.

Although beliefs about God may differ widely across cultures and individuals, the fundamental yearning for connection, meaning, and moral guidance is a universal human experience.

Faith molds our identities, provides solace, and instills hope amidst the uncertainties of existence. Ultimately, the relationship between faith and God is both deeply personal and profoundly communal. It mirrors the rich and diversity of human experiences and aspirations, uniting us in our shared search for purpose and understanding.

> *"Faith is permitting ourselves to be seized by the things we do not see."*
>
> Martin Luther King Jr.[25]

Faith instills humility by fostering a profound awareness of God, that we are not the center of the universe but a special creation in it. It encourages learning from failures and setbacks, nurturing resilience and building a growth mindset. By fostering a sense of community, faith connects us, promoting mutual support and understanding.

Moreover, faith supports spiritual growth through practices of reflection and introspection, helping us to gain a deeper understanding of ourselves in relation to others and to God. These elements collectively cultivate a humble, grounded perspective, enriching our journey toward self-awareness, enlightenment, and our identity.

Faith bestows upon us the strength to endure adversity, assuring us that our struggles are not in vain. Faced with seemingly insurmountable obstacles, faith empowers us to rise above our fears and uncertainties, placing our trust in the boundless wisdom and providence of God.

> *"God has already done everything He's going to do. The ball is now in your court. If you want success, if you want wisdom, if you want to be prosperous and healthy, you're going to have to do more than meditate and believe, you must boldly declare words of faith and victory over yourself and your family."*
>
> Joel Osteen[26]

Faith is prayer in action. It is your daily conversation and relationship you cultivate with God. Faith means trusting that God has an extraordinary plan for your life journey.

God wants you to have an abundant life, a life of freedom, but it takes you to initiate your success in motion. Your journey will experience trials, challenges, and failures, but these perceived setbacks are really setups designed to fortify the foundation for your ultimate success. Faith empowers you to focus on today while having the confidence that God is carefully orchestrating your tomorrows.

If you're feeling a void and know something is missing, then invite God into your life. He wants the best for you, an abundant life, in return, He wants nothing more than a relationship with you. He wants to be part of your life as an active participant in your successes and be there when you experience failure too. Ask God to join you in your journey in Finding JOY. He wants to answer the door when you knock.

Your Love Journey

"We need to love ourselves first in all our glory and imperfections."

John Lennon[27]

Love is the most powerful emotion that we show ourselves and give to others in our quest to Finding JOY. However, self-love often proves to be one of the most challenging emotions to cultivate. It's important to be kind to ourselves.

Contrary to misconceptions, self-love is not about being self-centered, narcissistic, or selfish. Rather, it is about recognizing your inherent value and treating yourself with the same kindness, compassion, and respect that you would offer to others and the world.

The importance of self-love cannot be overstated, as it plays a pivotal role in your overall well-being and quality of life. It serves as the foundation for personal growth, fosters healthy relationships, and paves the way for a fulfilling and meaningful existence.

> *"Love yourself unconditionally, just as you love those closest to you despite their faults."*
>
> Les Brown[28]

You are the reflection in the mirror staring back, a reminder that you must give yourself grace and allow space for personal growth. By practicing self-love, you inherently affirm your value and cultivate a deep sense of self-respect. Your self-respect becomes the cornerstone of positive, healthy self-esteem and unwavering confidence in your ability to overcome challenges and help others.

Self-love empowers you to navigate life's challenges with remarkable resilience. It fortifies your ability to rebound from setbacks, failures, and disappointments. It also strengthens your intrinsic value not to be dictated by external circumstances but by your continual growth and journey forward. Embracing self-love means recognizing your value, regardless of the hurdles you encounter, and fostering an unwavering sense of purpose that propels you through life's ups and downs.

> *"Self-care is never a selfish act; it is simply good stewardship of the only gift I have, the gift I was put on earth to offer to others."*
>
> Parker Palmer[29]

When you love the person in the mirror, it establishes a benchmark for the treatment you anticipate from others. Why would you expect any less from others?

Self-love empowers you to cultivate healthier, more authentic relationships. By approaching interactions from a foundation of self-confidence, rather than a need for validation or approval, you foster deeper and more meaningful connections in our journey.

By embracing self-love, you not only nurture your own well-being, but also serve as a powerful role model in your friendship circle. This act of self-compassion highlights the significance of self-care and self-acceptance, illustrating that a fulfilling life stems from a foundation of inner respect and kindness, and it all starts with you.

> *"You've got to love yourself first. You've got to be okay on your own before you can be okay with somebody else."*
>
> Jennifer Lopez[30]

Genuine self-love involves embracing yourself completely, acknowledging both your strengths and your imperfections. This holistic acceptance is the basis of nurturing healthy relationships and leading a fulfilling life. It inspires you to practice self-compassion, honor your individuality, foster a positive self-image, and cultivate your identity in Finding JOY.

Dedicate Daily YOU Time

Dedicating time each day to enhance and love the individual you see in the mirror is crucial to Finding JOY. By meditating, exercising, reading uplifting books, and developing a comprehensive self-improvement program, you honor and cherish the unique value you bring to the world.

In our vast universe, you are truly special and irreplaceable. Take care of your body, a precious gift on loan from God, and shield your mind from the negativity that society often propagates. In doing so, you become a beacon of positivity in our world. Strive for personal perfection not just for yourself, but to contribute to the betterment of the world around you. Let love be the force that conquers hate in you.

> *"Love yourself first and everything else falls into line. You really have to love yourself to get anything done in this world."*
>
> Lucille Ball[31]

The Journey of Lady Gaga

There are numerous inspiring stories of people who have journeyed from self-adversity to self-love, discovering a deep appreciation and acceptance of their true selves. In this transformative process, they have found their purpose, recognized their intrinsic value, and embraced their own greatness. A great example that comes to mind is Lady Gaga's journey.

Stefani Germanotta, widely known as Lady Gaga, has captivated the world with her extraordinary music, avant-garde fashion, and distinct persona. Despite her outward bravado, she has privately battled with depression, anxiety, and feelings of inadequacy.

At the beginning of her musical career, she faced relentless rejection and harsh criticism from the music industry, which significantly impacted her self-worth and mental well-being. As her fame skyrocketed, the pressure to uphold an impeccable image intensified, leading to increased self-doubt.

In addition to these challenges, Lady Gaga has grappled with chronic pain from fibromyalgia and the weight of emotional trauma, often feeling overwhelmed by these burdens. Over time, she shifted her focus toward cultivating self-love and self-acceptance, coming to understand the vital importance of inner validation rather than constantly seeking external approval.

> *"It doesn't matter who you are, or where you come from, or how much money you've got in your pocket. You have your own destiny and your own life ahead of you."*
>
> Lady Gaga[32]

She began to focus on her mental and physical health by attending therapy, meditating, and setting boundaries in her work and personal life. Lady Gaga accepted her flaws and used her art to express her pain and recovery. In her Netflix documentary *Gaga: Five Foot Two*, she shared her struggles openly, showing that even the most successful people can feel vulnerable.

Lady Gaga's dedication to self-love became a key part of her career. She turned her experiences into powerful music, like the hit song "Born This Way," which became an anthem of self-acceptance for many. Her message was clear: Love yourself as you are despite your struggles or insecurities.

In her interviews and acceptance speeches, Lady Gaga often talks about the importance of self-love, encouraging her fans to be kind to themselves and embrace their uniqueness. She is a strong advocate for mental health and founded the *Born This Way Foundation* to help young people dealing with low self-worth and mental health issues.

> *"At the end of the day, you won't be happy until you love yourself."*
>
> Lady Gaga[33]

Lady Gaga's story shows that self-love means accepting all parts of ourselves, including the flaws and scars. By fully loving herself, she has inspired millions to do the same, proving that true beauty and strength come from within. You can't be a value to others if you don't value yourself.

Your Journey of Consistency

One of the most important snacks to pack in the Igloo before your journey is a bottomless can of consistency. Without this travel snack you will be driving in circles, going nowhere fast, getting frustrated at not seeing any progress, let alone your destination.

> *"It's not what we do once in a while that shapes our lives. It's what we do consistently."*
> Tony Robbins[34]

At the heart of progress lies consistency. It's not about achieving perfection; it's about showing up consistently, putting in the effort, and making gradual improvements. Through regularity, you cultivate habits, discipline, and the resilience necessary for enduring success. This also enhances your self-confidence and self-reliance, as each incremental step reflects your commitment to yourself and to your new journey. Keep in mind that remarkable accomplishments are the result of the accumulation of daily, consistent steps. Commitment to your journey is the first step of consistency.

> *"Consistency is the key to success. You have to consistently work hard, never giving up and believing in yourself to reach your goals."*
> Brian Tracy[35]

Consistency also helps in creating a sense of structure and routine, which can reduce frustration and stress. It can also increase productivity, which leads to a sense of accomplishment. Moreover, it allows for continuous learning and adaptation, enabling you to refine your strategies and approaches over time. By prioritizing consistency, you not only work towards your goals but also build a sustainable path to long-term achievements and reinforce a growth mindset.

The Journey of Angela

A great example of consistency combined with a growth mindset is Angela's journey. About sixteen years ago, I got a call from a lady who was interested in buying an office building. Well, that day in August 2008 started my friendship and journey with Angela and her husband.

Angela's journey reveals an incredible life story. She was born and raised in China amidst adversity in an oppressive political climate, devoid of freedom and personal liberty, which ultimately gave her fortitude and a fighting spirit. She was born just before China's Cultural Revolution in 1966. The revolution main purpose was to preserve Chinese socialism and to eliminate capitalism and personal freedoms from Chinese society. The Chinese cultural revolution imprisoned her father, a highly educated and accomplished civil engineer, into a re-education camp doing hard labor. This subsequently led to his death due to depression, poor nutrition and lack of adequate medical care, leaving her family destitute.

Despite this family tragedy, Angela's sheer determination and intellect resulted in her being admitted to college to study nursing at the young age of fourteen! She subsequently obtained her nursing degree and worked in a government-run hospital. Even at her young age, she knew her life was meant for greater purpose and value. Uncertain about what the future would hold she was hoping for just a sliver of opportunity to knock on her door.

As fortune would have it, that opportunity came in as an exchange program to work in Saudi Arabia. When she saw the program, she jumped at the opportunity knowing she would have to leave her family and may not see them again. Her faith in herself was stronger than her fear of the unknown. The beginnings of a growth mindset!

After completing her contract in Saudi Arabia, and not wanting to return to communist China, Angela then relocated to Thailand. She arrived with little money, no job, knowing no one and not knowing the language. In spite of that, she very quickly and successfully obtained employment, and within a few months became a co-owner of a local business. While in Thailand she became fluent in the Thai language.

In the mid-nineties, Angela recognized another opportunity to relocate to America to work at an infusion pharmacy managing a small nursing staff. After a year with the infusion pharmacy, she had another opportunity to move to Los Angeles. Upon hearing this news, the owner of the pharmacy asked Angela to stay and gave her an offer she couldn't refuse to become the owner of the nursing business side of the infusion pharmacy. This was a great opportunity for her.

Now this is where Angela's journey became life changing. When she took over the nursing business, she only had a couple of nurses on staff and about twenty-five patients. Angela's entrepreneurial drive took over and she started to build the business. This was about the time I got that fateful call from Angela looking for an office building to house her new business.

At the end of the day, Angela took this fledgling home health business and built it to over five hundred medical staff of nurses and doctors with offices throughout California, including over a thousand patients. But the story doesn't end here! With her dedication, consistency, and clear vision of her business plan with many HMO service contracts, she received several offers to buy her business. Well, one offer came in for millions of dollars, and she said yes!

This was a culmination of a lifelong dream, pure determination, and a growth mindset to experience complete life freedom from her beginning in China. But her growth mindset would not allow her to stop and say this is good enough. She and her husband bought some land and started a "hobby" vineyard. When Angela told me that, I knew her hobby vineyard would become a major winery! What do you think happened? The hobby vineyard turned into Twin Rocks Estate Winery with many first-place wine awards and is one of the top estate wineries in Northern California. The property grounds are immaculate, the estate event center is spectacular, and the wine is award-winning!

Angela stands in testimony to what Finding JOY is all about: finding your purpose and increasing your value to live life in ultimate freedom. As Eric Worre said, "Freedom is not free!"36 and Angela's story is devoid of excuses to reach her freedom. She was focused and did the work unafraid and fearlessly with an unstoppable attitude because she knew she was destined for a greater life of freedom from her childhood beginnings in China.

Angela journey represents a person who valued their life and time above all else. Like many Finding JOY success stories, she did not give into fear or let excuses lead her life. She built a growth mindset by experiencing oppression at an early development age in China that triggered gratitude for freedom and unstoppable attitude for success.

Journey of YOU

"Life isn't about finding yourself. Life is about creating yourself."

George Bernard Shaw[37]

The Journey of YOU is a profound choice. It's your unique life expedition. You're the captain of your ship on how you spend your time and resources to reach the destination you charted. Your destination becomes predetermined by the choices you make and actions you take every day. Consistency in action is progress toward your destination. Even if you decide to relinquish control and let life's currents dictate your ship's direction, you have, in essence, chosen your life destination by default.

Ultimately, the direction of your life is your sole responsibility. As you reach your life destination and the end of your journey, you will either be filled with gratitude or burdened with regret.

> *"You cannot change your destination overnight,*
> *but you can change your direction overnight."*
> Jim Rohn[38]

Finding JOY serves as your essential syllabus, the comprehensive curriculum for the mandatory course of Life 101. This transformative resource equips you with the tools to cultivate a fulfilling and prosperous life brimming with achievements by fostering self-development in mindset, attitude, brand and identity.

Finding JOY encourages deep introspection and self-evaluation, offering a roadmap to navigate from your current state to your envisioned future, all grounded in your purpose to build value and find time freedom.

You can't alter the events of your past, but you have the power to shape your present and future. If you've had enough of struggle and are sick and tired of being sick and tired, then it's essential to release the negative baggage, the stinkin' thinkin', the toxic associations, and those life issues that hold you back from finding your bright light, your greatness, your abundance.

> *"All successful people men and women are big dreamers. They imagine what their future could be, ideal in every respect, and then they work every day toward their distant vision, that goal or purpose."*
>
> Brian Tracy[39]

Life is too short and too precious to allow any issue, any situation, or any person to derail your life from your life's purpose, your greatness. Guard your time fiercely, and cultivate a positive, growth mindset and a grateful attitude brimming with passion, vitality, and goodwill.

The greatest investment you can make is in yourself. Just like any investment you may make be it real estate, stocks, bonds, commodities, 401K, business, or your house, by far the most important investment you can make in anything is YOU. Finding the main premise in JOY is perfecting the person you are and your present station in life. So don't be cheap on the most important investment you possess - your time to find your purpose. This investment takes love, respect, daily maintenance and consistent updating.

Finding JOY is a complete introspection of each aspect of the total package you present to the world and how you want the world to react to you. Each aspect is our internal journeys to how we develop and perfect our mindset, change, time, value, friendship, identity, attitude, fear, failure, success and growth. These journeys are our roadmap to a fearless, positive life, a life of success and abundance.

> *"It doesn't matter where you are coming from. All that matters is where you are going."*
>
> Brian Tracy[40]

You are now ready to go! The journey is going to be awesome! The car is in the driveway, the snacks are packed, and the key is in the ignition. The only thing missing is your commitment to turn the key to consistently drive every day to your ultimate destination, the destination you were born to become. It's a wonderful life when you can live fearlessly while unfortunately most are mired in struggle, discontent and regret.

Add the 'Journey of You' matrix to your car dashboard as a quick guide to stay focused, keep your eyes on the road, and fuel your determination to reach your destination.

"Journey Of You" Matrix			
Life Events	**Focus**	**Intention**	**Question**
Career & Contribution	Retired, mentoring, consulting	Share wisdom, legacy work, give value	Am I contributing with purpose?
Relationship, Your Friendship Circle	Spouse, family, grandkids, friends, associations	Strengthen bonds, support loved ones, build your tribe	Am I present with those who matter most?

Health & Wellness	Energy, fitness, health awareness	Stay active, eat well, be wellness mindful	Am I caring for my health span?
Lifestyle & Life Freedom	Travel, downsized, near family, recreational toys	Comfortable, peaceful living, enjoyment	Does my home life reflect my values?
Growth & Mindset	Reading, education, hobbies, spiritual life, mindset	Keep learning, stay curious, self development	Am I growing personally & making an impact?
Fun & Leisure	Travel, nature, arts, games, time freedom	Enjoy life, try new things, expand your boundaries	Am I making time for myself and feeling grateful?
Finances & Stability	Income, budgeting, peace of mind	Stay secure, give back, free from struggle, increase time value	Am I financially free with no debt worry.
Purpose & Reason	Faith, clarity, build legacy	Inspire, give back, reflect, life direction	What legacy do I want to leave?

C'mon! Are you ready?! Get your sunglasses! Your future looks bright! You may have to pull over every now and then at a rest stop or service station to get refreshed or get directions or to fill your tank. Just remember, our JOY Community is here to refresh your enthusiasm, give you life directions, and fill your tank with motivation. We are here to help with your life success in *Finding JOY: The Journey Of You.*

Congratulations! You are well-equipped to hit the road on your journey to an ultimate life. Our Joy Community is excited to work with you to keep you committed to finding your value, purpose and freedom.

> *"When your dream is bigger than you are, you only have two choices: give up or get help."*
>
> John C. Maxwell[41]

Reach out. We want to help you in your life journey. If you are seeking mentorship, life coaching, or seminar trainings, then consider our future speaking events or the Finding JOY workbook. You can also browse our JOY T-shirts and other fun stuff at our website, or scan the code on the next page. Let's do this journey together because it is more fun than traveling alone!

> *"No one lives long enough to learn everything they need to learn starting from scratch. To be successful, we absolutely, positively have to find people who have already paid the price to learn the things that we need to learn to achieve our goals."*
>
> Brian Tracy[42]

Through the pages of "Finding JOY... Journey Of You", you've rediscovered your story, defined your purpose, reclaimed your voice, raised your value and reconnected with the power that's always been within you. But this journey has been guiding you somewhere even deeper. The real breakthrough is "Finding YOU". Now it's time to rise, expand, and build "**Y**our **O**wn **U**niverse". If you're ready to take that next step, I invite you to join our JOY Community and continue with me in my next book - "Finding YOU... Your Own Universe".

Journey Rest Stop 12

1) Why is frustration a great motivator for change?

2) What health changes do you plan to make or incorporate into your daily life? What is oxidative stress, and why is it important to your health? (Go to www.FindingJOY.us, join our JOY Community and click on "Science" tab to get your free health guide to reduce your oxidative stress naturally, blood test proven.)

3) What is your growth plan to build your future self now?

Journey Thought

"If something's important enough, you should try. Even IF the probable outcome is failure."

Elon Musk[3]

www.FindingJOY.us

As I always say…

"Procrastination always stalls your destination."

So Don't Wait!
Be Part of Our JOY Community

Scan the code & sign up TODAY!

Your new life journey is waiting!

Let's do this Journey together.

www.FindingJOY.us

Finding JOY Notes

NOTE[1]: The quotes within the pages of this book are hints and clues from highly successful entrepreneurs, mentors, and life leaders to help you in your new life journey to keep in mind as you encounter resistance from some of your closest associations and friendships. Cherish these quotes as mantras for your life direction. The insecure may urge you to stay where it's safe, not because it's best for you, but because they fear what they've never dared to pursue. The herd offers comfort, but never liberation. True freedom begins at the edge of the familiar. It's time to say goodbye to the herd. Stop struggling within your means and start living the life of your dreams.

Your journey is to find the life you were meant to live, the purpose you were meant to develop and the value you were born to give. Never stop your journey. Never give up. This new journey you are embarking upon is about JOY...

The Journey Of You

 .

Book Cover

1.   Usher [@Usher]. (2023, January 29). *"Success is about dedication. You may not be where you want to be or do what you want to do when you're on the journey. But you've got to be willing to have vision and foresight that leads you to an incredible end."* [Tweet]. X. https://x.com/Usher/status/1619758448627040258

Introduction - Your Journey Starts Now

1.   London, Jack. *The Call of the Wild.* 1903.

Chapter 1 - Journey of Mindset: What's on Your Mind?

1. Hill, Napoleon. *Think and Grow Rich*. The Ralston Society, 1937.
2. Chanel, C. (n.d.). *"Don't spend time beating on a wall, hoping to transform it into a door."* [Quote]. Retrieved from https://www.harpersbazaar.com/fashion/designers/g32971271/best-coco-chanel-quotes/
3. Brown, L. (n.d.). "Life has no limitations, except the ones you make." [Quote]. Retrieved from BrainyQuote.com
4. Bezos, J. (n.d.). *"Life's too short to hang out with people who aren't resourceful."* [Quote]. Retrieved from https://www.businessinsider.com/amazon-ceo-jeff-bezos-quotes-2015-7
5. Brown, L. (n.d.). *"You must remain focused on your journey to greatness."* [Quote]. Retrieved from BrainyQuote.com
6. Ford, H. (n.d.). *"Whether you think you can or think you can't, you're right."* [Quote]. Retrieved from BrainyQuote.om
7. Dweck, C. S. (2006). *Mindset: The new psychology of success.* Random House.
8. The American Heritage Dictionary of the English Language. (n.d.). Mindset.
9. Dweck, C. S. (2006). *Mindset: The new psychology of success.* Random House.
10. Dweck, C. S. (2006). *Mindset: The new psychology of success.* Random House.
11. Sikiru, S. (2014). *John C. Maxwell's quotes: 450 inspirational and motivational quotes by John C. Maxwell.* CreateSpace Independent Publishing Platform.
12. Dweck, C. S. (2015, December 16). *Carol Dweck explains the 'false' growth mindset that worries her.* MindShift. Retrieved from KQED interview.
13. Dweck, C. S. (n.d.). *"You try something, it doesn't work, and maybe people even criticize you. In a fixed mindset, you say, 'I tried this, it's over.' In a growth mindset, you look for what you've learned."* [Quote]. Retrieved from BrainyQuote.com
14. Diamandis, P. H. (2014, June 20). *The abundance mindset.* Forbes. Retrieved from https://www.forbes.com/sites/peterdiamandis/2014/06/20/the-abundance-mindset/
15. Eastwood, C. (Actor). (1973). *Magnum Force* [Film]. Warner Bros.
16. Dweck, C. S. (n.d.). *"With a fixed mindset, you're so worried about how smart or talented you are, you don't take on challenges. You don't try new things."* [Quote]. Retrieved from BrainyQuote.com

17. Dweck, C. S. (n.d.). *"You can't just declare that you have a growth mindset. Growth mindset is hard."* [Quote]. Retrieved from BrainyQuote.com

18. Maxwell, J. C. (n.d.). *"Growth demands a temporary surrender of security. It may mean giving up familiar but limiting patterns, safe but unrewarding work, values no longer believed in, and relationships that have lost their meaning.""* [Quote]. Retrieved from BrainyQuote.com

19. Proctor, B. (n.d.). *"The only limits in our life are those we impose on ourselves"* [Quote]. Retrieved from Goodreads

20. Dweck, C. S. (n.d.). *"Praise your child explicitly for how capable they are of learning rather than telling them how smart they are."* [Quote]. Retrieved from BrainyQuote.com

21. Dweck, C. S. (2010). *Even geniuses work hard. Educational Leadership*, 68(1), 16–20. Retrieved from ASCD

22. Dweck, C. S. (n.d.). *"If parents want to give their children a gift, the best thing they can do is to teach their children to love challenges, be intrigued by mistakes, enjoy effort, and keep on learning."* [Quote]. Retrieved from Goodreads.com

23. Dweck, C. (2012, June 19). *Stanford University's Carol Dweck on the growth mindset and education.* OneDublin.org. Retrieved from OneDublin.org

24. Maxwell, J. C. (n.d.). *"If you don't change the direction you are going, then you're likely to end up where you're heading."* [Quote]. Retrieved from Goodreads.com

25. Kiyosaki, R. (n.d.). *"It's time to start thinking differently about money and debt and start the healing process—and the process toward wealth and freedom. Freedom from bad debt can get you started."* [Quote]. Retrieved from BarinyQuote.com

26. Brown, L. (n.d.). *"If you put yourself in a position where you have to stretch outside your comfort zone, then you are forced to expand your consciousness."* [Quote]. Retrieved from Addicted2Success.com

27. Dweck, C. S. (2006). *Mindset: The new psychology of success.* Random House.

28. Robbins, T. (1991). *Awaken the giant within: How to take immediate control of your mental, emotional, physical and financial destiny!* Free Press.

Chapter 2 - Journey of Change: Let's Change It Up!

1. Churchill, W. S. (n.d.). *"To improve is to change; to be perfect is to change often."* [Quote]. Retrieved from Goodreads.com

2. Brown, L. (n.d.). *"Too many of us are not living our dreams because we are living our fears. Life has no limitations, except the ones you make."* [Quote]. Retrieved from Goodreads.com

3. Jobs, S. (2005, June 12). 2005 *Commencement Address at Stanford University*, Retrieved from https://news.stanford.edu/2005/06/14/jobs-061505/

4. Robbins, T. (n.d.). *"Change happens when the pain of staying the same is greater than the pain of change."* [Quote]. Retrieved from Goodreads.com

5. Towery, J. (2021). *Your powerful, changeable mindset.* Stanford Report. Retrieved from https://news.stanford.edu/stories/2021/09/mindsets-clearing-lens-life

6. Kennedy, J. F. (1963, June 25). *Speech at Paulskirche, Frankfurt.* Retrieved from https://www.oxfordreference.com/display/10.1093/acref/9780191843730.001.0001/q-oro-ed5-00006245

7. Rohn, J. (n.d.). *"We are the average of the five people we spend the most time with."* [Quote]. Retrieved from https://www.businessinsider.com/jim-rohn-youre-the-average-of-the-five-people-you-spend-the-most-time-with-2012-7

8. Brown, L. (n.d.). *Align yourself with people you can learn from, people who want more out of life, people who are stretching and searching and seeking some higher ground in life.* [Quote]. Retrieved from https://www.bravethinkinginstitute.com/blog/life-transformation/favorite-les-brown-quotes

9. Welch, J. (n.d.). *If you're the smartest person in the room, you're in the wrong room.* [Quote]. Retrieved from https://globalleadership.org/articles/adam-grant-jack-welch-even-smart-leaders-make-these-mistakes/

10. Obama, B. (2008, February 5). *Super Tuesday Speech.* Chicago, IL. Retrieved from https://www.nytimes.com/2008/02/05/us/politics/05text-obama.html

11. Wilson, R. (n.d.). *"I truly believe in positive synergy, that your positive mindset gives you a more hopeful outlook, and belief that you can do something great means you will do something great."* [Quote]. Retrieved from BrainyQuote.com

12. Towery, J. (n.d.). *Your powerful, changeable mindset.* Stanford Report. Retrieved from https://news.stanford.edu/stories/2021/09/mindsets-clearing-lens-life

13. Branson, R. (n.d.). *"If somebody offers you an amazing opportunity but you are not sure you can do it, say yes – then learn how to do it later."* [Quote]. Retrieved from Goodreads.com

14. StatPearls. (n.d.). *Neuroplasticity.* [Internet]. StatPearls Publishing. Retrieved from https://www.ncbi.nlm.nih.gov/books/NBK557811/

15. Brown, L. (n.d.). *"You are the only real obstacle in your path to a fulfilling life. When your why is big enough, you will find your how."* [Quote]. Retrieved from https://www.inspireyoursuccess.com/les-brown-quotes/

16. Twain, M. (n.d.). *"The two most important days in your life are the day you are born and the day you find out why."* [Quote]. Retrieved from https://alicehocker.com/quote-worthy/

17. Brown, L. (n.d.). *"Forgive yourself for your faults and your mistakes and move on."* [Quote]. Retrieved from BrainyQuote.com

18. Kiyosaki, R. (n.d.). *"If you want to go somewhere, it is best to find someone who has already been there."* [Quote]. Retrieved from https://medium.com/@rahulsonwanshi3/powerful-quotes-from-robert-kiyosakis-rich-dad-poor-dad-14f0bd65a9eb

19. Brown, L. (n.d.). *"If you set goals and go after them with all the determination you can muster, your gifts will take you places that will amaze you."* [Quote]. Retrieved from BrainyQuote.com

20. Dweck, C. S. (2006). *Mindset: The new psychology of success.* Random House.

21. Hill, N. (1937). *Think and grow rich.* The Ralston Society.

22. Tracy, B. (2001). *Maximum achievement: Strategies and skills that will unlock your hidden powers to succeed.* Simon & Schuster.

Chapter 3 - Journey of Time: Do You Have a Minute?

1. Tolkien, J.R.R. (1954). *The Fellowship of the Ring.* George Allen & Unwin.

2. A. Chown, M. (2013). *The edge of space: A journey to the farthest reaches of the universe.* Chicago Review Press.
   B. NASA. (2018). *Parker Solar Probe: Fastest spacecraft ever launched.* Retrieved from https://www.nasa.gov/content/nasas-parker-solar-probe

3. Armstrong, N. (1970). *First on the Moon: A voyage with Neil Armstrong, Michael Collins, and Edwin E. Aldrin, Jr.* Warner Books.

4. Hawking, S. (1988). *A brief history of time: From the big bang to black holes.* Bantam Books.

5. Bradbury, R. (1950). *The Martian Chronicles.* Doubleday.

6. Osteen, J. (2004). *Your best life now: 7 steps to living at your full potential.* Warner Faith.

7. Proctor, B. (n.d.). *You were born rich.* (p. 72). Life Success Publishing.

8. Proctor, B. (n.d.). *The art of winning.* Life Success Publishing.

9. Disraeli, B. (1880). *The life and speeches of Benjamin Disraeli* (Vol. 1). Henry Colburn.

10. Ziglar, Z. (n.d.). *See you at the top.* Pelican Publishing.

11. Brown, L. (n.d.). *Live your dreams.* Fawcett Columbine.

12. Brown, L. (n.d.). *"Life takes on meaning when you become motivated, set goals and charge after them in an unstoppable manner."* [Quote]. Retrieved from BrainyQuote.com

13. Brown, L. (n.d.). *Live your dreams*. Fawcett Columbine

14. Brown, L. (n.d.). *"Accept responsibility for your life. Know that it is you who will get you where you want to go, no one else."* [Quote]. Retrieved from BrainyQuote.com

15. Penn, W. (n.d.). *"Time is what we want most, but what we use worst."* [Quote]. Retrieved from Goodreads.com

16. Komisar, R. (2000). *The monk and the riddle: The education of a Silicon Valley entrepreneur* (p. 154). Harvard Business School Press.

17. Ferriss, T. (2007). *The 4-hour workweek: Escape 9-5, live anywhere, and join the new rich.* Crown Publishers.

18. Shaw, G. B. (n.d.). *"Life isn't about finding yourself. Life is about creating yourself."* [Quote]. Retrieved from BrainyQuote.com

19. Robbins, T. (1991). *Awaken the giant within: How to take immediate control of your mental, emotional, physical and financial destiny!* Free Press.

20. Jobs, S. (2005, June 12). *Steve Jobs' 2005 Stanford commencement address* [Speech transcript]. Stanford News. https://news.stanford.edu/2005/06/14/jobs-061505/

Chapter 4 - Journey of Value: What's the Value of Your Time?

1. Peck, M. S. (1978). *The road less traveled: A new psychology of love, traditional values and spiritual growth.* Simon & Schuster.

2. Jobs, S. (2005, June 12). *Steve Jobs' commencement address at Stanford University.* Stanford University. https://news.stanford.edu/2005/06/12/steve-jobs-commencement-address/

3. Dyer, W. (2009). *Excuses Begone! The Power of Thinking Without Limits.* Hay House.

4. Sandburg, C. (n.d.). *"Time is the coin of your life. It is the only coin you have, and only you can determine how it will be spent. Be careful lest you let other people spend it for you."* [Quote]. Retrieved from BrainyQuote.com

5. Brown, L. (1992). *Live your dreams.* Simon & Schuster.

6. Carlin, G. (2004). *When will Jesus bring the pork chops?* Free Press.

7. Worre, E. (2014). *Go pro: 7 steps to becoming a network marketing professional.* Success Books.

8. Robbins, T. (1991). *Awaken the giant within: How to take immediate control of your mental, emotional, physical and financial destiny!* Free Press.

9. Worre, E. (2014). *Go pro: 7 steps to becoming a network marketing professional*. Success Books.
10. Tolkien, J. R. R. (1954). *The fellowship of the ring*. George Allen & Unwin.
11. Maldonado, C. (2019, June 25). *The real reason you're not going to retire isn't because you're not frugal enough*. Forbes. https://www.forbes.com/sites/camilomaldonado/2019/06/25/the-real-reason-youre-not-going-to-retire-isnt-because-youre-not-frugal-enough/?utm_source=chatgpt.com
12. Proctor, B. (2004). *You were born rich*. Proctor Gallagher Institute.
13. Robbins, T. (2014). *Money: Master the game: 7 simple steps to financial freedom*. Simon & Schuster.
14. Rohn, J. (1992). *The art of exceptional living*. Nightingale-Conant.
15. Hopkins, B. (n.d.). *"If you don't know your own value, somebody will tell you your value, and it'll be less than you're worth."* [Quote]. Retrieved from BrainyQuote.com
16. Kiyosaki, R. T. (2008). *Rich dad's increase your financial IQ: Get smarter with your money*. Warner Business Books.
17. Brown, L. (1992). *Live your dreams*. The Les Brown Institute.
18. Worre, E. (2014). *Go pro: 7 steps to becoming a network marketing professional*. Success Books.
19. Maxwell, J. C. (1998). *The 21 irrefutable laws of leadership: Follow them and people will follow you*. Thomas Nelson.
20. Worre, E. (2014). *Go pro: 7 steps to becoming a network marketing professional*. Success Books.
21. Rohn, J. (1992). *The art of exceptional living*. Nightingale-Conant.

Chapter 5 - Journey of Friendship: Are You Friend or Foe?

1. Rohn, J. (2007). *Jim Rohn's philosophy for successful living*. Sound Wisdom.
2. Brown, L. (1992). *Live your dreams*. William Morrow and Company.
3. Robbins, T. (1991). *Awaken the giant within: How to take immediate control of your mental, emotional, physical and financial destiny!* Free Press.
4. Page, L. (n.d.). *"Our objective is essentially to organize the world's information and make it universally accessible and useful."* [Quote on Google's mission]. Retrieved from https://about.google/
5. Keller, H. (1927). *My religion*. Doubleday, Doran & Company.
6. Burg, B. (2002). *Endless referrals: Network your everyday contacts into sales*. McGraw-Hill.
7. Winfrey, O. (n.d.). *"Surround yourself with only people who are going to lift you higher."* [Quote]. Retrieved from https://www.oprah.com/

8. Rohn, J. (2007). *Jim Rohn's philosophy for successful living.* Sound Wisdom.

9. Ford, H. (n.d.). *"My best friend is the one who brings out the best in me."* [Quote]. Retrieved from https://www.ford.com/

10. King, M. L. Jr. (2001). *The papers of Martin Luther King, Jr. Volume VI: Advocate of the social gospel.* University of California Press.

11. Ziglar, Z. (2000). *Over the top.* Thomas Nelson.

12. Wooden, J. (1997). *Wooden: A lifetime of observations and reflections on and off the court.* McGraw-Hill.

13. Hardy, B. (2020). *Personality isn't permanent: Break free from self-limiting beliefs and become who you were meant to be.* Penguin Life.

14. Dyer, W. (2004). *The power of intention: Learning to co-create your world your way.* Hay House.

15. Bennett, R. T. (2016). *The light in the heart.* Inspired Life Publishing.

16. Winfrey, O. (2014). *What I know for sure.* Flatiron Books.

17. Seuss, D. (1978). *I can read with my eyes shut!* Random House.

18. Brown, L. (1992). *Live your dreams.* Doubleday.

19. Meyer, J. (2002). *Battlefield of the mind: Winning the battle in your mind.* FaithWords.

20. Schuller, R. H. (1983). *Tough times never last, but tough people do!* Hallmark Press.

21. Kessler, R.C., McGonagle, K.A., Zhao, S., Nelson, C.B., Hughes, M., Eshleman, S., Wittchen, H.-U., & Kendler, K.S. (1994). *Lifetime and 12-month prevalence of DSM-II-R psychiatric disorders in the United States.* Archives of General Psychiatry, 51, 8–19.

22. Hofmann, S. G., Asnaani, A., Vonk, I. J., Sawyer, A. T., & Fang, A. (2012). *The Efficacy of Cognitive Behavioral Therapy: A Review of Meta-analyses.* Cognitive Therapy and Research, 36(5), 427-440. https://doi.org/10.1007/s10608-012-9476-1

23. Colier, N. (2019, April 15). *Negative thinking: A dangerous addiction.* Psychology Today. Retrieved from https://www.psychologytoday.com/intl/blog/inviting-monkey-tea/201904/negative-thinking-dangerous-addiction

24. Tseng, J., & Poppenk, J. (2020). *Brain meta-state transitions demarcate thoughts across task contexts exposing the mental noise of trait neuroticism.* Nature Communications, 11, Article 4670. https://doi.org/10.1038/s41467-020-17255-9

25. Proctor, B. (2004). *You were born rich.* HarperCollins.

26. Osteen, J. (2004). *Your best life now: 7 steps to living at your full potential.* Free Press.

27. Ziglar, Z. (1975). *See you at the top.* Pelican Publishing.

28. Osteen, J. (2004). *Your best life now: 7 steps to living at your full potential.* Free Press.

29. Rohn, J. (1993). *The five major pieces to the life puzzle.* Success Publications

30. Helmstetter, S. (1986). *What to say when you talk to yourself.* Pocket Books.

31. Darwin, C. (1869). *The correspondence of Charles Darwin (Vol. 17).* Cambridge University Press.

32. Kopecko, T. (2025). *Finding Joy, Journey Of You.* Best Seller Publishing

Chapter 6 - Journey of Identity: I'm Sorry... Who Are You?

1. Jung, C. G. (1953). *Modern man in search of a soul.* Harcourt, Brace & World.

2. Gallagher, S., & Proctor, B. (2010). *Thinking into results: Accelerating your personal and professional success.* Proctor Gallagher Institute.

3. Trump, D. J. (2008). *Trump never give up: How I turned my biggest challenges into success.* Wiley.

4. Lao Tzu. (2006). *Tao Te Ching (S. Mitchell, Trans.).* Harper Perennial Modern Classics. (Original work published circa 6th century BCE)

5. Osteen, J. (2014). *You can, you will: 8 undeniable qualities of a winner.* FaithWords.

6. Angelou, M. (n.d.). *"If you are always trying to be normal, you will never know how amazing you can be."* [Quote]. Retrieved from Goodreads.com

7. Pike, K. L. (1967). *Language in relation to a unified theory of the structure of human behavior.* The Hague: Mouton & Co.

8. Williams, S. (n.d.). *I've grown most not from victories, but setbacks. If winning is God's reward, then losing is how He teaches us.* Retrieved from https://medium.com/be-bold/ive-grown-most-not-from-victories-but-setbacks-serena-williams-b5dc720003f6

9. Auliq-Ice, O. (n.d.). *"Your identity is like a fingerprint; it is unique to you, and it leaves an impression on everything you do."* [Quote]. Retrieved from Goodreads.com

10. Social Cognition Center Cologne. (2019). *Competition is crucial for social comparison processes in long-tailed macaques (Macaca fascicularis).* Scientific Reports, 9(1), 1-10. https://doi.org/10.1038/s41598-019-39647-0

11. Musk, E. (2015). *Elon Musk: Tesla, SpaceX, and the quest for a fantastic future.* Harper Collins.

12. Jordan, M. (2009, September 11). *Hall of Fame induction speech.* NBA.com. Retrieved from https://www.nba.com/bulls/news/jordanhof_speech_090912.html

13. Buffett, W. (n.d.). *"It takes twenty years to build a reputation and five minutes to ruin it. If you think about that, you'll do things differently."* [Quote]. Retrieved from Brainyquote.com

14. Jordan, M. (n.d.). *"You must expect great things of yourself before you can do them."* [Quote]. Retrieved from Goodreads.com

15. Ecko, M. (2009). *Unlabel: Selling you without selling out.* Portfolio.
16. Bezos, J. (1997). *The Bezos letters: 14 principles to grow your business like Amazon.* Bezos Letters Publishing.
17. Peters, T. (1997). *The brand called you.* Fast Company, (10), 83–90. Retrieved from https://www.fastcompany.com/28905/brand-called-you
18. Citroen, L. (2013). *Reputation 360: Creating power through personal branding.* AMACOM.
19. Aristotle. (n.d.). *On the soul* (R. D. Hicks, Trans.). The Internet Classics Archive. Retrieved from http://classics.mit.edu/
20. Maxwell, J. C. (2010). *The 15 Invaluable Laws of Growth: Live Them and Reach Your Potential.* Thomas Nelson
21. Tracy, B. (2004). *Create Your Own Future: How to Master the 12 Key Reasons for Success.* AMACOM.
22. Ziglar, Z. (2000). *See You at the Top.* Pelican Publishing
23. Jordan, M. (n.d.). *"My attitude is that if you push me towards something that you think is a weakness, then I will turn that perceived weakness into a strength."* [Quote]. Retrieved from Brainyquote.com
24. Meyer, J. (2006). *Battlefield of the mind: Winning the battle in your mind.* Hachette Book Group.
25. Shaw, G. B. (n.d.). *"Life isn't about finding yourself. Life is about creating yourself."* [Quote]. Retrieved from Brainyquote.com
26. Rohn, J. (n.d.). *"The major value in life is not what you get. The major value in life is what you become."* [Quote]. Retrieved from https://www.jimrohn.com
27. Brown, L. (n.d.). *"Define your priorities, know your values and believe in your purpose. Only then can you effectively share yourself with others."* [Quote]. Retrieved from Goodreads.com
28. Jobs, S. (2005, June 12). *Steve Jobs' commencement address at Stanford University.* Stanford University. Retrieved from https://news.stanford.edu/report/2005/06/14/steve-jobs-commencement-address-0614/
29. Mandela, N. (n.d.). *"Money won't create success, the freedom to make it will."* [Quote]. Retrieved from Goodreads.com
30. Jobs, S. (n.d.). *"I think money is a wonderful thing because it enables you to do things. It enables you to invest in ideas that don't have a short-term payback."* [Quote]. Retrieved from Goodreads.com
31. Kiyosaki, R. T. (2000). *Rich dad poor dad: What the rich teach their kids about money that the poor and middle class do not!* Warner Books.
32. Hardy, B. (2018). *Willpower doesn't work: Discover the hidden keys to success.* Perennial.
33. Ford, H. (n.d.). "Quality means doing it right when no one is looking." [Quote]. Retrieved from Goodreads.com

34. Brown, L. (n.d.). *"Life takes on meaning when you become motivated, set goals and charge after them in an unstoppable manner."* [Quote]. Retrieved from Goodreads.com

35. Jobs, S. (n.d.). *"Be a yardstick of quality. Some people aren't used to an environment where excellence is expected."* [Quote]. Retrieved from Goodreads.com

36. Ziglar, Z. (1993). *See you at the top: 25th anniversary edition.* Pelican Publishing.

37. Maxwell, J. C. (2001). *The 15 Invaluable Laws of Growth: Live Them and Reach Your Potential.* Thomas Nelson.

38. James, L. (2018, July 17). *LeBron James opens up about his future in Hollywood and his new media company.* The Hollywood Reporter. Retrieved from https://www.hollywoodreporter.com

39. Brown, L. (1994). *Live your dreams.* Hyperion.

40. Brown, L. (2006). *It's Not Over Until You Win: How to Become the Person You Were Meant to Be.* Grand Central Publishing.

Chapter 7 - Journey of Attitude: Is Your Glass Half-Empty or Half-Full?

1. Holtz, L. (2006). *Wins, Losses, and Lessons: An Autobiography.* Penguin Books.

2. Ziglar, Z. (2007). *See You at the Top: 25th Anniversary Edition.* Pelican Publishing.

3. Ziglar, Z. (2000). *See You at the Top.* Pelican Publishing.

4. Brown, L. (1992). *Live your dreams.* William Morrow and Company.

5. Maraboli, S. (2013). *Life, the truth, and being free.* Better Today Publishing.

6. Maraboli, S. (2013). *Life, the truth, and being free.* Better Today Publishing.

7. Musk, E. (2012, July 13). *The real iPod: Elon Musk's wild idea for a 'Jetson tunnel' from S.F. to L.A.* The Atlantic.

8. Musk, E. (2014, March 16). *Interview on innovation and failure.* Retrieved from https://spacex.com

9. SpaceX. (2023, April 20). *"With a test like this, success comes from what we learn, and today's test will help us improve Starship's reliability as SpaceX seeks to make life multi-planetary"* [Quote]. SpaceX https://x.com/SpaceX/status/1649046293489254402

10. Musk, E. [@elonmusk]. (2023, April 20). *"Congrats, SpaceX team, on an exciting test launch of Starship! Learned a lot for our next test launch in a few months!"* [Tweet]. X. https://twitter.com/elonmusk/status/1649050306943266819

11. Musk, E. (n.d.). *"When something is important enough, you do it even if the odds are not in your favor."* [Quote]. Retrieved from Goodreads.com

12. Maxwell, J. C. (2000). *Failing forward: Turning mistakes into stepping stones for success.* Thomas Nelson.
13. Ziglar, Z. (1975). *See you at the top.* Pelican Publishing.
14. Rogers, W. (n.d.). *"A man only learns in two ways, one by reading, and the other by association with smarter people."* Retrieved from Goodreads.com
15. Morin, A. (2015, April 17). *The 3 components of mental strength that will help you succeed.* Forbes. https://www.forbes.com/sites/amymorin/2015/04/17/the-3-components-of-mental-strength-that-will-help-you-succeed/
16. Bennett, R. T. (n.d.). *The light in the heart: Inspirational thoughts for living your best life.* Roy T. Bennett.
17. Jobs, S. (1996, February). *Steve Jobs: The Next Insanely Great Thing.* Wired. Retrieved from https://www.wired.com/1996/02/jobs-2/
18. Einstein, A. (n.d.). *"Creativity is seeing what others see and thinking what no one else ever thought."* [Quote]. Retrieved from Brainyquote.com
19. Lynch, D. (2014, December 9). *His mission to change the world through meditation.* The Huffington Post. Retrieved from https://www.huffpost.com/entry/david-lynch-meditation_b_6272336
20. Moyers, B. (n.d.). *"Creativity is piercing the mundane to find the marvelous."* [Quote]. Retrieved from Brainyquote.com
21. Judd, N. (n.d.). *"Your body hears everything your mind says."* [Quote]. Retrieved from Brainyquote.com
22. American Heart Association. (Jan 2021). *Psychological health, well-being, and the mind-heart-body connection: A scientific statement from the American Heart Association.* Circulation, 143(10), e763–e783. https://doi.org/10.1161/CIR.0000000000000947
23. Myss, C. (1996). *Anatomy of the spirit: The seven stages of power and healing.* Harmony Books.
24. Kimmel, P. L., Cohen, S. D., & Weisbord, S. D. (2022). *Well-being and health in kidney failure: A scoping review.* Seminars in Dialysis, 35(2), 93–103. https://doi.org/10.1111/sdi.13036
25. Rohn, J. (n.d.). *"Take care of your body. It's the only place you have to live in."* [Quote]. Retrieved from Goodreads.com
26. Levy, B. R., & Bavishi, A. (2018). *Survival advantage mechanism: Inflammation as a mediator of positive self-perceptions of aging on longevity.* The Journals of Gerontology: Series B, 73(3), 409–412. https://doi.org/10.1093/geronb/gbw035
27. Tracy, B. (n.d.). *"If you achieve all kinds of things in the material world, but you lose your health or your peace of mind, you get little or no pleasure from your other accomplishments."* [Quote]. Retrieved from https://www.caryobgyn.com/21-quotes-to-inspire-healthy-living/

28. Anderson, G. (1999). *The 22 non-negotiable laws of wellness: Feel, think, and live better than you ever thought possible.* HarperOne.

29. Meyer, J. (1997). *Battlefield of the mind: Winning the battle in your mind.* Warner Faith.

30. Dalai Lama. (n.d.). *"Let go of negative people. They only show up to share complaints, problems, disastrous stories, fear, and judgment on others. If somebody is looking for a bin to throw all their trash into, make sure it's not in your mind,"* [Quote]. Retrieved from Goodreads.com. Quote is attributed to Dalai Lama but not verified.

31. Banks, T. (n.d.). *"Stop saying these negative things about yourself. Look in the mirror and find something about yourself that's positive and celebrate that!"* [Quote]. Retrieved from https://www.azquotes.com/quote/17677

32. Peale, N. V. (1987). *You can if you think you can.* Simon & Schuster.

33. Hill, N. (1937). *Think and grow rich.* The Ralston Society.

34. Winfrey, O. (2005). *What I know for sure.* Flatiron Books.

35. Kent, G. (n.d.). *"Be careful not to let a negative social media life attract you to a dark way of thinking."* [Quote]. Retrieved from Goodreads.com

36. White, D. (n.d.). *"The amount of negativity I hear on a daily basis is unbelievable. But that's the kind of stuff you have to tune out, focus, stick with your vision and keep plugging every day."* [Quote]. Retrieved from Brainyquote.com

37. Osteen, J. (n.d.). *"Nothing happens to you; it happens for you. See the positive in negative events."* [Quote]. Retrieved from Brainyquote.com

38. Proctor, B. (1984). *You were born rich.* Life Success Productions.

39. Lucas, G., Brackett, L., & Kasdan, L. (Writers), & Kershner, I. (Director). (1980). *Star Wars: Episode V - The Empire Strikes Back* [Film]. Lucasfilm; 20th Century Fox.

40. Emerson, R. W. (2000). *The essential writings of Ralph Waldo Emerson.* Modern Library.

41. Lucas, G. (Writer & Director). (2005). *Star Wars: Episode III - Revenge of the Sith* [Film]. Lucasfilm; 20th Century Fox.

42. Schuller, R. H. (n.d.). *"Negative thinking is subtle and deceptive. It wears many faces and hides behind the mask of excuses. It is important to strip away the mask and discover the real, root emotion."* [Quote]. Retrieved from Brainyquote.com

43. Gordon, J. (2008). *The no complaining rule: Positive ways to deal with negativity at work.* Wiley.

44. Rowling, J. K. (2003). *Harry Potter and the Order of the Phoenix.* Scholastic.

45. Rowling, J. K. (n.d.). *"I would like to be remembered as someone who did the best she could with the talent she had."* [Quote]. Retrieved from Goodreads.com

46. Business Insider. (2020, June 2). *What Is J.K. Rowling's Net Worth? Here's How She Spends Her Fortune.* Business Insider. Retrieved from https://www.businessinsider.com/jk-rowling-net-worth-spending-harry-potter-2020-6

47. Tracy, B. (2009). *Reinvention: How to make the rest of your life the best of your life.* AMACOM.

48. Dyer, W. W. (2006). *Inspiration: Your ultimate calling.* Hay House.

49. Winfrey, O. (2014). *What I know for sure.* Flatiron Books.

50. Sandburg, C. (1978). *The Complete Poems of Carl Sandburg.* Harcourt Brace Jovanovich.

51. Hatfield, E., Cacioppo, J. T., & Rapson, R. L. (1994). Emotional contagion. Cambridge University Press.

52. Fredrickson, B. L. (2009). *Positivity: Top-notch research reveals the 3-to-1 ratio that will change your life.* Harmony Books.

53. Covey, S. R. (n.d.). *"Trust is the glue of life. It's the most essential ingredient in effective communication. It's the foundational principle that holds all relationships."* [Quote]. Retrieved from Goodreads.com

54. Angelou, M. (2009). *Letter to my daughter.* Random House.

55. Holtz, L. (n.d.). *"Virtually nothing is impossible in this world if you just put your mind to it and maintain a positive attitude."* [Quote]. Retrieved from Brainyquote.com

56. Brown, L. (n.d.). *"You are the only real obstacle in your path to a fulfilling life."* [Quote]. Retrieved from Brainyquote.com

57. Berlin, I. (n.d.). *"Our attitudes control our lives. Attitudes are a secret power working twenty-four hours a day, for good or bad. It is of paramount importance that we know how to harness and control this great force."* [Quote]. Retrieved from Brainyquote.com

58. Moore, J. (n.d.). *"The most important thing you'll ever wear is your attitude."* [Quote]. Retrieved from Goodreads.com

Chapter 8 - Journey of Fear: What's Got You Scared?

1. Kipling, R. (1923). *The collected works of Rudyard Kipling.* Doubleday.

2. Poorvu Center for Teaching and Learning. (n.d.). Public speaking for teachers I: Lecturing without fear. Yale University. Retrieved February 6, 2025, from https://poorvucenter.yale.edu/teaching/ideas-teaching/public-speaking-teachers-i-lecturing-without-fear

3. Hill, N. (1937). *Think and grow rich.* The Ralston Society.

4. Bovee, C. N. (n.d.). *"We fear things in proportion to our ignorance of them."* [Quote]. Retrieved from AZQuotes.com

5. Cerebral. (n.d.). *Conditions we treat: Phobias*. Retrieved from https://www.Cerebral.com/conditions-we-treat

6. McVie, C. (n.d.). *"I had the feeling every time I was on a plane everyone was going to die. It was a horrible phobia. A stupid one."* [Quote]. Retrieved from Brainyquote.com

7. ten Boom, C. (n.d.). *"Worry does not empty tomorrow of its sorrow, it empties today of its strength."* [Quote]. Retrieved from Goodreads.com

8. LaFreniere, L. S., & Newman, M. G. (2020). *Exposing worry's deceit: Percentage of untrue worries in generalized anxiety disorder treatment.* Behavior Therapy, 51(3), 413–423. https://doi.org/10.1016/j.beth.2019.07.003

9. ten Boom, C. (n.d.). *Clippings from My Notebook*. Barbour Publishing.

10. Brown, L. (1997). *Live your dreams*. HarperCollins.

11. Byrnes, J. F. (n.d.). *"Too many people are thinking of security instead of opportunity. They seem to be more afraid of life than death."* [Quote]. Retrieved from https://vernonlwilliams.com/54-empowering-quotes-to-help-you-conquer-your-fears/

12. Boone, L. E. (n.d.). *"Don't fear failure so much that you refuse to try new things. The saddest summary of a life contains three descriptions: could have, might have, and should have."* [Quote]. Retrieved from Brainyquote.com

13. Trump, D. J. (1987). *Trump: The art of the deal*. Random House.

14. Tracy, B. (n.d.). *"You begin to fly when you let go of self-limiting beliefs and allow your mind and aspirations to rise to greater heights."* [Quote]. Retrieved from AZQuotes.com

15. Schultz, H., & Yang, D. J. (1997). *Pour your heart into it: How Starbucks built a company one cup at a time.* Hyperion.

16. Robbins, A. (1986). *Unlimited power: The new science of personal achievement.* Simon & Schuster.

17. Worre, E. [@ericworre]. (n.d.). *"It's not enough for you to remove limiting beliefs from your life. You must replace them with empowering ones."* [Instagram post]. Received from https://www.instagram.com/ericworre/reel/DAJ1yVStTzi/

18. Ash, M. K. (n.d.). *"Don't limit yourself. Many people limit themselves to what they think they can do. You can go as far as your mind lets you. What you believe, remember, you can achieve."* [Quote]. Retrieved from BrainyQuote.

19. Emerson, R. W. (n.d.). *"Fear defeats more people than any other one thing in the world."* [Quote]. Retrieved from BrainyQuote.

20. Robbins, T. (2014). *MONEY Master the Game: 7 Simple Steps to Financial Freedom.* Simon & Schuster.

21. Robbins, T. *"Change happens when the pain of staying the same is greater than the pain of change."* [Quote]. Retrieved from Goodreads.com.

22. Worre, E. (2013). *Go pro: 7 steps to becoming a network marketing professional.* Network Marketing Pro, Inc.

23. Brown, L. (n.d.). *"You must remain focused on your journey to greatness."* [Quote]. Retrieved from BrainyQuote.

24. Branson, R. (2014, July 7). *My top 10 quotes on opportunity.* Virgin. Retrieved from https://www.virgin.com/branson-family/richard-branson-blog/my-top-10-quotes-opportunity

25. Tracy, B. (n.d.). "Successful people are always looking for opportunities to help others. Unsuccessful people are always asking, 'What's in it for me?' [Quote]. Retrieved from BrainyQuote.

26. Kennedy, J. F. (n.d.). *"There are risks and costs to action. But they are far less than the long-range risks of comfortable inaction."* [Quote]. Retrieved from BrainyQuote.

27. Maraboli, S. (2009). *Life, the truth, and being free.* Better Today Publishing.

28. Robbins, T. (1986). *Unlimited power: The new science of personal achievement.* Free Press.

29. Lucado, M. (2009). *Fearless: Imagine your life without fear.* Thomas Nelson.

30. Brown, L. (n.d.). *"You have to be willing to allow the person you are today to die so that you can give birth to the person you are meant to become."* [Quote]. The BJJ Mental Coach. Retrieved from https://www.thebjjmentalcoach.com/blog/you-need-to-read-what-les-brown-wants-to-teach-you

31. Canfield, J. (n.d.). *"All too often we're filled with negative and limiting beliefs. We're filled with doubt. We're filled with guilt or with a sense of unworthiness. We have a lot of assumptions about the way the world is that are actually wrong."* [Quote]. Retrieved from AZQuotes.com.

32. Brown, L. (n.d.). *"Life has no limitations, except the ones you make."* [Quote]. Retrieved from Goodreads.com.

33. Proctor, B. (2012, November 14). *"Science and psychology have isolated the one prime cause for success or failure in life. It is the hidden self-image you have of yourself."* [Facebook]. Retrieved from https://www.facebook.com/OfficialBobProctor/posts/science-and-psychology-have-isolated-the-one-prime-cause-for-success-or-failure-/10151234161334421/

34. Williamson, M. (1992). *A return to love: Reflections on the principles of "A Course in Miracles".* HarperCollins.

35. LaFreniere, L. S., & Newman, M. G. (2020). *Exposing worry's deceit: Percentage of untrue worries in generalized anxiety disorder treatment.* Behavior Therapy, 51(3), 413–423. https://doi.org/10.1016/j.beth.2019.07.003

36. Proctor, B. (n.d.). *"Faith and fear both demand you believe in something you cannot see. You choose."* [Quote]. Retrieved from Goodreads.com.

37. Author Unknown. (1999, January). *Clinton's a compartmentalizer— Are you?* The Observer. Retrieved from https://observer.com/1999/01/clintons-a-compartmentalizerare-you/

38. Clinton, B. (n.d.). "Sometimes when people are under stress, they hate to think, and it's the time when they most need to think." [Quote]. Retrieved from BrainyQuote.com

39. Carnegie, D. (1948). *How to stop worrying and start living.* Simon and Schuster.

40. Carnegie, D. (n.d.). *"Inaction breeds doubt and fear. Action breeds confidence and courage. If you want to conquer fear, do not sit home and think about it. Go out and get busy."* [Quote]. Retrieved from Goodreads.com

41. Proctor, B. (n.d.). *"Clearly understand that the only limitations you will ever have are the limitations you impose upon yourself. You truly do have infinite potential."* [Quote]. Retrieved from AZQuotes.com

42. Einstein, A. (n.d.). *"Assumptions are made and most assumptions are wrong."* [Quote]. Retrieved from AZQuotes.com

43. Emerson, R. W. (n.d.). *"Fear defeats more people than any other one thing in the world."* [Quote]. Retrieved from BrainyQuote.com

44. Bovee, C. N. (n.d.). *"We fear things in proportion to our ignorance of them."* [Quote]. Retrieved from AZQuotes.com

45. Canfield, J. (n.d.). *"Everything you want is on the other side of fear."* [Quote]. Retrieved from AZQuotes.com

Chapter 9 - Journey of Failure: Why Try… Nothing Works!

1. Einstein, A. (n.d.). *"Failure is success in progress."* [Quote]. Retrieved from BrainQuote.com

2. Brown, L. (n.d.). *"Accept responsibility for your life. Know that it is you who will get you where you want to go, no one else."* [Quote]. Retrieved from Goodreads.com

3. Robbins, T. (1986). *Unlimited power: The new science of personal achievement.* Free Press.

4. Henderson, N., Benard, B., & Sharp-Light, N. (2007). *"Resiliency in action: Practical ideas for overcoming risks and building strengths in youth, families, and communities (2nd ed.)".* Resiliency In Action.

5. Itzler, J. (n.d.). *"You have to learn to get comfortable being uncomfortable. You have to be willing to get out of your comfort zone and push your limits."* [Quote]. Retrieved from BrainQuote.com

6. Ziglar, Z. (n.d.). *"It's not the situation, but whether we react negative or respond positive to the situation that is important."* [Quote]. Retrieved from BrainyQuote.com

7. Allen, W. (n.d.). *"If you're not failing every now and again, it's a sign you're not doing anything very innovative."* [Quote]. Retrieved from AZQuotes.com

8. Goldsmith, O. (1762). *The citizen of the world: or, letters from a Chinese philosopher residing in London to his friends in the East* (Vol. 1, Letter VII). London: Printed for George and Alex Ewing.

9. Rooney, M. (n.d.). *"You always pass failure on your way to success."* [Quote]. Retrieved from AZQuotes.com

10. Brown, H. J., Jr. (n.d.). *"If you're doing your best, you won't have any time to worry about failure."* [Quote]. Retrieved from AZQuotes.com

11. Harari, O. (2003). *The leadership secrets of Colin Powell* (p. 164). McGraw-Hill.

12. Maxwell, J. C. (1987). *Be all you can be: A challenge to stretch your God-given potential* (p. 45). Victor Books.

13. Ford, H. (n.d.). *"Failure is simply the opportunity to begin again, this time more intelligently."* [Quote]. Retrieved from BrainyQuote.com

14. Edison, T. A. (n.d.). *"I have not failed. I've just found ten thousand ways that won't work."* [Quote]. Retrieved from Goodreads.com

15. Churchill, W. (n.d.). *"Success consists of going from failure to failure without loss of enthusiasm."* [Quote]. Retrieved from Goodreads.com

16. Maxwell, J. C. (n.d.). *"Without failure there is no achievement."* [Quote]. Retrieved from BrainyQuote.com

17. Wooden, J. (n.d.). *"Failure is not fatal, but failure to change might be."* [Quote]. Retrieved from Goodreads.com

18. Musk, E. (n.d.). *"If something's important enough, you should try. Even if the probable outcome is failure."* [Quote]. Retrieved from BrainyQuote.com

Chapter 10 - Journey of Success: Which Way to Success Street?

1. Lovell, J. (n.d.). *"There are people who make things happen, there are people who watch things happen, and there are people who wonder what happened. To be successful, you need to be a person who makes things happen."* [Quote]. Retrieved from BrainyQuote.com

2. Hill, N. (1928). The law of success (p. 112). The Ralston University Press.

3. Forbes, M. (n.d.). *"Failure is success if we learn from it."* [Quote]. Forbes. Retrieved from https://www.forbes.com/quotes/6315/

4. Trump, D. J., & Kiyosaki, R. T. (2011). *Midas touch: Why some entrepreneurs get rich—and why most don't* (p. 45). Plata Publishing.

5. Carnegie, D. (n.d.). *"Develop success from failures. Discouragement and failure are two of the surest stepping stones to success."* [Quote]. Retrieved from BrainyQuote.com

6. Greenfield, J. (n.d.). *"Don't just do something because it's a trendy idea and will make you a lot of money. The reason I say that is because any kind of venture involves going through difficult times. If you're doing something you are passionate about and really believe in, then that will carry you through."* [Quote]. Retrieved from BrainyQuote.com

7. Hill, N. (1937). *Think and grow rich*. The Ralston Society.

8. King, B. J. (n.d.). *"A champion is afraid of losing. Everyone else is afraid of winning."* [Quote]. Retrieved from BrainyQuote.com

9. Honda, S. (n.d.). *"Success is 99 percent failure."* [Quote]. Retrieved from BrainyQuote.com

10. Brothers, J. (n.d.). *"Success is a state of mind. If you want success, start thinking of yourself as a success."* [Quote]. Retrieved from Goodreads.com

11. Maxwell, J. C. (n.d.). *"Success is due to our stretching to the challenges of life. Failure comes when we shrink from them."* [Quote]. Retrieved from https://www.instagram.com/johncmaxwell/p/DDnf5p4SNS_/

12. Worre, E. (2013). *Go pro: 7 steps to becoming a network marketing professional*. Network Marketing Pro, Inc.

13. Worre, E. (n.d.). *"There will always be a good reason to quit and there will always be a good reason to keep going. Decide what kind of person you're going to be."* [Quote]. Retrieved from Addicted2Success.com

14. Hilton, C. (n.d.). *"Success seems to be connected with action. Successful people keep moving. They make mistakes, but they don't quit."* [Quote]. Retrieved from BrainyQuote.com

15. Ziglar, Z. (n.d.). *"You were designed for accomplishment, engineered for success, and endowed with the seeds of greatness."* [Quote]. Retrieved from BrainyQuote.com

16. Kroc, R. (n.d.). *"Luck is a dividend of sweat. The more you sweat, the luckier you get."* [Quote]. Retrieved from Goodreads.com

17. Mandela, N. (n.d.). *"Money won't create success, the freedom to make it will."* Retrieved from https://www.britannica.com/list/nelson-mandela-quotes

18. Edison, T. A. (n.d.). *"Many of life's failures are people who did not realize how close they were to success when they gave up."* [Quote]. Retrieved from BrainyQuote.com

19. Kiyosaki, R. T. (n.d.). *"The size of your success is measured by the strength of your desire; the size of your dream; and how you handle disappointment along the way."* [Quote]. Retrieved from Goodreads.com

20. Trump, D. J. (n.d.). *"What separates the winners from the losers is how a person reacts to each new twist of fate."* [Quote]. Retrieved from Inc.com https://www.inc.com/peter-economy/21-donald-trump-quotes-to-inspire-your-success-and-happiness.html

21. Hill, N. (1937). *Think and grow rich.* The Ralston Society.

22. Maxwell Leadership. (2024, September 15). *Effective Ways to Grow Your People* [Audio podcast episode]. In Maxwell Leadership Podcast. Maxwell Leadership. https://www.maxwellleadership.com/podcast/maxwell-leadership-podcast-grow-your-people/

23. Maxwell, J. C. (n.d.). *"Growth is the great separator between those who succeed and those who do not. When I see a person beginning to separate themselves from the pack, it's almost always due to personal growth."* [Quote]. Retrieved from BrainyQuote.com

24. Schwarzenegger, A. (2009, May 15). *Dr. Arnold Schwarzenegger's 6 Rules of Success Full Speech.* Singju Post. Retrieved from https://singjupost.com/dr-arnold-schwarzeneggers-6-rules-of-success-full-speech-transcript/

Chapter 11 - Journey of Growth: Are You Still Growing?

1. Goggins, D. (2018). *Can't hurt me: Master your mind and defy the odds.* Lioncrest Publishing.

2. Brown, L. (n.d.). *"You cannot expect to achieve new goals or move beyond your present circumstances unless you change."* [Quote]. Retrieved from BrainyQuote.com

3. Schwarzenegger, A. (n.d.). *"For me, life is continuously being hungry. The meaning of life is not simply to exist, to survive, but to move ahead, to go up, to achieve, to conquer."* [Quote]. Retrieved from Goodreads.com

4. Maxwell, J. C. (2012). *The 15 invaluable laws of growth: Live them and reach your potential.* Center Street.

5. U.S. Census Bureau. (2022, February 24). *Census Bureau releases new educational attainment data.* U.S. Department of Commerce. Retrieved from https://www.census.gov/newsroom/press-releases/2022/educational-attainment.html

6. Rohn, J. (n.d.). *"If you don't design your own life plan, chances are you'll fall into someone else's plan. And guess what they have planned for you? Not much."* [Quote]. Retrieved from Goodreads.com

7. Maxwell, J. C. (2012). *The 15 invaluable laws of growth: Live them and reach your potential.* Center Street.

8. Brown, L. (n.d.). *"All of us need to grow continuously in our lives."* [Quote]. Retrieved from BrainyQuote.com

9. Maxwell, J. C. (2012). *The 15 invaluable laws of growth: Live them and reach your potential.* Center Street.

10. Maxwell, J. C. (2012). *The 15 invaluable laws of growth: Live them and reach your potential.* Center Street.

11. Brown, L. (n.d.). *"If you put yourself in a position where you have to stretch outside your comfort zone, then you are forced to expand your consciousness."* [Quote]. Retrieved from BrainyQuote.com

12. Maxwell, J. C. (n.d.). *"The unsuccessful person is burdened by learning, and prefers to walk down familiar paths. Their distaste for learning stunts their growth and limits their influence."* [Quote]. Retrieved from BrainyQuote.com

13. Tracy, B. (n.d.). *"No one lives long enough to learn everything they need to learn starting from scratch. To be successful, we absolutely, positively have to find people who have already paid the price to learn the things that we need to learn to achieve our goals."* [Quote]. Retrieved from BrainyQuote.com

14. Rohn, J. (n.d.). *"Formal education will make you a living; self-education will make you a fortune."* [Quote]. Retrieved from Goodreads.com

15. Mackay, H. (2004). *Dig your well before you're thirsty: The only networking book you'll ever need.* Business Plus.

16. Hill, N. (1937). *Think and grow rich.* The Ralston Society.

17. Vance, A. (2015). *Elon Musk: Tesla, SpaceX, and the quest for a fantastic future.* HarperCollins.

18. Trump, D. J., & Schwartz, T. (1987). *Trump: The art of the deal.* Random House.

19. Tracy, B. (n.d.). *"Invest three percent of your income in yourself in order to guarantee your future."* [Quote]. Power Quotations. Retrieved from https://www.powerquotations.com/quote/invest-three-percent-of-your

20. Rohn, J. (n.d.). *Become The Person Who Naturally Attracts SUCCESS - Jim Rohn* [Video]. YouTube. https://www.youtube.com/watch?v=VCI5iA_lXx8

21. Brown, L. [@thelesbrown]. (2019, January 9). *"Just because Fate doesn't deal you the right cards, it doesn't mean you should give up. It just means you have to play the cards you get to their maximum*

potential" [Facebook Post]. Facebook.
https://www.facebook.com/thelesbrown/posts/10157821966369654/

22. Brown, L. [@thelesbrown]. (2019, January 9). *"Perfection does not exist - you can always do better and you can always grow."* [Facebook Post]. Facebook.
https://www.facebook.com/thelesbrown/posts/10157889130739654/

23. Maxwell, J. C. (n.d.). *The Leading Edge: The Importance of Changing Your Mind.* John Maxwell Team. Retrieved from https://johnmaxwellteam.com/the-leading-edge-importance-of-changing-mind/

24. Kennedy, J. F. (1961, September 25). *Address before the General Assembly of the United Nations.* John F. Kennedy Presidential Library and Museum. https://www.jfklibrary.org/archives/other-resources/john-f-kennedy-speeches/united-nations-19610925

Chapter 12 - Journey of YOU: It's a Wonderful Life!

1. Brown, L. (n.d.). *"You must remain focused on your journey to greatness."* [Quote]. Retrieved from BrainyQuote.com

2. Brown, L. (n.d.). *"If you take responsibility for yourself, you will develop a hunger to accomplish your dreams."* [Quote]. Retrieved from BrainyQuote.com

3. Rohn, J. (n.d.). *"The worst thing one can do is not to try, to be aware of what one wants and not give in to it, to spend years in silent hurt wondering if something could have materialized... never knowing."* [Quote]. Retrieved from BrainyQuote.com

4. Rohn, J. [@OfficialJimRohn]. (2014, January 6). *"The major value in life is not what you get. The major value in life is what you become."* [Facebook Post]. Facebook.
https://www.facebook.com/OfficialJimRohn/posts/10152708774430635/

5. Brown, L. (n.d.). *"Life takes on meaning when you become motivated, set goals and charge after them in an unstoppable manner."* [Quote]. Retrieved from BrainyQuote.com

6. Rohn, J. (n.d.). *"Take care of your body. It's the only place you have to live."* [Quote]. Retrieved from Goodreads.com

7. Gupta, S. (2021). *Keep sharp: Build a better brain at any age.* Simon & Schuster.

8. A. Centers for Disease Control and Prevention. (n.d.). *Chronic diseases in America.* U.S. Department of Health & Human Services. Retrieved from https://www.cdc.gov/chronic-disease/about/index.html
B. Centers for Disease Control and Prevention. (2025). *Preventing chronic disease: Public health research, practice, and policy.* U.S. Department of Health & Human Services. Retrieved from https://www.cdc.gov/pcd/issues/2025/24_0149.htm

9. CDC "Physical Activity Basics," December 20, 2023, https://www.cdc.gov/physical-activity-basics/guidelines/adults.html.

10. Boersma, P., Black, L. I., & Ward, B. W. (2020). *Prevalence of multiple chronic conditions among US adults,* 2018. Preventing Chronic Disease, 17, Article 200130. https://doi.org/10.5888/pcd17.200130

11. Khan, S., & Gadaleta, D. (n.d.). *Regain Be Gone: 12 Strategies to Maintain the Body You Earned After Bariatric Surgery.* Everand.

12. Książkiewicz, K. (2021). *Oxidative stress and its role in cancer.* Journal of Cancer Research and Therapeutics, 2021 Jan-Mar Postępy Higieny i Medycyny Doświadczalnej, 75, 442–450. https://pubmed.ncbi.nlm.nih.gov/33723127/

13. Pall, M. L., & Levine, S. (2015). *Nrf2, a master regulator of detoxification and also antioxidant, anti-inflammatory and other cytoprotective mechanisms, is raised by health promoting factors.* Acta Physiologica Sinica, 67(1), 1–18.

14. Kensler, T. W., Wakabayashi, N., & Biswal, S. (2007). *Cell survival responses to environmental stresses via the Keap1-Nrf2-ARE pathway.* Nrf2-signaling pathway and cytoprotection. Integrative and Comparative Biology, 50(5), 829–843. https://doi.org/10.1093/icb/icq034

15. Harman, D. (2009). *The aging process: Major risk factor for disease and death.* Proceedings of the National Academy of Sciences, 71(11), 4685–4689. https://doi.org/10.1073/pnas.71.11.4685

16. Hicks, J. (2014, March 15). *Move over hackers, biohackers are here.* Forbes. https://www.forbes.com/sites/jenniferhicks/2014/03/15/move-over-hackers-biohackers-are-here/

17. Edelman, M. W. (1986, March 30). *Fighting for kids is a full-time job.* Interview with MLK. Cleveland Plain Dealer, p. 21.

18. Osteen, J. (n.d.). *"Faith is about trusting God when you have unanswered questions"* [Quote]. Retrieved from BrainyQuote.com

19. Bernard, A. R. (Host). (2020, June 29). *Denzel Washington discusses his spiritual journey* [Interview]. In A.R. Bernard Instagram Live Series. Instagram.

20. Dowd, M. (2021, December 9). *Denzel Washington: A leader commands respect.* [Interview]. The New York Times. https://www.nytimes.com/2021/12/09/movies/denzel-washington-macbeth.html

21. Scott, A. O., & Dargis, M. (2020, November 25). *The 25 greatest actors of the 21st century (so far).* [Interview]. The New York Times. https://www.nytimes.com/2020/11/25/movies/25-greatest-actors-actresses.html

22. Washington, D. (2015, May 9). *Commencement address at Dillard University* [Speech]. Dillard University, New Orleans, LA.

23. McKirdy, E., Olarn, K., & Berlinger, J. (2018, July 11). *Thai cave rescue: The full story.* CNN. https://www.cnn.com/2018/07/11/asia/thai-cave-rescue-full-story-intl/index.html

24. Bethune, M. M. (n.d.). *"Without faith, nothing is possible. With it, nothing is impossible."* [Quote]. Retrieved from BrainyQuote.com

25. Luther, M. (n.d.). *"Faith is permitting ourselves to be seized by the things we do not see."* [Quote]. Retrieved from BrainyQuote.com

26. Osteen, J. (2004). *Your best life now: 7 steps to living at your full potential.* Warner Faith.

27. Lennon, J. (n.d.). *"We need to love ourselves first in all our glory and imperfections."* [Quote]. Retrieved from AZQuotes.com

28. Brown, L. (n.d.). *"Love yourself unconditionally, just as you love those closest to you despite their faults."* [Quote]. Retrieved from https://www.thegoodtrade.com/features/self-love-quotes/

29. Palmer, P. J. (2000). *Let your life speak: Listening for the voice of vocation.* Jossey-Bass.

30. Lopez, J. (n.d.). *"You've got to love yourself first. You've got to be okay on your own before you can be okay with somebody else."* [Quote]. Retrieved from BrainyQuote.com

31. Ball, L. (n.d.). *"Love yourself first and everything else falls into line. You really have to love yourself to get anything done in this world."* [Quote]. Retrieved from BrainyQuote.com

32. Gaga, L. (n.d.). *"It doesn't matter who you are, or where you come from, or how much money you've got in your pocket. You have your own destiny and your own life ahead of you."* [Quote]. Retrieved from Goodreads.com

33. Gaga, L. (n.d.). *"At the end of the day, you won't be happy until you love yourself."* [Quote]. Retrieved from https://www.entrepreneur.com/leadership/10-lady-gaga-quotes-to-inspire-you-to-be-your-authentic/299540

34. Robbins, T. (n.d.). *"It's not what we do once in a while that shapes our lives. It's what we do consistently."* [Quote]. Retrieved from Goodreads.com

35. Tracy, B. (2017). *Million dollar habits: Proven power practices to double and triple your income.* Gildan Media.

36. Worre, E. (2021, June 10). *Freedom is not free* [Video]. YouTube. https://www.youtube.com/watch?v=ACIllkoJULg

37. Shaw, G. B. (n.d.). *"Life isn't about finding yourself. Life is about creating yourself."* [Quote]. Retrieved from Goodreads.com

38. Rohn, J. (n.d.). *"You cannot change your destination overnight, but you can change your direction overnight."* [Quote]. Retrieved from https://www.success.com/10-unforgettable-quotes-by-jim-rohn/

39. Tracy, B. (n.d.). *"All successful people men and women are big dreamers. They imagine what their future could be, ideal in every respect, and then they work every day toward their distant vision, that goal or purpose."* [Quote]. Retrieved from Goodreads.com

40. Tracy, B. (2002). *Create your own future: How to master the 12 critical factors of unlimited success.* Wiley.

41. Maxwell, J. C. (n.d.). *"When your dream is bigger than you are, you only have two choices: give up or get help."* [Quote]. Retrieved from BrainyQuotes.com

42. Tracy, B. (n.d.). *"No one lives long enough to learn everything they need to learn starting from scratch. To be successful, we absolutely, positively have to find people who have already paid the price to learn the things that we need to learn to achieve our goals."* [Quote]. Retrieved from BrainyQuotes.com

43. Yahoo Finance. (2024, May 1). *Elon Musk admits, 'I really didn't think Tesla would be successful...'* [Article].Yahoo Finance. Retrieved from https://finance.yahoo.com/news/elon-musk-admits-really-didnt-202140580.html

NOTE[2]: The quotes obtained in Finding JOY were retrieved on or before January 2025 from the sources detailed in the citations and references above.

"Your JOY is within you,

Your journey is before you,

Your legacy is your destiny,

Go find your JOY and

change the world."

Ted Kopecko

www.ingramcontent.com/pod-product-compliance
Lightning Source LLC
Chambersburg PA
CBHW071703120626
46550CB00001B/84